D0522130

THE WORM FORGIVES THE PLOUGH

THE WORM FORGIVES THE PLOUGH

BOOK 1 · WHILE FOLLOWING THE PLOUGH

INTRODUCTION BY
MICHAEL HOLROYD

JOHN STEWART COLLIS

BARRIE & JENKINS
LONDON

Book I: *While Following the Plough* was first published by
Jonathan Cape in 1946. It was republished together with
Book II: *Down to Earth* under the title *The Worm Forgives the
Plough* by Charles Knight in 1973.

This edition published in 1988 by
Barrie & Jenkins Ltd
289 Westbourne Grove, London W11 2QA

British Library Cataloguing in Publication Data

Collis, John Stewart, 1900-1984
The worm forgives the plough.
Book 1: Following the plough
1. England. Rural regions. Social life,
1940-1946. Personal observations
I. Title
942.084'092'4

ISBN 0-7126-2060-5

Typesetting by
SX Composing Ltd, Rayleigh, Essex.
Printed in West Germany by
Mohndruck, Gütersloh

The typefaces used in this edition are called 'Joanna' and
'Pilgrim' and were both designed by Eric Gill.

CONTENTS

BOOK I: WHILE FOLLOWING THE PLOUGH

PART ONE: A FARM IN SOUTH-EAST ENGLAND

PART TWO:
A FARM IN SOUTH-WEST ENGLAND

INTRODUCTION

'From the hour of my birth she hated me,' John Stewart Collis wrote of his mother. '... Ours was not a united family ... Beautiful as were the garden and surroundings at Kilmore, there was no peace or happiness to be observed or felt.'

Jack, as he was called, had been born at this house on the border of County Dublin and County Wicklow in 1900. His father was a Dublin solicitor, physically fearless but unadventurous in mind and spirit. 'My father did not get on with my mother and I do not recall a single pleasant hour they spent together in my life time,' Jack wrote in his autobiography. He respected his father but did not feel close to him. He could not feel close either to his sisters or to his elder brother Maurice who was to become well-known as an industrious non-fiction writer. In the neurotic family atmosphere 'a film of pain and bewilderment separated me from them.'

But he was emotionally tied to his twin brother Robert, later to be one of the world's leading paediatricians. A shadow, however, existed between them. It had been a difficult confinement for their mother, late in her life, ending with severe labour pains, and Robert, the second twin, was born somewhat narcotised. When after a long struggle he started breathing and was handed to her, now changed from blue to pink, 'her maternal love poured out to me,' Robert Collis wrote. 'The other twin, Jack, was forgotten and hardly seen for several days. From that moment she accepted me and rejected my brother.' Her exclusion of the elder twin from her life appeared like some motiveless malignity and was painful to see. 'I was never taken up in my mother's arms and kissed,' Jack wrote. He never received a word of endearment or an act of kindness from her. He learnt to accept as normal her offers of second helpings at meals to Robert 'but not me,' and her loving goodnights to him as she passed by his own bedroom without a word. 'She could not help herself.' His unhappiness was so penetrating that he suffered a virtual loss of memory before the age of nine.

His memory began when he left home for his preparatory school in Bray and his later schooling at Rugby in England. His formal education here was pitifully inadequate. 'I was a prime sample of classroom-fodder,' he admitted: 'unawakened, unoriginal, unprecocious.' In later years he would turn from being an unquestioning victim of school-knowledge into a passionate inquirier after personal knowledge. This process had already begun at Balliol College, Oxford, to which he gained entry with some judicious cheating at Latin Unseen. Here he perfected a technique for discovering something valuable within a system that was largely useless to him. He had already fallen under the spell of Shakespeare and been beguiled by the word-music of Tennyson. He also taught himself to understand the principle of prose structure by reading Macaulay. Above all things he warmed to the spoken word. 'I hankered after oratory,' he remembered. The chief gain he derived from Oxford was the practice of public speaking and the acquiring of a style. At the Oxford Union he not only heard Asquith, Chesterton, Lloyd George and W.B. Yeats speak, but also scored many oratorical successes himself.

After coming down from Oxford he briefly entered a theological college. He imagined himself as a great preacher. But there had been another process at work in him. Riding his motor bicycle into the countryside each afternoon to examine his faith, he discovered that 'the more I looked at Nature, the less I needed theology. The more I loved the fields and skies the less I liked Doctrine.'

In London he managed to supplement an annual allowance of £150 from his father by writing for A.R. Orage's *New English Weekly* and Lady Rhondda's *Time and Tide*, as well as by teaching for the Workers' Educational Association and the Extra-Mural Department of the University of London. Much of this time he passed at the British Museum Reading Room where he continued the process of self-education and the search for a satisfying philosophy of life.

He also married. 'I met my wife in London and got married after a week.' But their married life with two daughters was oppressed by poverty during the 1930s. 'The financial problem was so appalling and so humiliating,' he records, 'that I could not even look at the flowers in spring so much did bills come between me and them.' His position was all the worse because he had been confident of success after the appearance of his first book, a perceptive study of Bernard Shaw whose work had become an 'inspiration to me' and whom he elected as a spiritual father. This had been published in 1925 and was well received. But his subsequent books over the next fifteen years, which included a dramatic dialogue, an autobiographical novel, a work of philosophy and a literary pilgrimage round England, were largely ignored. They all testify to Collis's rigorous programme of reading at the British Museum and an untiring quest to find his own voice and the form in which to use it.

He found both in the Second World War during which his wife and daughters were evacuated to America and he began work as an agricultural labourer. His six years of agricultural experience gave him the maternal love he needed from the land. 'I had got what I wanted at last,' he wrote, 'a complete participation in the ordinary work of the world.' It was as if a state of well being, native and near to him from which he had been mysteriously sundered, now took possession of him.

These years marked a turning-point in Collis's career. 'I had a great literary chance to bring together the Fact, the Idea, the Process and the Person, he wrote. '. . . Here was material upon which I could impose form.' The great work he fashioned from these experiences united his psychological and physical needs with the knowledge and training he had gained from the British Museum. 'The Reading Room days had not been entirely barren,' he was to write. 'There also I had sown; there also I had reaped to some extent.' But it was also true, as Richard Ingrams comments in his affectionate *memoir* of Collis, that until 1940 he 'bore the marks of someone who had spent too much time in the British Museum Reading Room, whose ideas about nature were derived, in part, from books by fellow-writers. Now he found himself in the open, face-to-face with the rough reality.'

The Worm Forgives the Plough is the collective title Collis eventually gave to the two volumes, *While Following the Plough* and *Down to Earth*, that arose from these years on the land. 'To work as a labourer on the land (not as a responsible farmer) had become a great desire of mine,' he explains. He swept away considerable obstacles and in 1940 went to live 'with my beloved dog Bindo' in an old empty house in the far corner of a farm at Stonegate on the Border of Kent and Sussex. The year he spent working here for J.G. Maynard forms the first part of *While Following the Plough*. Overcoming still more obstacles he then achieved his ambition to be a ploughman by going to a farm at Tarrant Hinton, near Blandford, in Dorset. This Farm, which 'was one of the most difficult I could have found anywhere and on that account one of the most interesting,' became the subject matter of the second part of this volume. Throughout these farming years he kept a diary and his habit of writing down what had happened at the end of each day helped to give this work its authenticity and vividness.

Nevertheless twelve publishers turned it down and even Jonathan Cape, which did accept it, demanded revisions. Richard Ingrams records that Collis was proud of the tactics with which he fended off this criticism. After an interval he returned the manuscript pretty well unaltered. But he thanked Cape for the substantial amendments they had suggested, and Cape replied that they were 'delighted with the improvements'.

While Following the Plough was published in 1946, *Down to Earth* in 1947, and the two were brought together as *The Worm Forgives the Plough* in 1973. Acclaimed on their appearance, they have now become accepted as classics. Before his death in 1984, Collis would sometimes revisit these farms and woods of the war years. 'I go past fields in all of which I have had business,' he wrote; 'I go through Tarrant Gunville and up to my wood and see how it is going on, and it always has gone on; and then up to the high road towards Shaftesbury till I come opposite Gore Farm and see my long field. There I stop – amazed that I can say, "I have ploughed that field."'

MICHAEL HOLROYD

PREFACE

'What made you go and work on the land?' I have so frequently been asked the question that perhaps an answer should be attempted. When a reason is completely obvious to oneself it is often difficult to explain it. Since 'because I very much wanted to' will not serve, I must be more explicit. While not refusing the term 'an intellectual' as applied to myself, since I believe in the Mind more than in anything else, I had hitherto regarded the world too much from the outside, and I wished to become more involved in it. The war gave me the opportunity. The previous war had left me as an Honorary Lieutenant in the Irish Guards, for it had stopped when I was at an Officer Cadet Battalion, and in 1940 I was offered an Army post. Since it was clear to me that I would be given some home job for which I should be entirely unfitted, I asked to be excused in favour of agriculture. This granted, I gained the opportunity of becoming thoroughly implicated in the fields instead of being merely a spectator of them.

I worked at this for nearly six years, a period which included much forestry, though I have not written of that experience in this volume. For the sake of unity I have restricted my narrative within given periods of time. My approach is one of genuine ignorance, and I have described many operations and implements as if the reader were as fresh to them as I was. Hence there is no instruction in this book; and I fear that my views tend to be as inconsistent as my moods, for my chief aim has been to present my physical and mental reactions regardless of their consistency, and to give a truthful picture of what I found in the agricultural world.

JOHN STEWART COLLIS

This book was written just before both the corn-rick and the hay-rick were deemed unnecessary by modern methods. The change of scene followed rather swiftly. Thus this book is about the last of its kind that can now be written in England.

J.S.C., 1973

PART 1

A FARM IN SOUTH-EAST ENGLAND

1

MY FIRST JOB

It was 16 April 1940. I could find no lodging close to the farm, but a friend did me the great service of putting me up at her cottage which was about thirty-five minutes' bicycle-ride distance. This meant rising in time to shave, breakfast, sandwich food for the day, and be ready to start out by six-thirty. I had always wanted something to force me up at this hour, this unsmirched hour of promise and of hope; and now I stepped out into a clear morning, with frost laid across the whole land, the air biting, and the hollows clouded. I arrived at the farm punctually, trying not to feel nervous and like a new boy at school. I gave up shyness some time ago when I realized that it was a form of self-consciousness and conceit, as well as being, like bad manners, a sign of ignorance of human nature; but to turn up into a completely new milieu – and not looking the part in person or clothes – to meet employers and employees and do something I had never done before, certainly made me apprehensive.

The foreman came out and shook hands and we walked across the farm towards some job that had been arranged for me. He was about thirty, non-rustic in appearance, quiet, accentless, pleasant, and exceedingly grave. We walked past some acres of fruit trees, for it was more than half a fruit farm, till we arrived at some ranks of apple trees. Their branches had been cut off and a new kind had evidently been grafted. My job consisted of dragging away and piling up the branches that lay on the ground.

The foreman went off and I was left alone at this my first job on the land. It was not very inspiring, but it was at least foolproof. I worked on for what I felt to be a very long time – nine hours to be exact, with one break, before the day was done. Already I began to ask at intervals what I discovered later is quite a famous question amongst agricultural labourers – *what is the time?* And after a few hours I began to feel lonely. This was a new experience and foreign to me; for complete isolation with a book is Solitude, a blessed state; but isolation with physical labour can be Loneliness, a very different thing. In the distance I could hear the chug of a machine (it was the spraying engine), a most welcome and important noise. I should have liked to get closer to it. Funny, I thought, that in the first few hours of labour on the land I should welcome the sound and long for the sight of a piece of machinery!

I had plenty of time to examine the grafting. Attached to the stumps where the branches had been cut off, were twigs about the size of a short pencil. Each was attached in a highly skilled manner, as if glued on by some black substance, and tied round with thread. The fore-

man told me that these apple trees were cookers and would require too much sugar to sell at a profit, so they were putting a sweeter apple on to the trees. I knew nothing whatever about grafting, and it surprised me that this could be done, now that I saw it in front of me.

When I had made some big piles of branches I was instructed to burn them, which I did. A pleasant task – for to reduce bulk to practically nothing, to make a hard thing soft, to cause substance to become insubstantial, is as interesting as making something out of nothing.

2

BROADCASTING ARTIFICIAL MANURE

After a few days my next job conducted me nearer the centre of the agricultural world: the spreading of artificial manure. Taking a horse and cart from the stable, Morgan (that was the name of the foreman) and I went across the farm to a far field which had been reserved for potatoes. It was a beautiful morning, and as we jogged along in the early sunshine with a wide view of the countryside and passed by a field of corn just coming up and looking more like a green light than a green object, I thought how pleasant it was to be here and to be doing this *as my job* – no longer to be looking at a horse and cart jogging through a field, but to be part of it now, to be *on the field* instead of a spectator of it. And I also reflected that if the countryman receives less pay than the townsman, he should not mind, since the latter ought to be compensated for his self-sacrificing denial of essentials.

We filled up with artificial at an old oast-house that served as a lower stable and barn. I had heard of artificial manure but that's about all, never seen it nor even considered what it looked like. Anyway, here was the stuff in front of me, neatly parcelled up in sacks of hundredweights and half-hundredweights. There were two kinds here, one a substance like very fine sand which I gathered was superphosphate, the other like salt which was potash. We loaded the superphosphate on the cart and brought it to the field, dropping the sacks at fixed intervals along the edge. This done we proceeded to broadcast it. The method was simple. We each filled a bucket, slung its rope over head and shoulder, and then holding the bucket steady with one hand, scattered the manure with the other at the rate of one handful to every second step as we advanced across the field. From a distance it would look the same as sowing grain.

A rather strong wind blew and the powder flew up into our eyes so frequently and so painfully that we had to give up and sow potash instead – which being much heavier and moister is

not blown about by the wind. Thus we sowed the potash walking forward and backward across the field, filling up our buckets at each end, for the rest of the morning and the whole afternoon. The ground of course was extremely uneven and I stumbled over the clods as I walked. I now remembered the word *clod-hopper*, the term of reproach reserved by townsmen for those who produce food, and I was interested to touch the reality. On account of my very early breakfast, with only a snatched bite since, I began to wonder if I could really last out till dinner. At length the great moment came when we knocked off, and then I experienced a pleasure in just *sitting down*, and in eating cheese, such as I have never known before.

After this I did a lot more manuring on my own for several days. One afternoon I sowed potash up and down twenty-five long rows of blackcurrant trees and plums. Up and down, filling my bucket at each end until eight sacks were empty, five hours had passed and it was

five-thirty. It struck me as qualifying for the term 'grinding toil'. I found these long afternoons something of an endurance test. Owing to laziness I possess a secret reserve of strength, and was not afraid that I wouldn't be equal to anything that turned up with regard to physical labour; but that afternoon's expedition, and subsequent work, seemed to me long drawn out. This opinion of mine, soon formed, never abandoned, I found held good for all labourers on the land not doing the more interesting jobs.

However, this particular job evidently left something to show for it, and to my amazement it made an impression on the foreman who remarked on it favourably the next day.

Continuing further at this I began to feel that it could now fairly be said that I was familiar with artificial manure – commercially spoken of as fertilizer. But at this stage I can put forward no opinion on the great Artificial v. Pure Compost problem. I have watched the waging of this

war with some care, but consider myself as yet too much a provincial in truth concerning this matter even to state a preference. Yet talking of schools of thought on the subject, it seems that should you live in the U.S.S.R. it would be wise to watch your step about this. Arthur Koestler in his *Darkness At Noon* says: 'A short time ago, our leading agriculturalist, B, was shot with thirty of his collaborators because he maintained the opinion that nitrate artificial manure was superior to potash. Number 1 is all for potash; therefore B and the thirty had to be liquidated as saboteurs.' Now in England if anyone disagrees with anyone else he doesn't get angry, he just says: 'That's a point of view anyway, old man.' This may not promote progress. Yet some of the thirty-one nitrate-supporters may have secretly wished that Number 1 – i.e. Stalin – was less un-English.

Without airing views on this subject I may add that one day, having been instructed to spread some artificial and to get the sacks, and not remembering whether it was potash or superphosphate that was to be used, I asked by a slip of the tongue: 'Which sort of *superficial manure* am I to use?' This was greeted with laughter by the boss who was not totally devoid of a sense of humour, and though a great supporter of these fertilizers, seemed to discern some slight element of justice or irony in this strange nomenclature.

3

MY FURROW

Presently I found myself back on the potato field broadcasting a final portion with 'super', while Morgan harrowed with a tractor, and the carter, a genial young Dane, ploughed open furrows for potato planting.

When the coast was clear later on I asked the carter if I might try my hand at ploughing a few furrows. I knew that he would be far from pleased at the request, but putting my pride in my pocket (a thing I do all my life at intervals with deliberation), and going on the principle that 'nothing dare, nothing do' I approached the ploughman. And as it is harder to refuse than to acquiesce in such things, he let me try. He said he would lead the horse (only one was being used) the first time, while I managed the plough. This was an easy way of starting. Even so I immediately felt in need of four hands, two for reins and two for plough. However, imitating this man's method, I put the reins over my head till they were held taut round the right shoulder and under the left arm. And since the horse was started and led by my companion I

reached the bottom of the field leaving behind a moderately straight furrow. It would be hard to make a complete bosh of this under the above condition. We returned to the other end again without marked mishap. Then I took over the whole thing. Now I would plough a furrow. It was a psychological necessity for me to plough a furrow – at last about to be fulfilled. I took up my position, and it only remained for me to proceed.

The horse refused to move.

I urged it forward, but it then moved sideways, upsetting the plough. And I spent some time in putting it into position again.

It then moved over the other side with the same result. I had not yet advanced a step. My psychological furrow still remained in the realm of the imagination.

Once more I got into position. This time we did really start, we did really move forward.

But after ten yards the horse swerved badly left. Using one hand for the reins, thus leaving only one on the plough, I pulled him round too much. Nevertheless we proceeded, but again owing to lack of rein control the horse went sideways and my furrow, after a few yards of near straightness, went west. Still, when I had reached the bottom the thing had been done. I had ploughed a furrow. It could hardly have been less straight, but a weight was lifted from my mind, for whatever geometrical terms might be necessary to describe my line, to me it was an Event – I had at any rate ploughed a furrow.

4

POTATO PLANTING: BROADCASTING SEED

A wet day now drew us indoors – into an old house, at a far corner of the farm, unoccupied and with no road to it. It was serving as a general store-house for artificial and potatoes and tools. We made use of the wet day to prepare the potatoes for planting. From a pile on the floor we sorted out the medium ones for planting, putting those that were too small on one side, and splitting the large ones to serve as two. So the Potato now came into my field of vision as a definite object on its own. Not being a garden or allotment man I had hitherto never looked at a potato save with my mouth, as it were. Now I decided to fix my eye on it and follow its act.

Early in May we assembled for planting. The personnel included all who worked on the farm: the boss (who, though frequently called away on another job at this period, was present at most of the important occasions), Morgan, the Dane, a general labourer called Arthur Miles and his wife, a land girl, and myself. We each took a row, filled buckets from sacks placed at intervals down the field, and planted the potatoes in the furrows at one foot distance from each other – which seemed to me a lot of room for them to play in. I was glad to put them in and let them get on with it. They have no beauty to recommend them, it is their performance we admire, and now they could start moving. But I soon lost interest in them and became much more concerned with my back. Since it is necessary to carry a bucket and to place each potato right down in the furrow as you advance, the back-strain is unexampled – in fact there is no other agricultural job so hard on the back. A machine-planter has been invented of course, and is much in use. And a good job too, thought I, many thanks and salaams to the benefacting inventor. 'So you are a believer in thorough agricultural mechanization, are you?' 'Pardon me, but I'm in no fit state to think it out – my back's aching too much. Empirically, as seen here regarding *this*, a machine seems excellent.' And I fear that machines come into the world, not following a principle, nor with an eye to future developments, nor in relation to the whole, but by fits and starts, one by one, each seeming splendid to those concerned. I have to admit that whatever views I might hold in the study concerning mechanization, on the field, from this labouring angle, I would cast a highly favourable eye upon any man who appeared with a potato-planter.

'What did you do today?' my friends often asked when I got home. 'Spread potash round the foot of fruit trees' was about all I sometimes could reply. Thus an accurate day-to-day account of life on a farm would be almost laughably dull – though I wish someone would do it if

only for the benefit of the romanticists. But spreading potash at the foot of fruit trees was in no way an irksome job. You simply filled your bucket and circled round each tree in the line, throwing down handfuls of the manure in a circle well away from the foot of the stem – for the roots which it is designed to reach are spread several feet outwards. There was thick grass round most of the trees which I dressed thus, and I wondered how much good I was really doing. I did not care, for I was not responsible. I was most happy and at ease in my non-responsibility. No farmer can be at ease hanging daily upon the response of nature to his decisions.

While on this manuring job one day I noticed that a certain attractively situated field with a long view was being sown with corn by Arthur Miles. This farm (a little less than a hundred acres) had not gone in for much arable work, the concentration being on fruit, hence it was not fitted out with much equipment for the former. The old method of broadcasting seed was

adopted. I saw that Arthur Miles, who seemed to do anything and everything, was engaged at this. And just as I had longed to put my hand on a plough, so again I felt the strongest desire to broadcast a field, or some of it, in creative contrast with broadcasting artificial. When the boss came round I asked him if I might take a turn. He was an understanding man and did not make fun of the awkward request. In fact he brought me up to the field and left me with Arthur Miles – though not going so far as to say anything to him about it. He just left me there. This made it a bit awkward. But again I overcame the resistance and he showed me how it was done. It is extremely concentrated work. You must walk straight and you must throw out the seed so as never to leave a patch uncovered. Thus, fixing your eye steadily upon an object at the end of the field, you start out, throwing the grain forward at every step. This means that the hand must work very quickly in seizing the grain from the bag or bucket slung by a strap over the shoulder,

and the arm must go out evenly and rhythmically with the legs – otherwise there will be gaps and patches when the corn grows.

It was exactly this steady synchronization that I found most difficult and I did a portion of the field none too well, and made Miles none too pleased. But I did do that portion and never in my life felt better employed. I was doing the oldest and most necessary work known to man. When you do it by hand there is the further attraction that not only are you doing something necessary for the life of mankind, but you are outside the Machine Age, so that even if the machines went up in smoke you would remain untouched and could continue to work across the field. And if we are moved by the poetry of tradition and the procession of time, remembering that a two-thousands-year-old Parable held up the image of the Sower at the self-same task, we shall be glad indeed, if only for a brief period in our lives, if only once, to do likewise and cast abroad these envelopes of life.

5

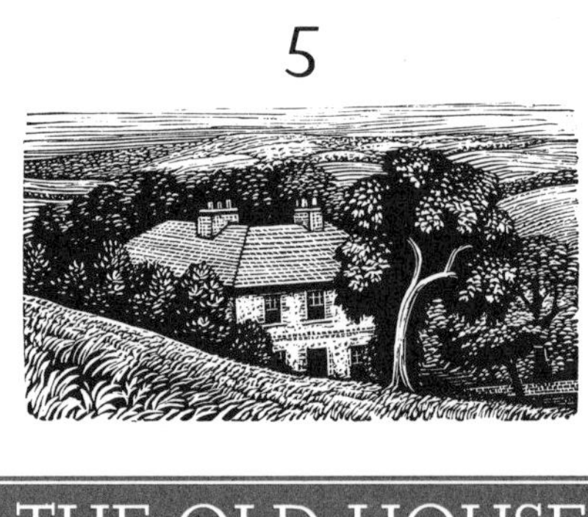

THE OLD HOUSE

Another wet day followed and I was sent to the old house to crunch potash. This chemical, lying up all winter, gets damper and damper, forming into hard lumps in the sacks. My job was to open the sacks, throw the potash on the floor, crunch it up into a fine powder and then re-pack it.

I carried on alone throughout the day at this, in the large old, empty house. Enormous beams, many doors, three stairways, attics, cellars – the whole empty save for the sacks of artificial, some broken chairs, one wash-basin, tools and potatoes, and in an upper room an enormous bedstead fitted with mattress.

At lunch-time – or, more properly, dinner-time – I went into this upper room. The bed certainly was formidable – one of those old Victorian 'beds like battlefields', as George Moore described them. There I had my meal, using the mattress as table and chair. This house was tucked away in a lost corner, far from any other house, with no road or even pathway to it. A lonely mansion at the best of times; on that day, that desolate room, one window stuffed up, one broken, one filled with cardboard, the wind whistling, the rain without and the damp within, I felt discouraged and inclined towards melancholy. I lay down on the bed, using my haversack as pillow, and, curling up, placed my overcoat over my body and head. The wind

rattled the panes and various doors banged, but I felt secure now and remote from the world, as if I had buried myself.

In spite of this I rose conscientiously after an hour and returned to the potash, and while crunching the strange white substance tried to grapple with the mystery of its action against the potatoes that I had put in the ground – and was irritated beyond measure by my ignorance.

The afternoon seemed remarkably long – longer than the usual longness. And no wonder, for my watch had stopped and I had worked two hours' overtime – for continuing to hear the distant chug-chug of the spraying machine, I thought it could not yet be five-thirty; but there had evidently been a pause for tea, and then on again. So that day my hours were from 5.30 a.m. when I rose, till 8 p.m. when I got back. Going home I remembered that I had to get some eggs (you could still get eggs at this time). After some searching up a hill I found the place and bought the eggs. The woman who gave them to me also gave me three small cakes gratis, for I had impressed her with 'a tired look'. This was encouraging. I seldom succeed in working either long enough or hard enough to look properly tired, and this was the first time in my life that a kind woman had taken pity on me as a worn-out man and given me three cakes.

If you have a fair distance to cycle to your work, then the question as to whether it is uphill going or coming back is of some moment – freshly considered every day. Is it better to have it downhill on the way to work? Yes, for as you always start out late you can arrive on time. But the return home! A slow push up a long slant is no pleasing prospect to the labourer who has achieved his 5.30 p.m. That was to be my experience later. Here, going home I started with a long swoop down, lovely in the evening but imperfect in the morning. However, I now asked the boss whether instead of doing this long bicycle journey every day I could live in the old house, putting into it the furniture which soon had to be taken out of a house in Kent, my wife having to go in another direction. This was agreed to. There was no road to the house, as I have said – only a railway line! No doubt it once had a fine approach to it: some of it dated back to the Elizabethan era, I believe. But any such approach had long since been abandoned, and the house itself forgotten and finally lost. Only in England, with its forty-seven million inhabitants, could you actually lose a house.

However, during certain months of the year there was a sufficiency of dry ground and even a track to make approach by lorry possible, even to the doorway. But of course in the eyes of furniture removers and tradesmen it was 'out in the wilds'. This latter phrase is frequently heard in twentieth-century England. 'You *are* out in the wilds!' people will say to anyone in the Home Counties living somewhere not on or very near a bus route, and perhaps two and a half miles from a railway station. Such is the imbecility to which industrialism can reduce a nation whose sons have travelled to the ends of the earth, pioneering and colonizing into the unknown and ruling millions of waves just for the fun of the thing.

Nevertheless I managed to persuade a firm to undertake this tremendous task. Unluckily, when the driver got near the house he left the hard track at one point and the van sank into swampy ground and had to be dug out. But in the end the furniture was carried into the house with amused condescension by the men.

I decided to occupy two rooms of the seven or eight – a large one upstairs, and the one underneath it, both supported by colossal beams. Thus beamed and buttressed by earlier centuries, I felt myself in a strong position. The ground floor of my bedsitting room upstairs was

uneven with age, as roughly wrinkled as the waves of the sea. Twelve beams crossed the ceiling from east to west, while a really fine one, besieged in vain by insects, crossed from north to south. The ancient cupboards, knotched and dented by the artillery of Time, might well have concealed alarming skeletons. The fireplace was so wide that you could have put a child's bed into it. The long latticed window looked across at the old oast-house, which in the declension of the sharp evening light had a wood-cut perfection about it. And the evening, after-tea sun came into the room – one of the most soothing of all Nature's effects. It was an ideal room, and all the time I was there I thought how I would hate to leave it when the time came. But there was a curious draught near the door. When you approached it, it became quite windy, almost hat-blowing-off, even when it was calm outside. The cause was obscurely connected with the peculiar exit. It opened on to two doors, one trap-door, and two stairways, and whichever one was

opened at this junction was banged by a cold tempest, the gale not coming from any certain direction but rather occupying a central typhoonish position. To complete this survey – the trap-door led to two separate attics which, like all attics, were utterly abandoned to despair. One door led to a bathroom, itself leading into a small room and it into another up two steps. The other door opened on to a commodious staircase and four big front rooms. While if you opened no door you could go down a steep back staircase leading to a scullery and one-time kitchen, now filled with sacks of potash. And then, should you wish to continue your odyssey, you could open a door in the corner of that and go down some stone steps to a cellar, damp and dungeoned as the Cells of Chillon. Many of these rooms, I sometimes felt, when in no lofty mood, would have been less lonely with a few ghosts.

Having installed myself here, it was suggested that I should have a meal per day with the

boss and family. 'Our chief meal of the day,' he said, 'is tea, at 5.30. What about coming in to that?' I gratefully accepted, at the same time wondering how that meal could be the chief one on a farm. Next day he told me that his wife preferred to make it dinner. The truth was of course that the midday meal was a real square one, and the other just tea; but he couldn't bear the thought of letting me have the dinner. His charming wife, however, wasn't standing for that. I have often noticed farmers' wives, before giving anyone anything, glance nervously to see if the husband is looking.

I had heard it said over and over again that 'Mother Earth' keeps men sane. This is so. But I have found from my own limited experience, and from a certain amount of note-comparing with others, that she makes all farmers, with few exceptions, go slightly off their heads. The above instance would easily find its counterpart, and shows to what a pass these men are brought by their unique struggle. I must add, if only to make the psychology of the thing more difficult, that this man did not charge me a penny rent for the house nor a penny for potatoes. He may have had ulterior motives, but I don't know what they were; and there it is, he charged me nothing, while at the same time he really could not bear serving a double-helping at table.

6

THE SPRAYING OPERATION

My services were soon called for at a new job – as assistant at the spraying of fruit trees. What we performed in this line was something wholly outside any previous experience of mine. Once or twice in my life I had sprayed; that is, I had taken a hand-syringe in the garden at home in childhood, put it in water, filled it, and squirted rose trees. But here was something colossal.

It might be thought that an apple or plum tree would bear fruit as satisfactorily as a gooseberry or black-currant bush, if left alone to a certain extent. This is too optimistic, it appears. The pear, the plum, but especially the apple, it seems, are open to the attack of hosts of enemies. First to the fungi: a fungus being a plant which does not prepare its own food but feeds on other plants. The apple tree lends itself as such food better than most, so it has to be protected against the Leaf Blight which is capable of despoiling all the leaves of whole orchards; against the Bitter

Rut, Black Rut, and the Brown Rut which devour their way into the fruit: against Rust which yellows the leaves and eats into the growing apple; against Scab which forms dark circular spots on the fruit and leaves. It must also be protected against a host of insect enemies; against the Aphis, an insect which, gathering in massed battalions, sucks the juices from leaf and blossom; against the Bud Moth which chooses the tree as good hatching ground in the crevices of the twigs so that the larvae can feed upon the foliage; against the Canker Worm, a caterpillar which, after feeding upon the tree, lowers itself to the ground by means of its self-produced thread; and against seven other kinds of moth and worm.

Such is the story, at any rate. How the unattended apple tree in your back garden manages to survive and produce fruit in considerable quantities would therefore seem something of a mystery. But it is not for me to question or even raise an eyebrow. My place is beside the spraying-machine. It consisted of a motor-pumping engine attached to a tank – the whole being mobile. A large tubular sucker (glorified hose-end) entered the tank which was filled with the spraying liquid, and a long coiling hose conveyed the spray to the place desired. I must say I took a fancy to this machine, partly because of its important noise while it chugged away pumping out the stuff; partly because it often went wrong, thus creating diversion and relaxation;. partly because of its dramatic filth and habit of leaking and spitting out green slime.

Its accompanying tank was filled with water, sulphur, and lime, a combination of such a poisonous complexion that even to look at it was mentally disturbing. Nor was I always in a position to keep my distance; for when the tank began to get empty and it became necessary to deal with the tubular sucker, it was like grappling with a vicious inhabitant of the first swamp. I have rarely handled an inanimate object that was more animated. It seemed bent on spraying me personally with its unspeakable juices.

My main task was to lug round the immense length of hose after Morgan who thus could hold a free lance with which to spray the trees when he went down the aisles. This was the most exhausting job I have ever had to do. It was like a solo tug-of-war of interminable duration. As the morning wore on and wore me down, dinner and its, as yet, appalling distance from realization, became too often and too painfully my sovereign thought. Morgan seemed entirely indifferent either to time or hunger – he never carried a watch and never appeared to be hungry. Luckily this endurance test was occasionally broken by the hose bursting at some point and sending up a high fountain of spray like a whale's jet, or the machine would go wrong, or the tank need refilling. And sometimes I sprayed also, both of us pulling the hose after us as best we could. It was anything but easy to spray effectively. No use just squirting a tree and passing on: the tree must be wet all over, on all the branches, and on both sides of every leaf; for an insect or fungus is not killed until the poison gets it – and does not accommodate a farmer by committing suicide. The direction of the wind was an important matter: it was necessary to see that it was blowing away from you, otherwise the lotion blew back upon your face . . . not itself in need of protection against fungus, scab, or blight.

Thus it goes on at this time of the year in all the big orchards of the country, hour after hour and day after day, an unceasing offensive against these enemies of table-fruit.

The refilling of the tank provided a species of light entertainment. The spraying-engine and the tank were mounted on the chassis of a Morris Oxford. When refilling time came we attached a tractor to the chassis and proceeded towards a pond, the engine of the spraying-machine

still chugging away. Morgan drove the tractor while I guided the platform, since the steering-wheel of the old car was still attached. We reached the pond and filled the tank with water, and then poured out two bucketfuls of the sulphur-lime liquid from a barrel, and added that to the tank. We were now ready to return to the scene of operation. The jolts and jerks caused by the exceedingly uneven ground made the liquid in the (now very full) tank splash about, shoot up, and pour down the back of my neck – the steering-wheel being between the tank and the tractor. Meanwhile the open radiator of the spraying-machine full of hot water splashed in a similar manner, going down the back of Morgan's neck and into my face. Thus we would proceed, the roar of both the engines and the double splashing of the waters providing a spectacle sufficiently disquieting in itself, you might fancy, to frighten away any enemies of the fruit.

'Will you have an apple, Mr Brown?'

'Thanks very much.'

'Oh dear, Bridget hasn't put any on the table! She must have forgotten to bring them up. I'll ring.'

'Please don't bother, it doesn't matter a bit.'

'But I particularly told her to put them on the table!'

Yet, before Bridget can bring them up, I, for one, am glad to realize what a lot must be done by God and man before she is even in a position to forget to 'put them on the table'.

7

MORGAN AND MILES

In spite of Morgan's extreme neglect of clock and absence of hunger, it was a pleasure to work with him. I thought at the time, and have frequently thought since, how impossible it would have been to have had a nicer foreman to start with. He was not in the least like the usual kind of foreman. He never lost his temper, never even raised his voice – it was quite phenomenal. He was a 'working man' but with no accent one way or the other. Almost totally lacking in class-consciousness. Very grave, respectable, correct, and ungossipy, but also with a sense of humour that lit up a peculiarly pleasant smile. There are so many classes within classes and grades upon grades in England that I am hard put to it to describe the social position of Morgan. His complete absence of accent or dialect was rather baffling. He had been the clever boy at school and could have taken scholarships and risen 'higher in the world', as it is called, but he had not liked schooling and had gone to Canada at first to farm – hence his wider horizon. He liked his work (not so common with land workers, I was to find). He was also fond of reading. This generally means, quite simply, reading novels. For many readers it is hardly known that there are any other books. And so it was with Morgan – a book was a novel. As he liked to mention books sometimes, I found it a bit awkward. Indeed I know few things more psychologically harassing than this kind of literary conversation, when one has seldom read any of the books mentioned and cannot name others that will convey anything. However, we managed somehow, and often he asked for a book. He never turned down a good one. I lent him a Hardy. He approved and said it was 'quite good'. He listened to book-talks by the B.B.C. and heard of *War and Peace*. I lent him my copy and he was not to be daunted. But he did not enjoy it. He confessed at intervals that he was 'wading through it'. (I wondered how many would have taken it on at all.) His paper was the *Daily Express* – and he quoted its opinions. Arthur Miles read *Picture Post* – 'very good value' he said. The boss read the *New Statesman* – and quoted its opinions.

Arthur Miles was a rough diamond. At many farms, it seems, there is one man who is 'always right', who 'knows everything', who puts everyone right and shouts loudly. An ordinary man might say 'You will find it in the shed' or 'You've got it the wrong way round', without undue emphasis or excitement. Arthur would yell the information in apparent fury. He was a tremendous blusterer. But an efficient blusterer, the regular handy man always called upon in difficulties for masterly improvisation.

In the agricultural world, I soon discovered, all sorts of problems must be solved on the spot, the difficulty must be got round somehow, there is no question of getting someone from outside to do it. Thus endless improvisation in the mending of breakages and the construction of suddenly essential gadgets. It is an agricultural habit of mind – foreign to the townsman. Wrestling with nuts and screws is an almost daily thing. Hence the agricultural labourer is an amateur mechanic (who afterwards went into the town and specialized). He is the first mechanic, the first man to 'conquer nature' just as he was the first man to get fed up with nature and to wall himself off from her by building the town. All things start on the land – not least the townsman, and most surely the mechanic. The idea that the engineer is a special kind of town-bred person was dispelled for me after a very short acquaintance with agricultural workers. Arthur always got round the difficulty somehow, provided he had a piece of wire. Your agriculturalist can do anything with a piece of wire – not a day passes but he saves some crisis with it. Arthur, with hands the size of spades, could twist the stuff about like twine.

He was a great master of language, though his mastery was confined to one word, beginning with b. It is a famous word, yet never reaching the status that would allow it to appear on the page, though it has long since lost its etymological significance. It is used equally as a noun, an adjective, or a verb. Dr Johnson, I think, described it in his *Dictionary* as '*a term of endearment amongst sailors*'. That is when used as a noun, one sailor calling another a b. On land it is used less as a sign of affection than in terms of music-while-you-work – an accompaniment. Swearing came as naturally to Arthur as leaves to a tree, and having command over all the possible variations in which the word could be used it came from his lips almost in terms of song – 'It's a b', 'well I'm b'd', 'he's a b', 'you can b off' . . . Once, when I heard him preserve silence for a few minutes on account of the proximity of the boss's wife, it seemed unnatural and disquieting, and I felt anxious for him until he started up again.

He roared out his council to everyone, including Morgan, *his* way being the right one, never allowing for two schools of thought even about potato planting. Morgan was careful to keep his temper, thus avoiding a pig-headed hold-up. Arthur's roaring at me was more extensive and violent – sometimes I thought he overdid it. But he possessed what is called 'a good heart at bottom' – which is by no means true of all men with rough tongues. He had another mood, perhaps later in the day, in strange contrast. He would be doing something in the lower stable, say; he would swing the door open slightly (it slowly went back on its hinges without needing any push) and would say as it swung back – 'Open Sesame'. I do not know what he thought the words meant, but with a gentle humorous expression he would give the door a little kick with his toe, saying – 'Open Sesame'.

Arthur's wife also worked on the farm. Like a number of women she was made of iron and capable of endless work. It was said of her also that at bottom she had a good heart. I think this geographical description was true enough. But I felt that she belonged to the category of those who would gain in amiability what they lost in virtue by having a bad heart at bottom and a hypocritical one on top. All women are more self-conscious than men, and many far more class-conscious. It blows from them like a wind. Arthur Miles 'didn't give a damn' for anyone or anything: 'I don't mind 'ow 'e is or wot 'e is' he'd say – and one liked him for it. Mrs Miles went on the same principle, but in a less engaging way. One of her minor pleasures was to work with some new land girl or amateur assistant. She would work at a pace impossible for the others to keep up, and shout at intervals (she never spoke, always shouted as if there was a gale on), 'How do you like wurking? This is *wurk*, you know!' All remarks addressed to her, whether in terms of the weather, the joke, the grouse, were answered by one sovereign rejoinder – 'You're telling me!'

8

THE THIRD DAY OF CREATION

A fortnight to three weeks having elapsed since I had broadcast seed with Arthur, I decided to have a look at that field. Hitherto I had always been too much of a Wordsworthian (not that I can ever bring myself to denigrate in any way the greatest of the nineteenth-century poets) and was content to see things only in the round, feeling that the scientific approach *is* to peep and botanize upon your mother's grave. But my chance had come to *see the particular*, now that I was personally implicated in it.

It was certainly true that in this instance I had little real idea of what precisely I should see. On approaching the field I saw a low green mist clinging to it, which turned out to be substance in the nature of grass, now covering what had been the brown surface of the field. I dug up a spadeful. We had sown a mixture of oats and peas. Those handfuls of round and oblong caskets that I had helped to broadcast had performed a peculiar act after leaving the hand and reaching the soil. Quite dead in the sack, it had seemed; but on touching the soil they had become animated, alive, and full of surprising moves. It were as if that little oat-seed, a tiny and inferior-looking piece of matter such as one might chip off a log, had been galvanized on being touched by Earth – making me think of gunpowder when touched by Fire. The envelopes had exploded. The pea seeds, those hard little balls like dented miniature ping-pong balls, had softened and shot downwards white webs and claws as long as my fingers, and shot upwards into the air a complicated system of green tubing and frills. The oat seeds, the shape of tiny fish, had performed a similar feat below and had sent up into the air long thin pieces of material like green ribbons. No matter how they had fallen on the ground or how they lay when they had fallen, they had all exploded in two directions only – down and straight up. None slanted, all preserved the perpendicular.

We glorify the present only when it has become the past. This is a recognized tendency in terms of history. It is equally true in terms of metaphysics. We imagine that Creation took place in the remote past. No doubt it did; but the same thing takes place today. The third Day of

Creation, as fabled in the book of Genesis, happens once every year no less certainly than the Sixth Day happens all the time. If this were not so the world would speedily dissolve. As I stand beside the rising corn I feel no need to have been present on the Third Day of the First Week, since I am witnessing the same thing. The same Force is at work, the same Voice obeyed. That which I would have seen then, I see now – sheer miracle, pure purpose. He who tries to dispose of this, uttering some mumbo-jumbo about 'chance' or 'mechanism' is the only real heretic, the only real atheist. All other denial, all other unbelief is mere speculation, and of no consequence. But this denial of clear witness is not speculation, and reveals the denier, not as a clever casuist, but as a stupid ass.

I have spent some time in the company of the philosophers and the priests, and have undertaken long journeys with them in search of the Absolute. It was all necessary. For only then could I understand that it was not necessary, and that if we will but look out of the window the answer is there. It is clear to me now that if we take the trouble to regard phenomena, with the eye, *not* of a child, but of an adult who weds intelligence with wonder, we shall soon find ourselves at ease with the Problem of Purpose and all the rest of it.

9

SOME FALLACIES

The orchards were now beginning to bloom. The Coxes, the James Grieves, the Beauty of Baths all appearing much more real to me than in the old days, already an ancient time left far behind, when an apple was 'only' a fruit which you bought for sixpence a pound, and an orchard just a pretty sight. Having opened the gate of labour I had suddenly stepped inside the world, and could see the objects with fresh eyes.

The spraying-machine had been put aside, of course, and my new job for a time was hoeing. The hoe, unlike the spade, having its knife-edge turned at right angles to the handle, allows you to thump it down into the ground while at the same time pulling it towards you – with the result that you can remove one or more weeds at each stroke. Still, it is not an inspiring job. I have met one or two people who liked it. But on the whole it is far from popular. Indeed, faced with many hours of it, there is a general agreement that it breaks the back and the mind. There is only one way by which it can be conquered – namely by good company. Absorbing conversation alone can overcome hoeing. And one can hardly expect to find that on the land.

Actually, the hoeing I did on this farm was the easiest and the least boring I have ever done. I had a good hoe, sharp and heavy (I never handled its like again). And the ground was soft. Hence one swoop easily removed the thistles and docks. Moreover, I worked not in an open field but between fruit trees. I have never since had a combination of similar qualities for softening the blows of monotony. At first I vastly preferred it to my recent tug-of-war with the hose. Nevertheless I soon began to wish I was doing something else.

This job, and the previous ones, brought me up against one of the fallacies concerning agricultural work held by the citizen of our mean cities. It is supposed that 'on the land' you have 'time to think', and that conditions are such that the mind can indulge quietly in wise expansive meditations in the open air. Certainly the place in which to think is the open air. But not during work. To be able to think *consecutively* about anything you must concentrate; and

there are few jobs on the land that you can do so automatically as to be free to really think. Perhaps hoeing should be one of these. For a short time it is. Then the body interferes with the mind. The back begins to ache. You become physically preoccupied. You become tired. And then the mind, instead of being able to concentrate upon something consecutively, indulges either in fatuous daydreams or nurses petty grievances or dwells upon the worst traits of one's least pleasant friends. At such times I have often been appalled at my mind and wondered if others could have such rotten ones. And if a Great Idea does descend, well, I stop working to take it in, and rest on my hoe, and look across the land (as a matter of fact I don't: I carefully gaze on the ground in case anyone is looking – for he who gazes towards the earth presents a less agriculturally reprehensible spectacle than he who looks towards heaven).

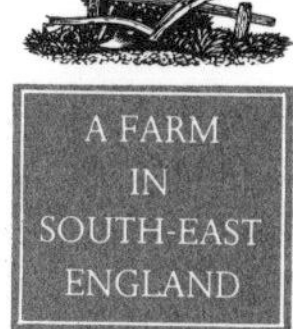

There is another fallacy, closely related. People say to me – 'It must be wonderful to feel perfectly fit, working on the land as you do.' I am fit enough, I suppose; but there is a misapprehension here. The best way to feel really fit is through games. A good game of tennis for two hours or a run for half an hour will give you a better feeling of physical well-being than a whole day's agricultural labour (with about three exceptions concerning the latter). In the former case you perspire and feel fine – and the mind often then moves with remarkable freedom. In agriculture you seldom perspire; you merely keep on keeping on, and at the end of the day do not feel amiably tired but somewhat exhausted – and the mind sticks fast. Neither hoeing nor other agricultural work is really conducive towards the formation of what is called 'a good figure'. Arnold Bennett went so far as to say that veteran countrymen resembled 'starved bus-conductors twisted out of shape by lightning'. (Did he mean *train-drivers?*) Still,

I think they match their surroundings better that way than if they stood up with the straightness of a soldier.

He who seeks happiness can find it in two ways. He can find it when the mind is absorbed and the body pleasantly active. This happens during certain games and during one or two agricultural activities. This pleasure is very great. He can find it also when the mind is absorbed and the body forgotten. This happens when reading a great book: on such occasions we as good as leave our bodies and go a journey without them. Few if any pleasures excel this. And the secret is that in both cases the ego is disposed of – quite forgotten. Conscious or not, that is the goal of everyone, to forget his ego, and to subdue the ego's two servile and obsequious slaves – the restless body and the wandering, lunatic mind.

Such are one or two of my reflections recollected in tranquillity after hoeing. But I would

not like it to be thought that I have any grouse against hoeing, against any job that has to be done. I was not seeking pleasure. And I got a good deal of satisfaction from a disciplinarian point of view. Self-discipline is splendid. I am all for it. But I cannot apply it without external pressure. It was now applied for me. I was forced to do what I could not force myself to do. And this was one of the things I wanted to do, which I neded to do if ever I were to understand and know the world instead of only 'knowing about' it.

10

MY DIFFICULTIES AS CARTER

The carter or horseman (the former term being the most usual but not so satisfactory) had to leave, and I took on the job. I was not wholly unfamiliar with horses from a riding point of view – and at one period could even jump without stirrups or reins and with a sword in my hand. All forgotten – along with horselore. And of cart-horses and harness I knew nothing whatever.

It was now a welcome change to start the morning rounding up the horses that grazed in the field adjoining the old house, and to bring them into the oast-house which served as the lower stable, where I groomed and harnessed them. One was easy to catch and hard to work with – Prince. The other was hard to catch and easy to work with – Beauty, a mare. Any moral? I found, however, that provided I brought out oats I could get hold of Beauty by her excellent forelock all right. It was no good simply going up with a bridle held behind the back, she was too wary. I never tried it that way, but always took a tray of oats which she always fell for, and then I could catch that substantial forelock and lead her into the stable easily enough with Prince following at her heels like a lamb. They were great friends, these horses, grazing together cheek beside cheek, nose by nose, mouth by mouth as they ate the grass – a sight so affecting that I couldn't bear to think of the day when one would be taken and the other left.

Incidentally, this method of catching Beauty was considered too elaborate. When others went to fetch her they only fell back on the bag of oats trick as a last resort, or did it one time and not the next. I remember reading how a man, having occasionally brought out oats to a difficult horse, and then only pretending to do so for several days on end, was suddenly kicked and killed, my sympathies being with the horse. Arthur was not good at catching Beauty. His blustering methods didn't work and the mare gave him a clean pair of heels. One day when I wasn't

using the horses Arthur had to fetch in Beauty for some purpose. As usual he went out, holding the bridle behind his back, and consequently couldn't get hold of her at all. As I happened to be in that direction I said I would get her, which I did (by a lucky stroke really, for I didn't take out any oats). Whereat he thanked me. This made me smile on the right side of my face for I was secretly both amused and gratified at the resourceful, efficient, always-right Arthur actually thanking *me* for doing something that he couldn't do himself.

He seemed to think that horses have horse sense. It is the custom to give your horse food while you harness and groom it. But Arthur on this occasion just chucked the harness on and gave her nothing – in order 'to teach the sod a lesson'. This seemed to me an inadequate psychological approach to a horse who can read little about crime and punishment, and in any case didn't learn the lesson.

When I came to deal with harnessing for the first time I was surprised at the weight of the harness. I found that the breeching and attendant straps were as heavy as a saddle. When I tried putting the collar on I found I had put the bridle on first. Having taken off the bridle, the collar still wouldn't go on – for the simple reason that you must *reverse* it while negotiating the head, which I had not done, thus following the example of Wordsworth who also failed in this matter. I was no more successful with the hames; I got them the wrong way round, and when at last I got them the right way round, I failed to pin them under the collar in a sufficiently tight notch. This done, I was now ready to put the horse into the cart. But I was not prepared for the difficulty of backing it straight between the shafts, nor for the weight of the cart when lifted up by one of the shafts, nor for the difficulties now confronting me in continuing the good work. For, having thrown over the long chain that rests on the breeching, and dodged under the

horse's neck to catch it on the other side, I missed it and it rolled back so that I had to throw it over again, all the time holding up the shaft with one hand while I went to the other side. And after this came the fixing of the remaining chains, all of which I put into the wrong notches.

I hadn't realized that so 'simple' a matter as harnessing a horse and putting it in a cart entailed so many moves. I found that the same held true regarding what must seem to the man on the road to be the elementary performance of going through a gate. Yet it is quite remarkably more easy to gatecrash than to make a smooth passage. The thing must be done skilfully if you don't want to knock into one of the posts. On the whole I wasn't too much a post-knocker, but this was due to the absence of many gates. There was something else more difficult than a gate. The track from the house-end of the farm went down an incline and up another. At the bottom

was a stream with a bridge over it. This bridge was narrow, breaking down, and with huge ruts near the edges. When it rained the mud was very thick on this clayey soil, and going over the bridge with a heavy load was extremely precarious. One wheel always fell into the rut at the very edge of the fenceless bridge, and in pulling the cart across the horse would generally lurch and slip. This bridge was in direct view of the house, and the boss often watched this part of my journey with some anxiety – lest we fall over and the horse be injured, he explained.

My next difficulty was the negotiation of sacks. The horseman has a great deal to do with sacks. All sorts of sacks, varying from half a hundredweight to two hundredweight, the potatoes or corn or artificial, must be continuously loaded up and carted somewhere. The loading of sacks is an easy job for two if done in the right way (hand linked with hand behind the sack), but not so simple for one. No use hauling the bag about in one's arms – you must get it on the back

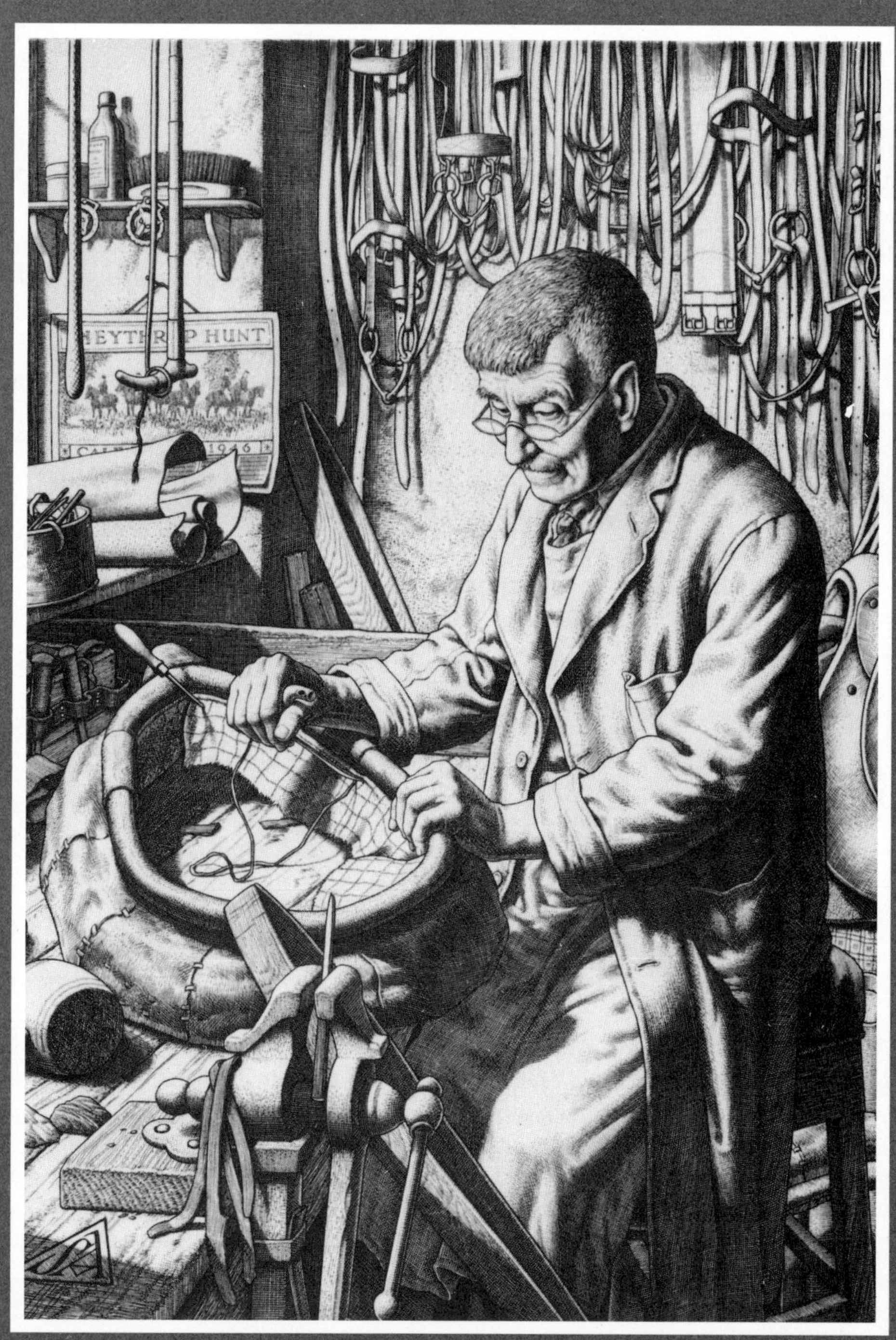
HUNT
1946

and high on the back. Once in that position the weight doesn't matter much. This is all right when you are taking them from the top layer of a well-built pile; but how about those on the ground? How about the stragglers, the sacks of superphosphate which when moved generally break and pour out the stuff? It was a job to elevate them . . . I was glad to learn that a loaded cart seen going quietly along has to be loaded first.

I never really became a good sack-lifter by myself. Beware of the phrase – 'It is all a question of knack.' It isn't. A certain kind of brute strength is just as much part of it, and although I am reasonably strong I was often surprised at the strength of others. One more thing about sacks, and I've done – namely unloading. I'll never forget how once I had to cart ten loads of potatoes from one end of the farm to the other and unload them in the barn in readiness for collection by a merchant. Believe it or not I just took the sacks out of the cart and *dumped them.* I was in a hurry, for the merchant was supposed to be arriving at a stated time, but it was ignorance of the first principle in all such operations – tidiness. It is as easy to unload and place the sacks in neat layers as to dump them in an unregulated heap, or nearly as easy, and much more satisfactory. But I didn't do so. '*Must* you put them down like that?' asked Morgan, when he saw them later. Until he said that, I hadn't noticed what the uncorrelated heap looked like. But he was so mild about it, though annoyed, that it made an impression on me never forgotten.

11

NEW VISION OF THE FIELD

Often, then, my day now started with getting a horse harnessed into a cart and then jogging across the farm to load up something. The morning young, the sun slanting, mist clinging to the ground, the bird in the tree, hope in the heart – the eternal, million-times repeated promise of the dawn. While jogging along at such times I often reflected upon some of the strange phrases in common use, so lightly spoke, so obsequiously swallowed by the multitude. We speak of the *cost of living*, without discomfort. It means that we must pay *money* to be alive, a definite fee for being in the world, with a heavy Entrance Fee. Everyone must *make a living* rather than make a Life. What is he going to *be*? it is asked of boys, for it is understood that it is not sufficient that he shall be *himself* – only a girl is permitted to say that she already *is*. I was not making a living at all well by jogging along here, but I could not help feeling Alive, the freedom of the fields, the freedom of the sky, the freedom of movement gratuitously bestowed upon me – far more

substantial than if I had been given the Freedom of the City of Birmingham, or had had pressed into my hands huge Atlantic Charters and other paper monuments to the perfidy of Man.

I had only been working on the land a question of weeks, but one morning as I went past the potato field I realized with what fresh eyes I now could see a field, this field. It was no longer just a bit of earth the beauty of which I perceived from the outside. I saw it a hundred times more clearly, it was a hundred times more real. For I had sown it with potash and superphosphate, I had walked up and down it endlessly, I had counted the minutes nearer the midday meal, I had tried to plough it, I had put down potatoes in the furrows. Already I was no longer an onlooker, a spectator, excluded as if by excommunication from its factual and actual existence. I no longer hung in the void, but had entered in at the door of labour and become part of the world's work in its humblest and yet proudest place.

12

HARROWING

I soon began to use harrows. Formerly, when I had walked across the farm I had continually come across strange-looking instruments at odd corners. Useless things thrown away, they seemed, old rusty chains and spikes with grass growing over them. They reminded me, somehow, of those awful crocodile-teeth traps that used to lie concealed in woods against poachers in the nineteenth century. But I found that these creatures were by no means dead. They were harrows – that is horse- or tractor-drawn rakes for breaking up the soil. There were the three main kinds here: the chain harrow or drudge, the spiked harrow or drag, and the spring tines harrow. Thus now I would go up to one of these rusty abandoned instruments, connect it with the horse-traces and bring it to life. A surprising transformation.

'Only a man harrowing clods . . .' Like many others I had read and loved that famous poem by Thomas Hardy called 'In Time of "The Breaking of Nations"'. To me just a picture in the mind, no knowledge of what harrowing entailed. Now actualized and made an absolute reality for me – my own job. And does the poem gain thereby? Mr Adrian Bell tells us that he had only been harrowing for a very short time before he began to find fault with the poem. *Only* a ploughman harrowing; that seemed to him all wrong (that deadly realm of 'only') while *half asleep as they stalk* seemed absurd. I find it difficult ever to say anything against Hardy (except with regard to *Tess*), but though the message of the poem perhaps requires that 'only', there seems to me now

no excuse for the 'half asleep'. From the road a number of agricultural jobs look remarkably quiet, serene, slow, and easy; but if you stand beside the man in question you may find that he is putting out all his strength, is moving quite fast, and is in anything but a serene state of mind. So with harrowing. I didn't find anything sleepy or serene about it. Not only is it impossible to walk with ease behind the harrow, since you are stumbling the whole time over the clods, but you can't *see* your work properly. You try to go straight across the field exactly beside your previous line, but you cannot see it without close inspection, and even when you do see it the horse is always standing you away from it, and in checking this you come back too much. Consequently you have the uncomfortable feeling most of the time that either you are going over ground already done or are missing out considerable areas. In short, it is exasperating. Certainly not something you can do half-asleep.

However, at first it did not matter to me in the least whether it was exasperating or not. Each thing I did was a new experience, equally interesting to me whether it turned out exciting or dull. And harrowing, above all, gave me great satisfaction. There is a special pleasure in doing something that brings one into line with all ages. While using this instrument I might just as well have been a contemporary of Virgil.

Nor is the profit small the peasant makes
Who smooths with harrows, or who pounds with rakes,
The crumbling clods; nor Ceres from on high
Regards his labour with a grudging eye;
Nor his, who ploughs across the furrowed grounds,
And on the back of earth inflicts new wounds,
For he, with frequent exercise, commands
The unwilling soil, and tames the stubborn lands.

Above, I have been thinking of harrowing the open fields. On this farm I also did a good deal, in fact a lot of harrowing and cultivating between fruit trees – using the horse-hoe (that is several reversed hoes or hoes attached to a tray), the spring tines, the chain harrow, and the leverage cultivator. With this last you can lever the instrument in such a way as to plough into the earth at the very foot of the trees without the horse being stopped by the outspreading branches. This was harder work than using the others, much strength being required to keep it in position; but since skill was also called for, it was most interesting.

The difficulty with the chain harrow was that in endeavouring to get it as near as possible to the foot of the trees as you went up and down the aisles, the pole of the harrow often caught on them if you were not careful, and barked the barks. This was highly reprehensible. A hideous gash was presented, clearly seen by the inspecting eye. On more than one occasion, having thus gashed a bark, I gathered some grass and then built it round the scar, thus hiding it!

I generally used two horses for this kind of harrowing – one in front of the other. There was often little enough space to turn them at the ends, but I managed somehow and was proud of the achievement. But on one occasion, when far away in a corner field, one of the horses backed on to the tines, the other became excited, and then both began to pull and kick. They stepped back over the traces which, together with the reins, became an involved mess.

The horses stopped their stamping. They became quite still. They might have been statues.

They were simply unable to move. The reins had got into such an extraordinary arrangement that, taut to breaking-point, they were held in opposite directions so that neither horse could move its head. The bit in Prince's mouth was pressing with an extremity of tightness against the rubbered lower lip. They made no sound – for the most striking thing about horses is their almost total dumbness.

It was a job to extract them. Not performed without some of the harness breaking. I was tying the several parts together with string when Morgan appeared. 'I'm afraid you haven't got a knack with horses, Collis,' was his comment. A beginner, I reflected, should not make an outstanding mistake or have an emphatic mishap; for the mistakes he has *not* made, and the mishaps he has *not* had, will make no impression, while the emphatic error will loom hideously over his head.

13

ABSENT-MINDEDNESS

The field that I most enjoyed dealing with was the potato field. First I harrowed away the lines and knocked the soil into small pieces; and when the potato-stems rose above ground, thus re-establishing the lines, I horse-hoed between them. A great deal of attention was given to potatoes on this farm – far more than I have seen anywhere else. Often enough, after a few hoeings, nothing more is done until late in the season when they are earthed up. Much more trouble was taken here. I did much horse-hoeing and a considerable amount of preliminary earthing up – the term used here was 'shinning'. For this I used the plough that turns a furrow on each side of it – ploughing the earth exactly as a ship ploughs the main. This was a grand job and I never tired of it, nor did it tire me since it made me sweat. It was not ploughing proper, but a close relation to it; and with the plough-handles to grasp and to guide, and the two horses, and a field to myself in a corner of old England, I felt the freedom of having extricated myself from the fetters of modern civilization – a civilization which, for the literary man, is a good working definition of hell.

Various land girls came and went on this farm. One of them was sent to assist me. She had been working with Mrs Miles and had been worn down by the effort to keep up with her. So she was given a change, and led my leading horse. She confessed that she was 'mad about poetry'. This was very cheering; for as we progress it becomes more common to meet a person

who writes bad books than who reads good ones. So we talked poetry, and I told her how I always hoped that in the course of my ploughing I would come upon a mouse, and thus be able to join with Burns who in November 1785 turned up the mouse that became immortal:

I'm truly sorry man's dominion
Has broken Nature's social union,
And justifies the ill opinion
  Which makes thee startle
At me, thy poor earth-born companion
  An' fellow mortal.

Before leaving the farm, my friend expressed the hope that I would meet my mouse. But I didn't.

During some conversation with her she said – 'You're so absent-minded they say.' I was surprised at this. The last thing I had ever allowed myself to acknowledge was anything in the nature of the 'absent-minded professor'. Later, I faced the matter and thought it out. Evidently I had been the subject of laughing commentary at the tea-table. Was it true after all? Come to think of it, it was true! In ordinary life I had always forgotten things and mislaid them to an astonishing extent. Carelessness shows up badly on a farm. I used to drop things. I would load so many sacks on the cart, and on arriving at the other end would find that two had simply dropped off. Looking round for them I would see, a long way off, a lump on the track! Or I would hang a coat on the hames, and again, at journey's end, would miss it. I had forgotten all about it and had quite failed to realize that nothing stands jerking about unless it is tightly tied on. But the worst instance of forgetting things was when one day, after the midday meal, I went right across to a field which I had to harrow – *without my horse*. This was recounted to me by the girl, who added that when I realized that I hadn't got the horse, I was seen running back madly. Now, no agricultural labourer is ever seen to run – except after rabbits at harvest. The spectacle of me (*a*) minus the horse and (*b*) running back to get it, had provided a sufficiently comic picture to raise a considerable degree of mirth.

I had another habit – one which particularly distressed the boss. When I went from one portion of the farm to another sitting upon the cart, I let the horse go its own pace and did not urge and hurry it on. This gave the impression of absent-minded lolling. Actually, my mind was present to a certain extent while I looked round and took the scene in. But you never know what may make a bad impression. One of the things that makes a bad impression, incidentally, is turning up late in the morning. I mean just a little late – you incur the odium of the other workmen, even more than of the boss. They can't stand anyone turning up late if they themselves are punctual. I was fairly punctual during all the time that I worked anywhere on the land, though I was always a good distance from the meeting place. At this farm I had a twenty-minute walk before reaching the upper part where we assembled. I shall never forget the Norwegian News (preceding 7 a.m.), the clock, as it were, against which I fought to get ready and be gone! But at one period, owing to an unfortunate remark made by Morgan about it not mattering if I got to the stable before 7.15 as the horses would be eating, I turned up at that time regularly. During this period Arthur Miles always seemed in a black, enraged mood towards me, I

ROWLAND HIL

BRIAN COOK — '40

couldn't make out why. It was not for a long time that I realized that it was due to my arriving at 7.15. He just couldn't bear it.

But to get back to my method of driving the horse and cart, I am not sure that Arthur's method had really anything more to recommend it. He was a great urger-on of horses. Yet his technique struck me as curious. As he drove Beauty along (a lazy mare) he would swear at her ceaselessly . . . 'What the hell are you doing? All right *go* into the ditch, I don't care, it's you that'll have to take the blank cart out not me, come on you blank sod or I'll be blank well blanked', and so on. These solicitations may have sounded as sweet nothings in the ear of Beauty for all I know (and certainly his tone was wholly lacking in either malice or cruelty), and it is fair to say that the mare responded to a perceptible degree. And it made a good show, suggesting the zeal and urgency that appeals enormously to any boss.

Sometimes a whole morning was spent in carting something to the station, and I fear it was wrong of me to have found this a delightful break. It took a good long time to get there, and one was paid just the same as for hard work. Human nature being what it is, the agricultural labourer loves earning easy money when occasion offers, such as going along to a station on a cart or when rain sends him indoors to a cushy job; while, human nature being what it is, the employer is intensely irritated by the same – for few employers give themselves psychological ease of mind by looking at the thing in the lump and regarding their wage payment as so much a year, instead of seeing it in pieces and feeling when a man is doing such and such a thing, '*it's not worth the money*'.

There was a pub along the road to the station, and on one occasion I stopped and had a drink. It struck me afterwards that this would have been regarded as incredibly reprehensible had it been known. I say it struck me afterwards for I was not acclimatized to my new milieu. The freedom of the more favoured professions, doctor, lawyer, writer, B.B.C. man, etc., is scarcely realized by their members: the weekly wage-earner who sells so many hours of his time is *owned* during those hours. Somehow I didn't get this clearly into my head at first. But before I was finished with the agricultural world as a labourer, I was keenly aware of a tense atmosphere if I stopped work for a few minutes to hold a conversation or even to pat my dog.

14

INDIGNATION OF MRS MILES

As carter, it was often my job to collect sacks of apples and centralize them. One day I was engaged in collecting a number of earlies from a certain portion of the apple orchards where Mrs Miles was working with a number of land girls and temporary assistants. The sacks were not always properly filled. Feeling full of beans that morning, I said to Mrs Miles in a jolly kind of way, and with what I imagined was an obvious acknowledgement of her as the overseer of the company – 'Mrs Miles, would you see that they fill up the sacks properly.' I had hardly finished the sentence when she flew into a rage. 'I don't take no orders from nobody!' she shouted very, very loudly. 'I'm not taking no orders from you, I only take orders from the boss,' she screamed seven times, as if I had said something mortally insulting to her. This silenced me properly, and I did not even attempt to start replies beginning with 'I only said . . .' knowing that it would be useless, and I went on my way without rejoicing. While she, I was later informed, continued to rail against me during the entire afternoon. In future I steered clear of any possible repetition of such behaviour, handling her with the respect one pays to a time-bomb which may explode at any minute.

All the same, she had one more shot at me, as it were, at a later date. I was engaged with a bill-hook on a hedge near a field where hoeing was in progress. Some friends of the boss, or rather neighbouring gentry, had come out to do 'a spot of work' for the afternoon – a pretty girl and a somewhat la-di-da young man. After about half an hour of hoeing they began to weary of well-doing, and resting on their hoes looked round the farm. Catching sight of me, a short distance away, I heard one of them ask idly – 'Who is that?' Mrs Miles, being present, answered, in

even louder tones than usual so as to make sure that I could hear – *'Oh that's nobody. He's only a workman here.'*

I could not help wishing that Mrs Miles could realize how completely she had failed to offend me. There is a certain type of intellectual, of which I am one, who suspects that his observations on life lack something vital, feeling uncertain as to the validity of reflections that owe nothing to experience of everyday work. So with me. Hence I had eagerly grasped at the opportunity of entering the manual working world. A man may do this and still feel an outsider and not accepted as a proper worker by the others. Thus it was with a real sense of satisfaction that I heard the tribute of Mrs Miles, and I was sorry that the irony of this was lost on her.

But it was easy to say the wrong thing to Mrs Miles. A young lady of the neighbourhood came in and worked quite regularly in the afternoons, knocking off at about four. Being a

middle-class girl of pre-war days she was brought up to be permanently out of work (though not receiving any dole). She came along now and hoed with Mrs Miles, going home at four. The afternoons always seem long and she was glad to knock off then. Being a very amiable person, I heard her say once to Mrs Miles when she was about to leave – 'I'm so sorry you have to go on till five-thirty, Mrs Miles.' This was, of course, a fearful psychological mistake, *'I don't mind!* said Mrs Miles in tones which combined intense indignation at the presumed commiseration, with amused contempt.

Anyway she was certainly a wonderful worker, worth her weight in gold to any employer – she belonged to the old-time type of woman who has always worked on the land, putting in an amount of work seldom witnessed nowadays. She had also another contribution which endeared her to the boss. She had an observant eye, and if anything seemed to have been

pinched, say some plums, she would report the same. The boss had carried the technique of 'being in hurry' almost as far as it would go; but, curiously, he forgot his urgency and would stand quite still and pleasantly absorbed if 'the tale' was being told, or if someone had a complaint to make about someone else.

15

THE JUDES THE OBSCURE

Most of the ends and sayings, saws and clichés, have their origin in agriculture, and it amused me to find them coming to life. Ploughing a lonely furrow. Putting your back into it. Doing the spade-work. Putting the cart before the horse. Separating the chaff from the wheat, the sheep from the goats. Spilling the beans. Stepping over the traces. Nipped in the bud. Getting the lie of the land. Having a harrowing experience. Barking up the wrong tree. Jogging along. A mere drudge.

The last-named is really another term for the chain harrow, which I often used on the grass between the fruit trees. The verb which rhymes with it so well, trudge, was certainly born on the land, and fitly describes the job of harrowing. After the interest of novelty had worn off I never took kindly to harrowing, it was too much of a trudge, too drawn out a clod-stumbling amble. The horse gave me the impression of hating it – though I may be wrong. It struck me forcibly, and to my surprise, that here was the job of jobs for a machine, a tractor. I think violent exercise suits me better than steady work, and on these harrowing occasions a certain weariness sometimes overtook me, and going home I often murmured to myself Gray's lines 'the weary ploughman homeward plods his way', wondering how exactly the line went, was it as above or 'the ploughman homeward plods his weary way'? but never having the energy to look it up.

On cheerless days I sometimes fell into a low mood and wondered what on earth I was doing there, and began to feel that by doing it I was not pulling my full weight for myself. Such moods gave me insight into the Judes the Obscure of the world. Of all the fundamentally necessary professions, the pursuit of agriculture is the most manly and the most worthwhile – about this there can hardly be two opinions. But it is not the job for Young Ambition, nor for a person potentially gifted at something else, nor for the very intellectually inclined. Luckily most people are not ambitious in a big way, nor specially gifted. Yet there are the Judes. One day when I was covering-over by harrow a freshly sown field, I recalled how in the old days the job of keeping the birds off was done by boys rattling a clacker for sixpence a day, and I remembered how

Hardy's Jude, in the hour of his greatest obscurity, standing in the ploughed field, clacker in hand, looked round and murmured – 'How ugly it is here!' It is a fine piece of realism. That field must indeed have seemed hateful in the eye of the small beholder, a torment of desolation, the veritable image of the awful monster that devours children – boredom. He must, he would escape it! He did. Thus in fiction. Not in life. I fell into conversation with a neighbouring labourer, a man exceptionally skilled with a team of horses that he could make follow him while he walked in front. I expected this man to say that he enjoyed his work and to sing the praises of horses versus machines. But no, he hated the life. He had been started on it very young, he told me. 'I didn't like it then,' he said, 'and I don't like it now.' He could have been a musician or singer. He played and sang in the village church and sometimes in the pub. But his talents had not been pronounced enough to allow him to make good his escape. The Judes of real life, the truly obscure Judes, are found at the end as at the beginning, in the field, by the side of the hill, not having achieved the exalted calamity of tragic failure.

16

A VIEW OF LITERARY PRODUCTION

The most exhilarating sight I saw this May, or for that matter during any May anywhere, was a big beanfield in bloom. It was a lovely sight for it was a superb crop, but perhaps I should write *smell*. I was ignorant that the bean-flower had such a magnificent scent. We sing the rose, we sing the honeysuckle; but a whiff from such a beanfield carries us further.

This field belonged to a neighbouring farm, and there was a right of way through it to the station. The farmer was an extremely friendly man and I often had a meal with him and his kind and generous wife. I do not know what he was like as an employer, but he was very human, and he resembled in person and ways my preconceived idea of the old-time farmer. He groused of course, and he 'made no money'; but he was not in a state of nervous tension; he was not in a hurry; he liked to stop and chat; a land girl who walked through his premises in a two-piece bathing-dress set him up for a week; and he enjoyed going to the Hippodrome on a Saturday.

One evening there was some talk of books and I happened to mention the existence of certain novelists who produced two books a year, regularly. I spoke as one shocked at this. He also was shocked, but for the opposite reason. 'Is that *all*?' he kept repeating. 'Surely with all that imagination they could turn out more than that!' This broadened my mind a bit. Life

is incredibly departmentalized, and we deceive ourselves if we think that others outside our department see us in the smallest degree as we see ourselves. The above remark of the farmer gave me the angle from which literary production is seen by many agriculturalists, no doubt. A farmer accustomed to produce vast quantities of corn, eggs, milk, roots, and bacon, which at given periods is all sold, eaten, and never seen again, assumes that literature is produced in similar perishable quantities, and that the author will turn out, say, ten books a month.

I said that I appreciated his point of view. The more so, I added, since there are far too many writers who accept the food that appears on the table without a conception of the skill, the ardours, and the devotion that makes its appearance possible. This was well received. But I could not help wondering what he would have thought if I had told him how Oscar Wilde, on being asked what he had done on a certain day, had replied – 'I spent the morning putting in a comma, and the afternoon in taking it out again.' We must hold that Wilde, in displaying such devotion over punctuation (it takes a great man to handle the comma: see Cobbett at one extreme, Shaw at the other, and Macaulay in the middle) thereby advanced the cause of Culture. But if I had spent the morning in putting down one seed-potato and the afternoon in taking it up again, it could scarcely be claimed that I had thereby advanced the cause of Agriculture. I went away that evening reflecting sadly upon the magnitude of the gulf that in this matter separated me from the farmer. I could understand his art, he could not understand mine, nor have a glimmering of what T.E. Lawrence meant by saying that he would rather write a great sentence than win a battle, nor appreciate why Churchill declared after an illness that though he was now strong enough to fight the Germans he was still too weak to paint a picture.

17

THE FARM IN LATE MAY

When I came to the farm there was little to see in the way of colour save various shades of wood and grass. How it had changed near the end of May! The old story – that which was brown turning green, that which was black seen as white: an old story, differing from all other tales, from all art, from all tricks, in that though repeated every year, it still surprises us, still calls for applause and praise.

The Grenadiers were just coming out, the Beauty of Bath in blossom, the Coxes in blossom – then over the hedge another field with James Grieves and Worcesters in blossom, while the

trees which had submitted to the grafting were budding on those branches. The dark hedges had become green. The corn was steadily rising. In a four-acre field into which were crowded black-currants, plums, gooseberries, blackberries, strawberries, and tomatoes, the bushes that began to change their appearance first were the black-currants. For some weeks in the midst of a general greyness their parallel green rows shone out with arresting distinctness. But at length the plum trees were in full bloom, and when I took the leverage cultivator up and down between the rows, the white petals fell upon the back of the perspiring horse and stuck there – a most decorative sight. Later, I spent some hours rescuing the miserable strawberry plants from under thistles and docks. Never did a poorer-looking plant produce so ostentatious a fruit as the strawberry. It looks well on a plate, but on the ground it looks absurd – the cultivated one, not the wild strawberry. The huge fruit, far too heavy for its frail stem, lies helpless

on the soil, and it is necessary to put straw under the berry to keep it from rotting – hence *strawberry*, I suppose.

Thus this field, which when the owner took it over eight years previously was barren, now was bursting with life. As I passed alongside of it on the cart, getting a good view of it as a whole, I often thought of the *latent power* that lay there till released and channelled by man. Nothing to see on that former dry and barren field, save tangled yellowish grass: yet holding within it the force to throw upward what I now beheld. A farmer is a liberator of the energy in the earth, ceaselessly creating what is good, and adding on a vast scale to the beauty of the world.

The boss here had built up all these orchards from scratch, and had battled successfully in the end through the lean years. It was a truly creative achievement. The struggle had left its mark upon him. Melancholy by nature, he was now, I think, inclined to detest the world. I did not

hear him say anything good of it or anyone in it. But he was obviously a man who held, or thought he held, ideas. He could be affable, if not courteous. Having had a bit of education, he rather enjoyed sometimes making me feel small in front of others over practical matters; but I could hardly blame him for that, and I marvelled at his patience with me during these green days of mine.

18

SCENE ON THE MEADOW

June is generally the great hay-making month. But as this was not a mixed farm, and it was only under the pressure of war that arable was being extended, our hay-making did not amount to much. In fact, there was only one field to cut. As Prince was often extremely difficult to manage with any unaccustomed instrument behind him, Morgan and Arthur Miles took over the horses with the idea of getting things going before I carried on. This turned out just as well. For Prince refused to move. He just would not pull the machine. 'I'll make the b move all right!' shouted Arthur, and laid on to his hindquarters with a stick. This did not make the slightest impression on the horse. 'You'll get what's coming to you, you sod!' bellowed Arthur again, this time attacking from the side. But the horse only stepped back on to the machine. Then Arthur, thundering at Morgan to get on to the seat and use the reins, made a frontal attack on Prince, striking his head and nose, until some blood began to trickle from the nostrils. Yet it had no effect, and I looked on at this quiet rural scene in the nice June morning with some interest, wondering who would win the battle of will-power. Of course the man did, and eventually the horse moved forward, and after a certain amount of preliminary unsteady going, he went quietly and I was ready to take over without mishap.

It was a rather miserable meadow, so I cannot pretend that I got much of a kick out of this new experience. Indeed the whole thing was hardly hay-making proper. Nor did we rick it. We carried it into the barn – one portion of the old oast-house.

During the loading-up I heard Arthur expand on the subject of modern wages and prices. 'The higher wages don't make no difference,' he said. 'We're worse off today, I reckon. Take baccy: twopence an ounce in the old days – now eightpence. Take boots: a fine pair for six shillings before – look at the price now. Take a suit: nice suit for twenty-five shillings in the old days. Now you can't get nothing for that.'

ROWLAND HILDER

And so on through a list. To which Morgan replied – 'Yes, but consider the laws and regulations these days. The wages are constant. A boss can't stand his men off. In the old days there was a well-paid foreman to keep the others down. On a wet day he would say to a man, "You can go home, *and play with the cat*". Or take piece-work. Think of the rates there. It depended upon the boss. I knew a man who used to say to a hedger, "Let me see now, perhaps I can manage a halfpenny per five yards", and then would add, "I dunno. *It's too much for a halfpenny, and too little for three-farthings*".'

I have since often heard variations on Arthur's reckoning on wages as good or better in the old days. It is quite a favourite theme amongst the older men. But I have never been able to swallow it. It is often downright contrariness – one might almost say it is nonsense. And if taken up on it, many are inclined to agree that it is nonsense – for though the agricultural labourer

tends to be a very pig-headed person with regard to views and practices, he is incredibly inconsistent in his thought and argument, often unsaying what he has just said in the most surprising way. This point is that though prices are so different today they are *not* commensurate with the rise in wages. And though in the old days labourers received a great deal of pay in kind, there was no definiteness about it, no absolute constancy, it depended upon the place (with regard to wood, for instance), and upon the boss, who always had you to that extent in his pocket. Finally, if you discount both the above considerations, the present wage puts the labourer into a far more dignified position than when he received a question of shillings as opposed to the pounds received by town workers. It is a psychological point of some importance. Not that I have any axe to grind on this or any other agricultural matter, and I should add that Mr Fred Kitchin, the author of that great book *Brother To The Ox*, opens his memoirs by saying that in his youth

'seventeen shillings went as far as two pounds in these days'. Also I have seen some formidable statistics on this subject produced by Mr H. J. Massingham which tell against my view.

But I am quite certain that if any of the present-day labourers were given the sudden option of going back to the old days, they would change their tune in a flash. I would be interested to meet the piece-working hedger who would like to go back to the boss who thought that while five yards' worth of work was too much for a halfpenny, it was 'too little for three-farthings', or to meet any labourer who would consider the old days as rose-coloured under foremen who could at any moment stand you off and say 'go home and play with the cat'.

19

WHILE THINNING, PICKING, PRUNING

The farmer who deals in corn can leave the situation in the hands of Nature for some months before harvest. The farmer who deals in fruit has to *thin out* his crop before it gets ripe and full. This was an eye-opener to me. When, for instance, the plum trees had become heavily weighted with rows of already large plums, it became necessary to do away with a large number of them. That is to say, you picked and threw down what seemed to be about two-thirds of the trees' fruit. It felt like appalling wastefulness, and went much against the grain to do it. Here was a branch hanging with dozens of excellent plums, all about the same size: and it was your business to snip away all that were closer together than two inches. Those remaining would grow, it appeared, into such fine plums that they would equalize the quantity of fruit that had been thrown away. Perhaps this was true; but it was impossible to believe it at this stage, and while engaged on the job, one felt – everyone new at it felt – a scandalous waster of nature's abundance. Yet custom stales. And I remember how a voluntary helper – a girl from the university – once became so doped and dazed by the work that I saw her thin *every plum* off one branch. An agonizing sight.

This thinning was a lengthy proceeding and went on for some weeks. To get it done at all many helpers were needed – another difficulty confronting the fruit-grower. For temporary labour is neither the easiest to get hold of, nor the most satisfactory. However, the boss was fairly strong on land girls. He was able to get some university students who came just for the thinning and the picking. Also he had one Land Army girl for milking (but there was only one cow) and other jobs; while he also employed another girl who was the daughter of a farmer,

and who in liveliness, guts and knowledge of literature was worth all the university students put together. She was strong but not hefty. In fact her figure left so little to be desired that she turned out in a two-piece bathing-dress, thus creating more sensation than the place could carry.

The university girls sometimes created a problem for Morgan. Not being afraid of getting the sack, they did not always keep the work going with that earnestness which is proper to agricultural proceedings. There were a number of pools on this farm surrounded by trees – very tempting places for a swim. One afternoon during working hours the girls decided to jump into one of these pools. Leaving their clothes on the bank, they began to enjoy a swim. Soon Morgan became aware of their disappearance, and at length, approaching the pond, spotted their clothes and then the swimmers. They were delighted. But he did not seem to appreciate the sylvan poetry and classic simplicity of the scene. Should he remove their clothes? he asked himself indignantly. It was clear that if he removed their clothes to a distance, or out of sight altogether, it would advance the cause of discipline. But would it advance the cause of morals? And was a diversion of this sort agriculturally advisable at this busy time? Being a very discreet man, he thought better of it – greatly to the disappointment of the multitude, amongst whom I must number Mrs Miles as well as myself.

If extra workers were needed for thinning the fruit, a great many more were necessary for the final operation of harvesting it in August. Seeing them all – perennial, professional fruit-pickers – I wondered how the owner could possibly make a profit after he had paid them all. This department of agriculture calls for a farmer of stout heart. He who deals with arable land can count upon a certain degree of harvest in the worst of seasons. He sows his seed and according to his skill in husbandry he will reap his reward. Luck, sheer luck may elevate or destroy the fruit-grower. The beauty of Spring, the whole parade of bloom and blossom, can change overnight into the whiteness of the flowers of frost. The spectacle of promise and bounty turns into a picture of blasted hope. This sometimes happens three years in succession. He can do nothing about it – no tarpaulin being large enough to spread over his farm at night.

First came the black-currant harvest. Enter crowds of women from round about, some of them pushing prams. They went at it hard all day, being paid so much a pound. They belonged to a very low-class stratum – a depressing crew, pale-faced, unhealthy-looking, truculent, their minds bent simply and solely upon l.s.d.; seeing nothing else in the fruit, absolutely nothing but so much l.s.d. There seemed no progress here from the similar kind of scene that Jack London used to write about in years gone by. However picturesque this sort of thing can be made to appear by a painter, the thing itself is pitiful, so charged with the harshness, not of life which all round is smiling and warm and beautiful with abundant increase, but of man's life, of man's narrowing down of life till there is nothing before his eyes but a few pieces of silver – which he can only get into his hands by doing work from which he robs all the enjoyment.

It was not a good black-currant crop this year, and the more truculent women demanded more money per pound since they couldn't pick the poor crop fast enough to make the turnover they expected. Since the boss was going to make less, he must pay them more – a good example, I thought, of the fraternal link between employer and employee in our democracy.

These outside fruit-pickers were all the more conspicuous since they were accompanied in their work by other strata of society. There were Arthur and Mrs Miles lording it after their

fashion. There was the boss at the receipt of custom, and Morgan filling up the van. There were the various girls in bathing attire contrasting forcibly with the heavily clothed pickers who, of course, regarded such dress as scandalous, since Nature herself is not seen by them, the human body when seen is a sore. And there were several other people who came in from round about to give a hand, including two who looked in for an hour, symbol of carefree leisure. All spoke, all behaved according to upbringing and chance in life. Marx was not wholly right. Everything is not caused by environment. But it is more than a half-truth. It is a three-quarter truth. And the more I see of people the more I see that they are for the most part what circumstances have made them, and the less I feel inclined to scoff or condemn, however little I seem to gild. Certainly this spectacle here was a neatly framed object lesson in the inequality of life. Also, I may add, a lesson in the equality of man – under the law of battle. At not infrequent intervals we all assembled in the ditch. For while we assisted at these old tasks upon the earth, a singular job was being performed in the sky by others. History was going on up there. England had again been challenged by the Hun, and her answer was being made above our heads. We witnessed an air battle twice daily. We enormously enjoyed the show. When the fall of metal became dangerous it was our *duty* to seek the ditch. These diversions considerably lightened our humble toil.

When the pickers had reached the plum harvest, my job was to prune the black-currant bushes. This means cutting away all the branches that had borne fruit, leaving the fresh shoots that had already grown up. For this purpose I used a long pincer-like shears with which I could reach down and cut right on the stool. As I went along I often came upon currants that had been left over by the pickers, a certain number of which I brought home every day, during which time I was freer, more completely free, from constipation, pardon my mentioning it, than I have been in the course of my life.

It was a lengthy but stimulating job. I made huge piles of the discarded branches, leaving behind the already renewed bushes which should repeat the work of the others next year. I find such well-known physical facts to be metaphysically most exhilarating. The ordinary is rather more extraordinary than the extraordinary just as the material is rather more immaterial than the immaterial, and it is surely the mark of an inferior mind to be moved to wonder by the exception instead of the rule. The rule beats the exception at its own game. It is not the rabbit out of the hat but the rabbit out of the rabbit that is so surprising. No phrase such as 'Nature's fecundity' is able to dismiss it. I confess it still stirs me at intervals, this the most conspicuous of all phenomena, the recurrent increase, the everlasting something out of nothing. Contrary to what one might expect. Granted, it is not quite something out of nothing: I'm surrounded by plums, apples, currants, hard and concrete substances miraculously appearing, but they are made out of earth, they are made out of air, they are the earth, they are the air – granted, but the circle is continued eternally, the washing is always taken in all round, yet no bankruptcy, no waste. The mind, made rotten by political economy, expects otherwise, fears waste. I still feel nervous when I throw away a piece of bread. But in Nature nothing can be lost, nothing wasted, nothing thrown away, there is no such thing as rubbish. It might be good for us if we threw things away a bit more, so that we might grasp that they cannot be destroyed – this, the first of the miracles of God.

As a matter of fact I see there is a tendency in some quarters to take this uneconomic and

metaphysical view of the matter. There is the famous case of the coffee growers in Brazil who in 1938 threw away six hundred thousand bags of coffee every month. That's the spirit.

About this time, several tons of Shoddy were delivered and deposited on the track beside the fruit trees. Previously shoddy had been merely an adjective as far as I was concerned. I had heard of shoddy goods or a shoddy person. I was interested to come upon the noun. It consisted of huge bundles of woolly material. It was the gleanings from cloth factories, fibres that had been thrown away, rubbish from the industrial angle. We proceeded to spread the stuff out, covering the ground between the trees with it as a species of manure. It was pleasant to see this 'rubbish' thus enter into a new mode of activity, and in obedience to the rule of eternal return, dedicate its action to the cause of Agriculture.

20

THRESHING SCENE

The small corn harvest was gathered simultaneously with the fruit, and as I did not take part in this to any complete extent, I shall say nothing about that operation in this place. But in early September I took part in my first threshing experience.

Since there was only one rick to do, it was not very elaborate. The old-time affair was used – the hired thresher with steam engine. We got going by about eight o'clock – and a few extra men came from outside to give a hand. The owner of the engine, having set the thing going, walked round looking on with a somewhat superior air. Indeed I was surprised to see how nearly he conformed to Hardy's description in *Tess* of the owner of the tackle who came to the farm that employed Tess. It was none of his business to lend a hand or in any way to take part in proceedings once he had started his engine. Occasionally he went to one of the bags and took a sample of the grain in hand and looked at it knowingly, then moved round rubbing the forefinger and thumb of his right hand in a thoughtful manner in order to cancel his absence of thought. It was clear that for him also 'the long strap which ran from the driving wheel of his engine to the red thresher under the rick was the sole tie-line between agriculture and him'.

There was no elevator and my place was at the shaft where the straw came out from the thresher, my job being to serve it to the rick-makers, Morgan and Arthur Miles. Quite enough of it came out to keep me engaged, and quite enough shreds went down my neck and back, since I had not grasped the necessity of a tightly buttoned shirt for this affair. There was no let-up for

hours, and owing to the prickling discomfort I began to feel it as an endurance test, for as the rick grew my handing up became increasingly harder; but I had no intention of giving any hint of fatigue, and in any case always rather enjoy that kind of thing. But I was quite blind to the scene as a whole, seeing nothing in fact but my own ever-falling straw.

In the interval for a morning meal, Mrs Miles, feeling the need for self-expansion, shouted (as usual as if against a high wind) – 'How do you like this *wurk*, Mr Collis, this is *wurk*,' etc., rather embarrassing everyone else as well as myself, I thought.

Before we knocked off, the remainder of the rick had to be covered with an old tarpaulin which we dragged out of the stable close-by. We unfolded it gradually, and as we did so more than one nest of mice came to light, mice large and small and tiny. They began to try and scuttle away, the baby ones running round helplessly. Arthur grabbed at them with his enormous

hands, catching two or three at a time. He squeezed them to death and stuck them in his waistcoat pocket. He disposed of a large number of them in this manner. He took a mouse, squeezed it between his forefinger and mighty thumb, stuck it in his pocket, then grabbed another, squeezed it and likewise stuck it into his coat or waistcoat until he was bulging with mice. At first I couldn't imagine the object of this collection. It turned out that they were for his cat at home. On returning he would call the cat to him and steadily produce mice from his person. Not so much for love of the cat, I gathered, as in order to encourage further research in this direction.

Before finishing for the day I made a typical beginner's *faux pas*. I left a prong lying on the ground. Arthur nearly stepped on it. And did he swear! Certainly he had every cause to do so. Failing to stick a prong upright and leaving it on the ground, is the sort of crazy thing beginners do, being blind to the extreme danger of such a thing.

21

WHILE POTATO-LIFTING

Time marched on. Each day seemed long, each week short. It was already autumn. What is the salient characteristic of autumn? The spiders' threads in the early morning frost. I am not thinking so much of the circular networks, marvellous as these are, hung along the gate; but rather the threads that are strung across everything, so that if you bend down till your eye is level with the field you can see a white veil over the whole expanse. They are everywhere, on everything. 'Do they drape the cannons in France?' asked Mr Ralph Wightman, true poet, in a striking image, the other day. To look down at these things is like looking up at the stars – we are baffled by quantity.

The time had come for potato-lifting. I was particularly interested in the potato field. I had been on it from the start, manuring, planting, harrowing, hoeing, shinning. At intervals I had examined the growth of the potatoes, minutely, from the appearance of the shoots that look like white worms coming out of the original potato, till down under, that one thing had produced many things, and sent up whole bushes which then flowered very prettily indeed in August – a lovely sight, strangely unsung. By which time the original potato, the cause of it all, having rendered up its virtue, had become a squashy bag of pulp.

A great deal of agriculture is simply common sense modified by experience. Thus, even if I assumed ignorance in the reader about potato-lifting, I know that without my help he could say in advance almost exactly what is done: first, the potatoes ploughed out; then the pickers with buckets each go up a row filling sacks already spread out at given distances along the lines; while at the same time a horse and a cart or tractor and cart take the filled sacks away. That is how one would imagine it is done: and that is how it is done. We did one thing here though, which I never did anywhere else since. The soil was very damp and the potatoes were clung with clay. Before we bagged them we went up the rows with a specially designed hand-fork which we used to dig the potatoes out of their clay covering, leaving them in heaps to dry.

This potato harvest calls for really dry weather. And one seldom gets it. We got plenty of rain. It was very clayey soil. Clay is not always called clay in the agricultural world; it is often called sand. A sandy soil means earth that is not very thick and cloggy. Clayey soil means thick stuff, with much mud in winter. It was the latter here. The mud was terrific. It clung to one like glue. I soon qualified not only as a clod-hopper but also as a clod-lifter. With such a soil potato-

lifting in rain provides considerable discomfort. It was so extreme in sheer wetness, slipperiness and muddiness that I enjoyed it.

Some extra hands came along for this job, also, casual labour sent out from the local labour exchange (foul official words all, 'hands', 'casual', 'labour exchange', containing the maximum of dehumanization). One was an actor. I worked beside him as we went up our respective parallel rows. There is nothing like conversation for making this kind of job go well. We talked about all sorts of things. We got on to psychologists for some reason. 'I hate their style and their outlook,' I said. 'I hate their motives,' he said. We soon turned to the theatre. 'What is the point in T. S. Eliot's *Murder in the Cathedral?*' I asked. 'Is it that egotism is always the real reason for our actions?' 'I believe the point is,' said he, 'that men do the right things for the wrong reasons.' At this point unfortunately our respective lines came to an end, and circumstances were such that we would not work together up two fresh rows, and so we parted. His name was Stanley Messenger, and I hope he is still posted somewhere in this world.

When he had gone I reflected upon how companionship depends upon what we have in our heads and not on what we have in our pockets. If one of us had been very rich and the other very poor it would have made no difference. The gulf between people is not one of money, it is one of mind. If I am working with a man who has nothing in his mind, with whom one can exchange no idea, no knowledge, no opinion, no witticism, then there is a real cleft between us far greater than anything that could be caused by class or money. All very obvious, perhaps. But I mention it because I continually have day-dreams of a time when lots of people would come out into the fields and love working with their hands, and also love working with the mind, their manly heritage, and make such jobs as these go quickly and delightfully. It will be a sad criticism of life if we have to say that such a dream is futile. Anyway I wouldn't ask much more than this of my Utopia – easier to come by, more worth coming by, than the honey-sweet Nowheres of the pseudo-poets.

HEDGING AND DITCHING

After this I took on a new job for the rest of the winter. There was much hedging and ditching to be done, and it was delegated to me. This opened up another field of labour for me. Hitherto, hedging and ditching were merely terms residing in the top floor of my head.

Now I could take them down and look at them. The hedges on a farm, or anywhere else, do not stay quietly dividing the fields. If left to themselves too long they invade the fields. During the agricultural slump nearly all the hedges on farms became neglected and out of hand. I have seen farms where shoots from hedges were advancing out into the fields in columns of fours. We are accustomed nowadays to statistics such as 'if everyone saved one lump of coal per day, this means a national saving of twenty thousand tons a year' or 'one old kettle given to salvage by every housewife means a squadron of Spitfires' or some such nonsense (if it is nonsense). In the same way the number of acres lost through neglected hedging might amuse a statistician's mind.

Whatever the national loss by such neglect, it is clear that hedges on any given farm soon get out of hand, growing far too high, straggling all over the place, and clogging the ditches. It is the job of the hedger to cut them down to about the height of his waist, to foster growth

where there are holes, to 'lay' them where they are too thin, and to clear the ditches beside them.

After due instruction I approached the hedges of this farm with the necessary implements – a bill-hook, a hook, and a slasher. I soon made an impression on them. No job has more to show for it. I would come to a great straggling growth with an accompanying ditch quite concealed under grass and hedge shoots, and presently I would have reduced a number of yards of it so that it was unrecognizable. A complete transformation of the scene. The whole character of the place changed, and beside the hedge, a neat ditch. As I went on at this, week after week, I felt I was making my mark on the farm. Especially at one place where a field sloped down to a river-bed. The hedge at the bottom came out several yards into the field, and my progress was almost like changing the landscape.

Incidentally, that river-bed was an eerie place. There was a sort of little glen running along at the bottom of two converging slopes. Indeed, except for its smallness it was a perfectly genuine glen, with trees and steep rocky clefts, at the bottom of which was a river-bed. But one thing was outrageously lacking. There was no river. During most of the year one could walk along the smooth, cliffed waterway. It was like going along a road where no traffic ever passed, where no man trod – a ghostly place, a haunted, silent, deadly lane.

At this job I was paid by the rod – that is, I did it as piece-work. I found that if I kept at it I was able to make about the same as being paid by the week in the ordinary way. But this was because Morgan gave me a generous cash measurement, not exactly on a par with the 'too little for three-farthings' man.

Doing work by the piece opened my eyes to the difference between Space and Time.

Philosophers are pleased to inform us that we live in a Space-Time Continuum and that both are the same thing. I do not question it. But I am free to say that in the agricultural world they are mighty opposites. When you are working by the hour, time drags. When you are working by the space, time flies. Doing piece-work you want to cover so much ground, so much space – and so time moves fast. If you have no Space to conquer but only Time – then time stands still.

Apart from this, hedging is certainly not a monotonous job, because each hedge is different and there is so much to show for the work. But even so one can have enough of a good thing, and not for worlds would I take on a roadman's life. I began to weary of hedges after I had done only a few; but to see nothing but hedges all your life, to hang perpetually on the periphery of agriculture, never in it, hedged off from it, and do the same thing every day, must be the devil of a business, especially in winter. I shall never again dash along the roads in a motor car without knowing just why the ditches and banks are so trim and neat.

There was plenty of firewood to be got out of these hedges, which came in very useful, for every week I could empty a cartful at my house, the boss not having the least objection to my doing so. The well from which I drew water was some distance from the house, a journey through two fields and over two fences. So I became 'a hewer of wood and a drawer of water'. That popular phrase, with the adjective 'mere' in front of it, suggests that here is the bottom rung in the ladder of life. Well, it may be. But if so, I cannot say that I want to climb the ladder much. I have no objection to these simplicities.

Still, I could have done with a bit of coal. But it was too much 'out in the wilds' for a delivery. So I had to cut down some trees also in order to get through the winter. Luckily the fire-

place was so big that I could put in long logs and thus save much cutting up. When they were too long to fit, I let them come out into the room. When I was behindhand in my cutting I sometimes sawed them in the fireplace in the evening while the fire was going. There were some very cold spells, and I became more than a hewer of wood, I became a hewer of water. I often didn't go to the well, and when the rain-water froze in the tub I had to axe it . . . However, space forbids further trivialities of this kind, for I am eager to get on to Part Two of this book, and offer the reader a change of scene.

PART 2

A FARM IN SOUTH-WEST ENGLAND

1

FIRST DAY

On the evening before the day I was due at the farm – the time being March 1942 – I unfortunately took something that disagreed with me, and felt ill at intervals throughout the night and no better at six o'clock the next morning. But feeling that I should stick to the engagement, I got up and cycled down (a twenty minutes' ride) to the farm, arriving punctually at seven.

I found no one in the farmyard. But soon the boss's son, a boy of fifteen, came out of the dairy and told me that I would find his father at the other dairy where there had been some mishap that morning. This meant a ride to a far portion of the farm, which was about a thousand acres. Very welcome, indeed a godsend, this ride, for in my present state I knew I would be actually sick if I did any work. So I took my time and in due course arrived at this other dairy where I found the boss. He instructed me to go and help the carter who was getting a load of hay from a certain rick. I didn't follow the geography of the instructions, but I gathered that it was necessary to go back the way I had come and then pass further on. But when I reached the farmyard again, I decided quite definitely to fail to find the carter, still feeling certain of sickness if I bent my body about in the slightest degree – which would be a maddening way of starting work at this new place.

So I went into the barn and sat down. It was a large barn, full of sacks of all sorts and for all purposes, some on the floor, some filled with artificial and others with corn. I saw more than one grain-grinder, and there was an engine with an extremely high funnel. One of the grinders had a good traditional air about it, for imprinted on it were the words – 'Patronized by Her Gracious Majesty the Queen, the late Prince Consort, and His Serene Highness the Viceroy of Egypt'. I sat down on one of the sacks, feeling very low, wondering what on earth I was doing here. I gazed round at the sacks, at the engine, at His Serene Highness, and out through the door into the paddock in the middle of which was a pool of water, to the left the stable, and straight ahead to a long shed in which were two wagons, a tractor, a drill, a binder, and some miscellanea. It was cold and raw, a drizzle coming down from the unbroken grey.

Here I remained for nearly an hour. Though not an inspiring hour, it saved my situation, for I was recovering and no longer felt that movement would undo me. So when the boss arrived and I had explained that I had missed the carter, I was ready for a job. There was a wagon

waiting to go out and I was told to get a load of hay. Did I know how to use a hay knife? I was asked, and had to reply in the negative – an annoying start. I joined the boy whom I had met earlier and we went along up a track, past several large fields, and across a down till we reached the hay-rick. We did not use the hay knife but took the hay from the top. My experience had been solely with a cart and I had never loaded a wagon, and I was surprised at the amount of stuff that one could put on to it. And when it came to fastening a rope round it I did not go about the fixing of it in the right way, and it was accomplished deftly by the boy who seemed very amiable. We brought the load down then and deposited it in the dairy.

The afternoon was spent in getting more loads and putting them in the stable-loft. This time I had a new companion, a young man called Dick, about twenty. He was very pleasant and friendly – an opinion I was never to change. We used the hay knife this time, an instrument

which I found needed a greater physical effort than any other I am familiar with. One of these days they will introduce a hay knife like a bread knife with teeth, let us hope. A haystack is simply a huge loaf for feeding cattle, and is cut just as one cuts an ordinary loaf, in slices. Not hacked away in bits and pieces. A half-cut stack should present a nice perpendicular wall on the cut side – then the rain won't hurt it.

Dick said that he had found hay very difficult at first, and still didn't like dealing with it (I have yet to find the labourer who finds it easy). He didn't make the slightest attempt now or at any other time to show off or to show me how to do a thing, or get a rise out of me, or put me right. That was his nature. It was also due to the fact that he did not like agricultural work and took no pride in it. He had been forced into agriculture – as so many cases – simply for the convenience of his parents. There were many other jobs he would have preferred, perhaps an

BRIAN C

engineering one of some sort. In the reaction caused today by the insolence, the folly, and the greed of many townsmen, there is a tendency for writers on country themes to assume that the countryman alone is splendid, the townsman a poor specimen. This view can be overdone. A man may loathe agriculture, have no love for the earth and no reverence for it, and yet be a superior human being to an ordinary countryman. In the same way it is superficial to suppose that the man who has dealings with animals, with sheep or cows or horses, is thereby more human or humanized than the man dealing solely with machines. The latter may be and often is more fully a human being than the former, who may be and often is most inhuman, callous, violent, and cruel.

2

UNROMANTIC VIEW OF AGRICULTURE

I continued on this sort of job for some days, either loading and unloading hay or spreading straw for the heifers. But my companion now was not Dick. It was the carter. He was a small man with a peculiar kind of stumping walk as if his legs were in some degree mechanical. His lower lip either hung down or closed over his upper lip. His tiny pale blue eyes glinted out from a red face. He spoke no word. He said neither good morning nor good evening. He answered no questions. He never said where we were going nor what we were about to do. I found this trying, as I did not then know that he was nearly as uncommunicative with everyone else. I thought that he harboured a special detestation for myself. And as a matter of fact, he did. But I did not realize to what extent this was true till one day when we were hitching a horse to a wagon and I was being slow with the chains on my side, he dashed round, fuming and hissing in a remarkable manner, snatched the chains out of my hand, connected them himself, and said that he would rather work by himself than with a blank like me. Again, we were fetching harrows one day from a field. I handed one up to him the wrong way round. He took it and flung it on the ground, muttering – 'I don't know why my old man keeps me!' I never knew when this sort of thing might happen, especially as it was never very clear what we were about to do next, and I am slow in the uptake in practical matters. Thus at any moment he might break out and wonder why his old man kept him (in view of the fact that the old man, i.e. the boss, thought fit to employ me).

Thus these early days were no picnic.

This carter was a man whose bite was worse than his bark. In fact he didn't bark at all, he only bit – suddenly. It was not long before I met the man on this farm whose bark was worse than his bite – the shouter, 'the man with the iron bellows' as Dick called him, the man everyone had to treat with circumspection. This was Robert, the shepherd.

Having loaded up a wagon of hay we went over to a field one day in which the sheep were being folded. Here we deposited it for the benefit of the sheep (I did not previously know that sheep ate hay). My dog was accompanying me as usual, but as we arrived in the field a great shout went up, for the shepherd's dog and mine had collided, and so I heard for the first time this man's famous voice. At the time I didn't know it was famous, and that his shouting at his dog *all* the time, whatever it was doing and wherever he went, was accepted by everyone as a normal and recognized phenomenon. But hearing it for the first time under these circum-

stances, I thought a crisis had occurred. However, this didn't last long, and I was soon standing beside the shepherd who was ready for a quiet chat as he weighed me up.

He was an elderly man. In his youth, he must have been uncommonly handsome. He was still very good-looking, strikingly so; completely rustic, his features, nose, cheekbones, set of eyes were yet at the same time aristocratically fine-shaped. Nor was this a passing fancy of mine; it struck me later whenever I caught him in profile on a rick. His eyes also, a pale-washed blue, were beautiful, except when they flared up in some outburst. And as I have already observed, his voice left nothing to be desired.

We chatted a little. We talked sheep. He said that there was a lack of milk in some of the ewes for no good reason, even when there were twins, and that when a lamb had to be put to a ewe that had lost one of its own lambs it was necessary sometimes to put the skin of the

dead lamb over the former. Trying to figure this out, I went on with the carter to the next item on the agenda which consisted of loading up some straw from a very tight rick. I couldn't get the stuff out easily, but the carter could! He dug his prong in and hauled out absolutely huge bundles – indeed, never before or since have I seen a more skilled or more powerful loader than this man.

I did not always work with him. There were five horses in the stable, and I frequently took out a horse and cart or wagon alone, either to distribute straw on the fields for the heifers, or to fill up from a dunghill and distribute it. It had not occurred to me before that so much work is done on a farm which is merely a question of preserving the *status quo*. Work going ahead which is not in terms of tillage or planting or harvesting, but just keeping things going. Yet of course a dairy farm's work consists chiefly in simply preserving the *status quo*.

April came in very coldly, and remained so for some time with a strong east wind blowing. The peaceless, ceaseless wind – how I hate it! If one were to give feelings to Nature, one would say that when the sun comes out she breaks into a smile, and that when the wind blows she is in a temper. Certainly I always feel the wind as a bad-tempered thing, especially a cold one, and my mind contracts in resisting it, and I can enjoy no pleasant, expansive thoughts when ruffled by its peaceless, ceaseless wave. And during the long afternoons in it on this job I would sometimes fall again into low moods, again wondering whether I had lost my way. 'Thin, thin the pleasant human noises grow, And faint the city gleams . . .' I would long for that city and a clean warm room. I will arise and go now, I would say to myself most unpoetically, and build me a town, far, far away from Nature and all her winds, where everything shall be artificial and where no man shall be comfortless nor cold for evermore!

I have no objection whatever to standing on a dunghill. There is no place where I am more content to stand. But for how long? That's the question. The dunghill today is rightly celebrated by poet, by prophet, and by priest. It is numbered amongst the highest riches of a land. I never feel better employed than when dealing with one. Thus engaged I can qualify for the approval of Sir Albert Howard and the tributes of statesmen, while also providing a perfect subject for a wood-cut. True. But consider the reality. It is 2 p.m. There are three and a half hours to go. There is an icy wind. Also a drizzle. There is no one to talk to, and if anyone does turn up there will be nothing to talk about. Though I am 'close to the earth' the dunghill soon ceased to be anything but an object, heavy and clogging. One wonders 'what is the time?' Alas – only 3.15!

3

'E

A farmer is called by his men either 'the boss' or 'the guvnor' or 'the master' (now out of date), or 'the old man' (regardless of age), or more often simply 'he'. He is never called 'the chief'.

At this farm he was sometimes called 'the boss', often enough 'the old man', generally 'He', or more properly, ''E', and sometimes merely 'the Van'. He used a second-hand butcher's van for getting about the premises and carrying oil and what not from one scene of operation to another. So one would hear – 'Look out, there's the van!' or 'I didn't see no van' when his whereabouts was doubtful. But on the whole he was designated simply as ''E' – ''E's coming!' It is as 'E that I think of him, and as 'E that I shall refer to him.

He was a man somewhere in the fifties. His eyes were impressive in their mildness, but his mouth was large and ugly, partly concealed by a stumpy moustache. You could recognize him a long way off by his walk. He took huge strides, head bent slightly down, like a man measuring a cricket pitch. That walk was very characteristic. There was no dawdling or diddling about with him: he never strolled; he never looked round quietly at the scene; he never took out a pipe nor smoked a cigarette, any more than he would be likely to drink a glass of beer, pat a dog, or say good night, good morning, or thank you. He was on the go the whole time, as if his life depended on it. When he was at all excited, or indeed when giving instructions, he waved his hands about almost like a man catching invisible balls. Though sturdy to a degree, he was obviously a man of nervous temperament.

He came of a farming family for generations back. He had climbed that famous 'farming ladder' by the only way it can be climbed – by ceaseless energy, relentless toil, and knowledge of the job. Starting with nothing, he now ran this large farm with full equipment. Men who rose by their own efforts in farming between 1900 and 1940, and did not fail during the agricultural depression, had to be unusual men. Whatever else 'E was he was not usual, and not small.

Having adopted a certain pace – a terrific pace – he meant to keep it up. He neither would nor could slow down a bit. ''E'll break up one of these days' they would say at intervals. He did not intend to lose a minute if he could help it – for time was money to him as certainly as to any business man. An atmosphere of hurry and almost of crisis prevailed whenever he was around; and he generally was around, for he was his own foreman. He was also one of his own labourers, so to speak, for he joined in anything and everything, no job was beneath him. In this way he got a tremendous amount of work out of his men, as he set the pace, and each person felt that he had his eye on him – and he had.

We assembled in the yard in the morning at 7 a.m. There was no question of a good morning any more than a good evening at the end of the day, nor any degree of cheerfulness. Life was too earnest for that. Orders would be given, and all dispersed in their several directions as quickly as possible out of his sight.

4

FULL-SCALE THRESHING

We did not always disperse in different directions, of course. There were combined operations even at this time of year. Quite a lot of threshing still remained to be done. (I used to imagine that threshing was an after-harvest affair, but bits of it are sometimes still waiting to be done in the following May!)

A corn rick is a bank in which the farmer has lodged about a hundred pounds. He draws the money when he feels inclined. But to get the cash out, as everyone knows, is a rather elaborate affair. I was to learn all about threshing at this farm.

The thresher is a machine which certainly holds the attention. Like a clear thought or a solved riddle, it looks perfectly obvious. And of course every invention is a clear Thought: every hard, concrete thing – chair, table, engine – was once as insubstantial as an idea. The threshing machine is informed with one comprehensive principle, namely to *shake* a series of trays with

holes in them, which are cunningly placed one above the other. And the outfit does shake to such purpose that each sheaf falls into six separate pieces; three kinds of grain – good, less good, and poor – flow out of exits at the rear; straw straggles out of a line of cradles in perpetual bobbing motion at the front; chaff pours out of a hole at the side; and at the bottom there is excreted the remaining bits and pieces from ear and stalk which are grouped under the term cavings. Such is the outline. As for the number of belts, I have never been able to count them without getting muddled. It is sufficient to say that here is a useful machine. Here is the right thing in the right place. Anyone 'against machines' should be invited to look at a thresher until it occurs to him that what he is against is simply the wrong thing in the wrong place. He will find few such things on the land, however many he may find in the town.

Plenty of time was spent in assembling the tackle – 'the menagerie' as they called it. Much

pulling and shoving about. First the thresher itself goes between two ricks – and when at last it is in the right spot it must be exactly level. A tractor (with special wheel for the purpose) is belted to it at the rear, while an elevator for depositing the straw is placed in front, with its own engine at its side.

Nine of us assembled to deal with this process of separation. The carter and Dick stood on it, on its deck, by the side of its hatchway or mouth into which the sheaves were let down, the carter performing that office, while Dick cut the string that held the sheaf together. Robert, the shepherd, stood under the elevator to make a rick with the straw deposited at his feet. 'E and myself got on to the now unthatched corn rick to deal out the sheaves. Harold, normally the tractor-driver, stood at the rear to deal with the sacks for grain placed under the exit pipe-mouths of the thresher. Jimmy, the lorry-driver and mechanic, presently appeared for loading

up. In the centre on the ground was a land girl to sweep up the cavings. That is generally considered too few for the job, since three or even four people are useful on the corn rick, and two or even three are helpful on the straw rick. Nine was all we could muster. A small staff for a farm of this size. The explanation is that the unit of work had greatly increased owing to the war, two hundred extra acres of downland having been ploughed up, while the housing accommodation did not increase in proportion.

The tractor was started up and we got going. My job was to feed 'E, who passed on the sheaves to Dick. This was my first experience of unpacking this tight parcel. I thrust my prong in to take out a sheaf, but nothing came. I couldn't move it. 'Let's have 'em!' said 'E. But at first I found great difficulty in letting him have them. With the beginner's instinct for starting by doing the wrong thing, I tried to take them out in an haphazard kind of manner, and found myself attempting to move the one I was half-standing on. A rick has been built in layers, and unless you unbuild in layers also you are lost, and so I had to improvise a technique for this immediately, and kept improvising techniques all day (as a matter of fact I have still no rule of thumb for this).

It was a windy day, the wind coming against us on the rick, so that the prickly dust flew into our faces, our eyes, and down our necks. By the middle of the afternoon I could hardly see out of either eye, while the stuff that had got down my neck, again owing to faulty buttoning, made me feel as if I were wearing an ascetic's hair-shirt. As the hours passed I occasionally glanced blurringly round to find a continually changing scene. Away to the left a yellow cliff had grown up, the straw stack, with a yellow mound beside it, the cavings; and over there at the other end bulging sacks now existed, filled with grain. And as other things rose, so I sank. At first high above the show, I was steadily sinking as I shovelled away my pedestal. But there was still a lot to be picked out and I couldn't believe I would ever get it all up this day – though it was known that 'E wanted to finish it. Another two hours passed and there was still some to deal with. Everyone by this time had turned chimney-sweep black, while the carter, not having shaved, and standing in the dustiest of all positions, offered an appearance that recalled earlier periods in the world's history. At length we had sunk to the very ground.

Having reduced the rick to its foundation, we stood on its bedding of straw. Under this were a number of rats. A ring was formed and everyone stood armed with a prong or shovel. Every second someone poked up a rat and slashed at it. Rats began to fly in the air like balls, one actually alighting on 'E's hat. Soon about twenty were disposed of. Then a large one escaped behind a horse-rake and ran under the straw rick. This did not ensure its escape. The carter dived down on his hands and knees beside the hole where it had gone, thrust in his arm, and in a second drew forth the rat in his ungloved hand. Waving it in the air by its tail, he smashed it down triumphantly on the horse-rake.

In the course of the next two weeks we finished off the remaining ricks. And we were joined by 'E's two sons, who though officially still at school, did a great deal on the farm. They were twins. In build they were not in the least like their father, being extremely slight and thin. Yet both, even in their teens, could do very nearly a man's work. They worked with the same rush and zeal as their father. One of them, Reggie, was gay spirited, the other, John, was earnest to a degree probably never surpassed. There are cases when farmers' sons are in the same position as boys without literary leanings who are forced to appreciate Shakespeare, thereby

acquiring a distaste for all things cultural. When farmers' sons have no leanings towards agriculture, I can conceive nothing more calculated to put them off it for ever than being forced to do it as soon as they can be of use, and forced to hear nothing but talk about it. However, by the nature of things this is rare. Certainly these boys had a decided liking and aptitude for agriculture and an equal abhorrence of anything cultural. They stayed away from school as much as possible to be on the farm. And that was very sensible. They had the one skill they were interested in, and they knew that miscellaneous knowledge, quickly forgotten, was absolutely useless to them. There was only one thing necessary to teach them to make them finally efficient at their coming profession, and that was not taught at their grammar school – namely manners. Very necessary when the time came to deal with men in their employment. But they had no exams in this, unfortunately. Thus their popularity with the staff was not marked.

Anyway the fact that they now turned up for threshing meant that I changed my position from being on the corn rick to that of Robert's assistant on the straw rick. This was a great improvement. There was much less dust and the job was easier. The golden river of straw flowed up the hill of the elevator and fell at my feet, needing only distribution. And now I rose while others sank. I could get a calm view of the general proceedings, the fat grain-sacks steadily multiplying, the sheaves diminishing, the straw increasing. The vastness of the mystery was so actual before the eye. That field there, sown less than a year ago with only a few sacks of seed: now all this straw coming up, all that grain flowing out. How well the cinema could show this sort of thing on a big fascinating scale, I reflected. It could show in quick succession, first the sowing, then the appearance of the light green shoots, darkening, browning, yellowing: then the carrying and ricking and threshing. To do it properly would no doubt be expensive, but hardly more so than the expense of some elaborate pictures evidently produced by infants.

My place on the straw rick also gave me a clear view of the well-known peculiarity about threshing. As soon as the tractor has been started up and the belts begin moving a curious change takes place in the situation. Up to now the human beings have had the matter well in hand, taking their time, fixing belts, and getting things ready. But as soon as the machines get going the atmosphere is changed. One gets the impression that the thresher is now more important than those who minister to it. It has evidently become alive. The first consideration of a living thing is food. To get food most creatures have to strain after it. Not so the thresher. It needs bread, certainly one rick a day, which is a fair-sized loaf: but all it has to do is to stand there while men feed it. And they mustn't let up for a minute. If the ever-open mouth doesn't get its sheaf in good time such a hollow roar comes up from the depths of the animal that its menials nervously hasten to hand up the food at double-quick time. Seen from the moon, as it were, the spectacle would look disquieting. If, quite ignorant of the existence of any machines, we turned a corner and suddenly came upon such a scene, it would be sufficiently surprising. There is nothing quite like it, this weird monster of man's conceiving, which, hour after hour, does really chew, digest, and pass out the very bread we eat.

5

DRILLING

The next operation in our sequence was the sowing of a hundred-acre field with barley. Hence I became familiar with the drill for the first time – the big Canadian double affair that drops artificial at the same time as grain. Mounted on two wheels, two separate long thin boxes are drawn across the field by a tractor. You open the lid of each box, pouring artificial into one and grain into the other. As the drill moves forward the two things trickle down through pipes to the earth, or rather, right into the soil. Thus you can sow with a drill in a strong wind and yet be sure of an equal distribution of seed throughout the field in parallel lines. Two men are necessary: one to drive the tractor, and the other to stand on the platform of the drill and keep an eye on the supply in the boxes and see that all is falling down according to plan.

Early in the morning we went out with wagon-loads of barley-seed and artificial on to the hundred-acre field. We had our own drill and also a hired one. These drills are nine feet wide; so that two going hard at it can cover plenty of ground in a few days.

We hung about at first in the cold wind, waiting for 'E who had not arrived; for though instructions had been given with regard to the end we were to start from, and which portion to do first, no one was clear about this, and no one would take the responsibility; nor was the extra man in charge of the hired drill fertile in suggestion, simply saying – ''E didn't tell me nothing about it.' No initiative was taken; nor did I ever find it taken even in the simplest matters at any time; it was always – 'Better wait for 'E.' Thus we stood about in the wind for some time.

At length the Van arrived and operations were set in motion at once. Taking it by portions, the two drills went round and round the given portion, stopping as they passed me for refilling with seed and manure – for I was the feeder. The carter stood on the platform of the hired drill, while 'E stood behind Harold, our tractor-driver. Since the circle round which the drills raced was a big one I had time enough to get the corn and the manure poured out into the bucket before they appeared, one closely following the other.

Just before dinner I was told to take a wagon and fill up with a dozen two-hundredweight bags of barley which were on another wagon beside a rick in a further field. This was the first occasion when I had to handle two horses (one in front of the other) drawing a wagon, thus when it came to backing the wagon so as to go neatly alongside the other wagon with the sacks on it, I found it anything but easy. A wagon is not at all like a cart; having four wheels, the first pair being on a swivel, backing becomes an art in itself – for if you do not go back straight you

will go mighty crooked! And if one horse does not behave properly and shies every time an aeroplane overhead fires at a target (our constant accompaniment), things are thus made no easier. Hence, by the time I had got my wagon alongside the other and had loaded up, it was well into dinner-time, and well past it when I was back on the drilling field. Being the sole feeder of the drills I couldn't very well stop for my food, and had to eat it as opportunity arose. We did not stop at five-thirty, and as no one had taken out any tea we did not stop for tea, but went on till seven-thirty. On this particular day – this has often happened with me – I had taken out far too little for dinner. Thus by five-thirty it became a real question of belt-tightening. I reached home by eight-thirty. Then did I enjoy *sitting down*! And did I enjoy my food! Pleasures normally denied me. Two simple and extreme joys missed by millions of men for no better reason than that they can sit down and eat when they like.

The next day the same thing happened during dinner-hour. I had to go right down to the farmyard to load up twenty sacks of artificial. Having arrived there, the question rose, how elevate them? It was simply solved. This farm was not lacking in equipment, and there was a sack-lifter in the barn. It is like a short ladder with one rung. You put it against your wagon, wheel a sack to it (there was also a sack-wheeler, for which many thanks) and let it slip on to that one rung which is on the ground; and then you turn a handle and force the rung upwards and tip your sack into the wagon.

So far so good. It only remained to go back with the load. Unfortunately I did not make a clean exit. I knocked down a gate-post. The reason for this was simple: in leading the front horse round out of the yard I walked on the right-hand side of the horse instead of the left, which is a mistake as elementary as walking too close to a horse – for which there is often

excruciating punishment from the hoof. I thought it advisable to make a general confession of this on my arrival on the field. 'E took it well, as he always took all such things. Harold thought it a great joke, saying that the carter would have to stand up there all night instead of the post. And even the carter himself only said – 'Christ!'

On we went again, my expedition having cost me the whole dinner-hour. I continued getting the buckets full with seed and artificial. In a current number of the *Farmers' Weekly*, artificial had been called 'little pills of comfort'. I quoted this to 'E who handed it on as a great joke – for he was far from being a surly man when things were going well.

As the circle grew smaller and smaller the tractors came round sooner and sooner. I did not now have to feed them each time, but all the same I was not always ready for them. Though much of the equipment had cost over four hundred pounds per item, there had been economy over buckets. They were too small for the job, it was the devil filling from a full sack. Also, the I.C.I. sacks were tied in a peculiar way and could only be opened in a trick manner – which sometimes failed and caused ill-spared delay. Rain loomed ahead and the pace was quickened.

From the road, I have no doubt, our scene looked leisurely and quiet. How different the reality, I reflected, now that I was in it. Everything in a hurry. Anxiety, hustle, nervous tension – anything but the serene rural atmosphere we hear of in books: more in the nature of a battle which by inadvertence may at any moment be lost. And from the field, how far away seemed the outside world that passed by on the road! We did not belong to it, and it knew nothing of us, cared nothing. Yet all its ways and all its tramping depended upon us; by us upheld in its trance and dream; by us made insolent and by us given power. I had come from that outside world, and many a time reflected here upon what now seemed the slack and sloping ease of city people whom I knew. But on this day, while here on this field anyway, I felt no desire to join them. Rather did I feel that I had escaped from the company of dream-walkers into the company of people who were awake and putting out all their strength, without which effort things can never be kept going. Here in the middle of this big field I at last began to feel really inside the agricultural world, part of it, one with it, and was well content to let the distant prancing devil's dance of nonsense, farce and folly fare without me.

The drills began to close in now, my patch becoming smaller at every round, until at last I was driven off it, and had to take up my position in a portion already sown, so that myself and my gear would not get in the way of the vehicles. Once when I had left a sack in the line of an approaching non-stop tractor, the carter leapt from the platform, rushed ahead, threw back the sack, and leapt on again – all for the benefit of his old man who could see the exhibition from close behind. At length the job was finished late in the evening of the third day, and we withdrew, leaving Nature now to get on with it.

6

SHEEP

While putting a sack of cake into the shepherd's hut – which resembled a bathing-box on wheels – I looked round inside. In certain respects it suggested a cloakroom. A line of lambskin coats hung from pegs. Wondering who wore these coats, I remembered how the shepherd had told me that he used them for disguising lambs who couldn't milk from their own mothers. Thus, if a ewe lost a lamb and another ewe wasn't giving milk, he put the latter's lamb to the ewe that had lost hers – first dressing it up in the dead lamb's skin. I wish I could have had an opportunity to watch this impersonation of a lamb in lamb's clothing.

My own liking for sheep is limited. As a flock they may fairly be said to be more pitiful than human beings. Their deplorable lack of self-possession and confidence, their perpetual hurrying and scurrying, their weak faces, their ceaseless maa-ing and baa-ing make one feel somehow they have got lost in evolution and are in a frightful state of anxiety about it.

Yet it is no wonder they feel bewildered and lost. Like so many creatures, they are now half created by Nature and half by man. The result is that they are now dependent upon us for everything – while we, of course, have to wait upon them hand and foot as we do on cows, the sheep-waiters being called shepherds and the cow-waiters being called cow-men. They have now so little control over their bodies that a slight hollow in the ground may make them fall over while grazing, and if they do fall over they cannot get up, and often die in twenty minutes. And we may be sure that it is not due to Nature but to us that they become the prey of worms.

There is very little that is romantic about sheep, though for some reason they enter both literature and painting in an idyllic manner not bestowed to an equal extent upon other stock, while it will be some time before the shepherd loses his poetic place. The 'milkmaid', now called a Land Army girl, is ceasing to make any strong appeal to the muse; but the shepherd is still conceived of a haze, for few people know what he actually does. They would be surprised if they knew how heavy a single hurdle is, and that a shepherd needs to be a particularly strong man since he has to move them continually, and carries from two to four at once (I know one who could carry eight). And he is seldom seen searching for a dear lost sheep and rejoicing over it when found more than over the ninety-nine others that did not go astray; he is more often discovered searching their bodies for maggots and finding plenty, whole rings of them worming their way through the wool, through the skin, through the flesh into the very bones – an

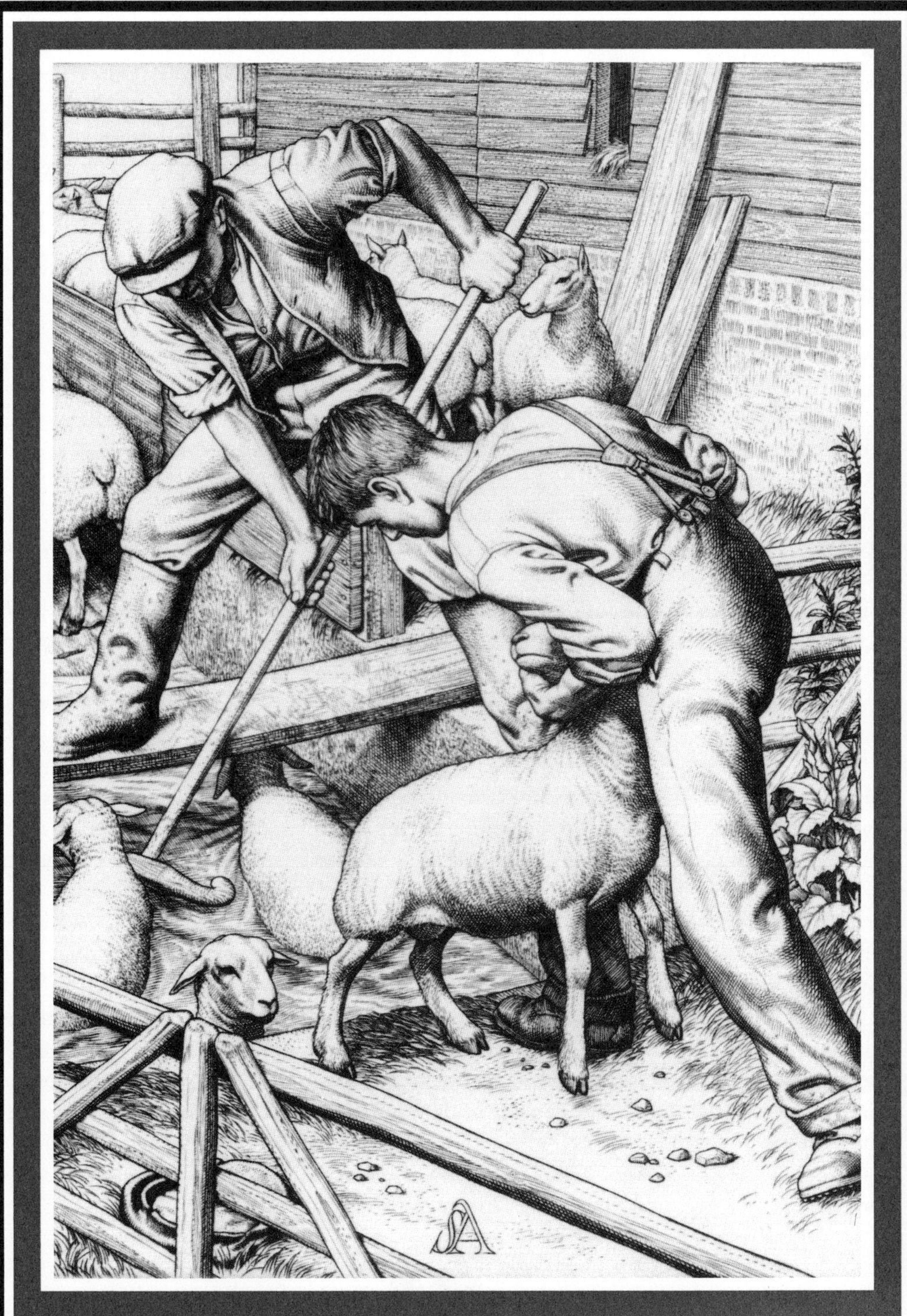

invasion which, if unchecked, will lead to hideous sores, huge patches of desolated flesh and red clefts in which are clearly seen the reeking ribs.

I write with some feeling about this, for though I had nothing to do with sheep at this farm, it is proper to mention here that I have since had occasion to lend a hand with them in the administration of pills, and also at dipping. It was a question of giving a hundred sheep four pills each (or rather four to the ewes and two to the lambs) against worms. Actually I failed to give a single pill to a single ewe by myself. It was all I could do to sit one up on its haunches, let alone open its mouth. We had them penned in a short space, so it was not difficult to catch hold of the lambs. But it was a game getting a several-hundredweight ewe into a sitting posture, and in my efforts to do so I frequently assumed that position myself, covered with the slobbering saliva of the sheep beside me whose agitated countenance betrayed ill-concealed dislike. The dipping was dirtier but slightly more easy. After penning up the flock beside the dip, it was only a question of catching hold of the sheep, lifting them over the step, and lowering them in. Several of the ewes were so bulky that I failed to lift them up the necessary distance. The splashings and general excitement relieved their bowels, and soon the floor became very slippery and their wool discoloured. What with that and the splashes from the yellow fluid, it was a job calling for very old clothes and a bath afterwards. All the same, contact with sheep, my mate assured me, is good for the health. He said that breathing sheep odour is the healthiest odour, and cures anyone in a low state. His wife's father was thus cured, and he went down again when he left sheep. His brother had to go to hospital after dealing with cows, then went to sheep and became strikingly well . . . So it seems doctors should not say – Go to the Riviera, but simply Go to sheep.

I allude to these operations since they served to clarify my mind with regard to sheep, and to take them out of the haze of half-perception. It was no doubt theoretically possible for Mary to have kept that small lamb; and when she went places it could possibly have accompanied her. But I wish we could have been told more about that phenomenal child's dealings with the lamb, for it seems to me now that her choice in pets must have been attended with grave disadvantages. Not that I question her existence. In 1938 my wife and I were in Germany, and had been journeying for a long time without meeting anyone or coming to any village: but at last we came upon a lonely house by the wayside. There was no sign of life anywhere. Then we saw, sitting on the steps and leaning against the closed front door of the house, a little girl about Mary's age as we imagine it. Beside her, with its head on her lap, was a sheep. It should have been a lamb, but it was an adult, quiet, unbleating sheep with an exceedingly amiable countenance. It gazed up towards Monica, and Monica gazed down towards it with her arms round its neck – a most peaceful, unhistoric scene. I say Monica, for my wife took a photograph of this companionship, and the girl gave her name as Monica and the sheep's name as Hans. She accepted a piece of chocolate; and as I left Monica and Hans, much appreciating their ideological position in the Third Reich, a deep voice, proceeding, it seemed from Hans, said – '*Danke schön, auf wiedersehen.*'

7

THE MACHINE-MILKER

My contact with stock here was confined to spreading straw for the heifers and dumping hay in the shed beside one of the dairies, which adjoined the pig run. Pigs are very attractive animals. When a body of them are all together, all snorting and making a general row, and you suddenly appear, silence will immediately fall on the assembly. Indeed, the attention is so encouraging that I have sometimes been tempted to emulate St Francis and preach them a sermon. Next to their intelligence I would place their cleanliness: they don't mind a bit of mud and appear even to eat it, but they are very clean in essentials. As for the sows – there we come upon great personalities, though often rather supercilious in countenance. The only thing about swine is that they scream when being hurt. We don't like this, so we call it squealing.

My journeys sometimes took me past the poultry. Took me past is right, for I don't stop to look at hens. 'The cold, greedy, completely egoistic eye of the hen,' as Ralph Wightman puts it, is enough to make anyone turn aside – not to mention that smell which suffocates the heart. Nor does the nosiness, the sniffing inquisitiveness of heifers appeal to me. Lie down for half an hour or leave a bicycle in a field with heifers at the far end, and sure enough in a short time the whole lot will come nosing round, and when driven off will presently come again exactly as if you were a magnet. Whereas cows will often regard you with indifference. There were some excellent cows in the dairies here, and there are few animals more comforting to stand beside than a sleek well-fed cow – or more mysterious and baffling. As for their cash value, I was surprised to learn that a really good one can fetch a thousand pounds. The truculent urban motorist who hoots his way through cows on the road would change his tune if he knew their money measure. It now amuses me to think how his jaundiced eye would moisten with greed if he found a thousand-pound cow blocking the path of his car (itself likely to fetch about thirty pounds). Probably he would raise his hat to it.

Both the dairies here were run on the basis of machine-milking. One was an ordinary cow-shed converted, the other a modern building constructed precisely for the purpose of machine-milking. These strawless, woodless, regimented stalls have a sad unhomeliness about them. To look at them when empty does really chill the heart. Nor is it possible to warm up when the work is in progress, and amidst the loud noise of the engine, you witness the red rubber fingers, the milk-pipes, and the truly mechanical nature of the proceedings.

Of course this way is no more illegitimate than the other. Cows were never made originally to be milked by hand, or to be milked by man at all. All that milk was not required. We have

created it. We have put those big bags of milk on the cow. Originally a cow, presumably, had about as much milk as a mare, and the teats were violently jerked by the calf. The hand is obviously an unnatural appliance here and, curiously enough, the machine appliance gets nearer to the original jerking of the calf's mouth – a machine, the ugliest of all, actually getting closer to nature! Of course this is a mere accident, a fluke, which is balanced by the heartlessness of the whole thing. Not necessarily heartless perhaps, for at bottom everything depends upon our attitude of mind; but it promotes the tendency to treat animals as if they were machines. 'I always tell my students,' said Professor McGregor to Mr Rolf Gardiner before an approving audience, 'treat a cow exactly as you would treat a tractor.'

As to whether the new method is better or worse than the old from a utilitarian point of view, I express no opinion. But if I go into a hall to hear a subject of this kind discussed by the knowledgeable, I know exactly what to expect. Two schools of thought will be advanced, each

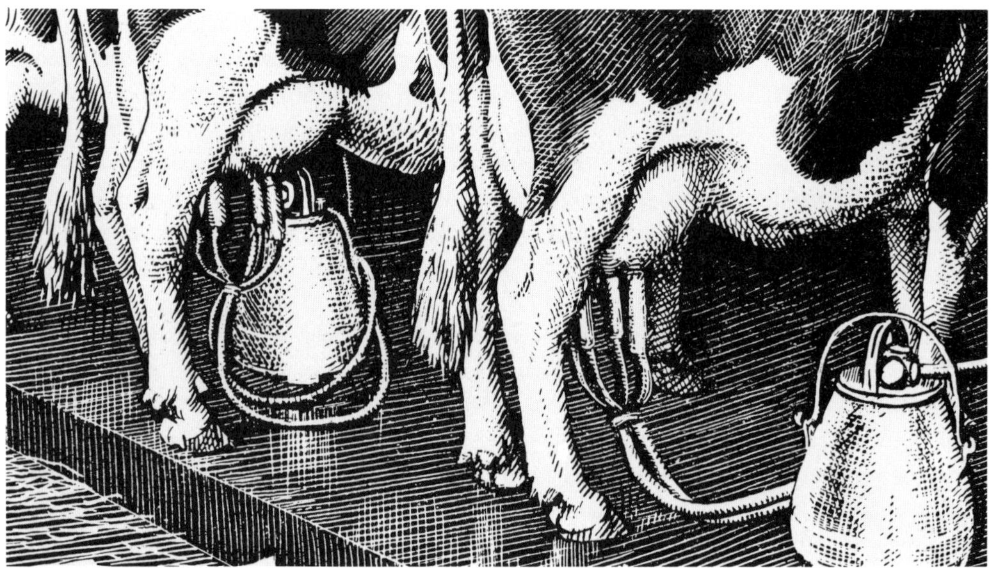

giving a convinced opinion backed by experience and particular instance. The argument will swing to and fro, and all to no purpose, for a new invention, when it satisfies an immediate need without obviously doing harm, always goes on its way without reference to ultimate aims.

Why is it so useful? Because it is an immense saver of time and labour – being able to milk twenty-five cows in an hour. A detached mind might contemplate the humour of this answer with some slight degree of amusement. Two things are saved: labour and time. So our question is – What is done with the saved labour? Either nothing at all, since labour-saving devices are coming in every day, or those relieved from hand-milking can theoretically (very theoretically) go now and make machine-milkers. Well, what is done with the time that is saved? Nothing whatever at the moment. We are quite unprepared to deal with this new uneconomic problem. The saved time is chucked away like a dirty piece of paper into the fire. The length of working

hours remains exactly the same for the labourers as before. There are fewer labourers, but their hours are the same amount; while the displaced workers (unless they *do* go and make machine-milkers) are paid a fee to keep away, called Unemployment Benefit or the Dole. These are the lucky ones, you may say, who have stolen a march on us and have entered the Leisure State in advance. The trouble is they don't seem to appreciate their good fortune.

But, it will be urged, since this saving of labour and time is all so unreal, what then is the reality? Quite simple – it saves *money*. The employer's money. There are few employers, many workers. But since power is always in the hands of the few, they can safely embark upon every new money-saving device.

We need not lose heart. It is all paving the way towards the Leisure State of the future. Always an optimist, I feel sure that we shall be economically ready and mentally fit for it in less than three hundred years.

8

TRACTOR V. HORSE

I cannot regard myself as a tremendous animal lover. I find them too baffling. I have sometimes looked searchingly into the eyes of a cow or a horse wondering what on earth it saw through its own dim windows, what it thought if it did think – hoping it didn't. I am a socialist at heart (also an aristocrat), and am inclined to extend my socialism to animals. So much so that I have to check myself sometimes from apologizing to one or other of them for my behaviour. It seems to me that they also should qualify for the ideal of Rights (there are no natural Rights). For this reason when I see a row of cows strung along the tubes of a machine-milker I feel that there is something deplorable about it – as if the cow itself were our invention.

For the same reason I welcome the tractor. Today horses get a thin time of it on the land. This is not always so, but it is so now in this transition period. There is no emphasis on the *care* of horses, and the young men (soon to be the old men) have no feeling for them. The emphasis is upon the tractor. It is a real machine-horse, and much more powerful, and can go anywhere and do anything that a horse can do. Horses could now be released from their slavery. This view will not meet with the approval of those who dislike machines and love the spectacle of horses in the field. I occasionally meet people who imagine that they are being poetical when they are

only being sentimental. They know nothing of the hardness of that rock from which the spark of poetry is struck. They cannot *see*. Hence the proverbial cruelty of your sentimentalist. He does not see a horse for what it is, a living creature in its own right, but only a picture of a horse; and is enchanted by the idea of that most pitiless of all victimizations – *cavalry*. And in this lesser matter of the horse versus the tractor he never dreams of taking into consideration the feelings of the horse.

My own view of machinery is not notable for consistency; but I welcome a machine which is in the right place, when it is full of use, *useful*; and not when we should use much less of it, when it is *useless*. It is unnecessary to go to extremes. Not long ago I saw the photograph of an interesting gentleman called Captain Roberts who had invented a motor car which came to him when he whistled for it, and of a man who had invented the means by which he could drive a

tractor while he stood at the corner of the field simply pressing a button. Such men have their place in our comedy and add to the gaiety of nations. But in practice they go too far.

Since the second tractor on the farm was not used by any definite worker, I seized the opportunity to use it myself. I am no engineer and not at all mechanically minded. Further, I lack a natural ingenuity and capacity for improvisation, both of which are called for constantly when dealing with agricultural equipment, mechanical or otherwise – though I now realize that ingenuity and improvisation are largely a matter of habit and experience. And though I had driven motor cars for some years, I had not bothered to form a mechanical sense, considering myself as a person who either knows or doesn't know a thing, and who therefore should not waste time in going into matters which can be dealt with by others. But I did not and do not regard machines and their workings as terribly mysterious or unknowable. A mechanic is only

an unglorified botanist. The chemical explosions that occur in the cylinders of an engine cannot be more difficult to deal with than the chemical explosions that occur in the parenchyma of a plant, and there is surely nothing more complicated about a piston than a pistil.

9

MISHAPS WITH TRACTOR

One must force the pace if one is ever to do anything, so when a favourable opportunity offered, I suggested to 'E that I should use the spare tractor. He agreed, and said that a given field needed rolling. He took me to the tractor, started it up, told me to drive off, while he stood on the step beside me. By a lucky chance I found the right gear and we went up to the roller. It was a three-piece roller, and not at the moment connected together, the two small rollers that are attached one on each side of the large one having been left beside it. Thus a good deal of turning and backing was necessary in order to couple them up and assemble the whole. I was lucky in my first backing and brought the coupling-pins exactly in line, but got it all wrong on the second occasion, having to go forward and back several times while 'E waited in irritation. Since the three pieces had been left haphazard and since I did not see at a glance where they should go and what moves I should make, and since I could not follow 'E's instructions, it took some time before I did what was required. But at length it was done and I was left to get on with the job.

After a very short time one roller came off. The coupling-pin had been loose and had jerked out. But I managed to find another pin in the box and assembled the roller-piece again, and continued without further mishap. It was a nice afternoon and seagulls swirled about like a species of day-fireworks. Time passed quickly. So far so good.

I was instructed to go when this field was done to a further one, a root field which had been folded by sheep, and needed knocking up with a cultivator. In due course I went there, found the cultivator, coupled it with the tractor without any query arising, and struck out. Since the method of cultivating is obvious and follows a simple rule of thumb, still so far so good. Then near the end of the day the tractor stopped. All that was wrong was that it had run out of paraffin oil. But as I had put in what I thought was a lot and had no idea how much it ate, I did not realize the cause of the stoppage, and kept urging it on. Then I tested the tank. There seemed to be a certain amount in it, and so I urged it on again for some jerky distance until at last I decided to

get some fuel and fill up. Even then it still went jerkily and I had to keep adjusting the choke (about which I understood little). When I left it in the evening I wondered how it would go next day.

I had cause enough to be apprehensive about this. For next day though it started up all right it would not pull the cultivator. It stalled each time at the strain. I was hopelessly held up. It was not firing properly; but – no one not knowing me will believe this – I did not examine the plugs! There was no rule of thumb for me, and I had no mechanical imagination, I could see no line of research for following out. At length the Van came rushing up, 'E leapt out in a flurry of annoyance, and Jimmy the mechanic who accompanied him whipped out a spanner and plug-twister from the box, and in a moment had taken out the plugs, held the dirty one up before us, cleaned it, put it back, and the tractor started up now and pulled properly – and the Van went off.

The tractor was a good type, an International, but it badly needed overhauling, having been looked after very badly and used now by one person then another. Thus it needed tender treatment. A slight pushing out of the choke at the wrong time would be sufficient to smudge the plugs. I did not know this. My rough treatment of the choke on the first day had done harm, and though the tractor now went again it did not pull well as the day proceeded. Next morning it was as bad as the previous one, and I broke a plug while screwing it out, and there wasn't a spare one. Hence more crisis. 'E's sons came out, saying 'Christ!' The Van appeared, saying 'Handy man! And look where you left the tractor last night – pointing *uphill!*' Learning thus at the cannon's mouth, as it were, it can be guessed that I picked up the tricks pretty fast!

Unfortunately there was always a new thing to pick up regarding this tractor. For the next thing was that it refused to start in the morning. I would leave it in the evening after it had been going all right, but next day it would not start. Even when I took out all the plugs and cleaned them, it wouldn't. One starts-up these tractors on petrol, then switching over to paraffin. It was not easy to lay one's hands on petrol here, and I was always in danger of running out of the small quantity I had in the little petrol tank before I could get started-up – in which case I would be floored again and have to face Van and boys saying 'Christ!' It was necessary to take the plugs to pieces and clean their insides (that was the secret) and I hadn't convenient tools for this at first. Thus you can imagine I had fun and games during these early days. My only merit in matters of this kind is that I don't make the same mistake twice – not on my life! Time certainly never dragged at all now. Indeed I hardly stopped for the morning meal of 'lunch', being too anxious to get on and make a show before something held me up, and in case the tractor wouldn't start again if I stopped it and let it get cold.

I was extricated from many of my early problems and mishaps by Harold, the chief tractor-driver. He was a leisurely chap who took things pretty calmly, though like everyone else, on catching sight of the Van approaching, would display an uncommon earnestness of demeanour and concentration of effort. Now in his late twenties he was already an old hand, having started very young and ploughed with horses long before he took on tractor work. It was clear that he had a good life on this farm and enjoyed it. But the most I ever heard him say was that he 'didn't mind the binder' and I think he 'didn't mind' ploughing. He never took any holidays. He was always about to do so, but never did. He could be very agreeable or very rough, as the mood took him. Robert, always ready to get a rise out of anyone or suddenly shout at anyone who

seemed fair game, never tried anything on with Harold. I knew it would not be wise to count on him helping me, but all the same he often did.

When I got a roller stuck in a gateway, for instance, he would come and help me through before the Van appeared. It was instructive to contrast his traditional and leisurely movements – still more those of Robert – with the movements of 'E. For example, the Van would rush up while I was using the cultivator, say; it was perhaps necessary to put on some new tines or shoes to the cultivator. 'E would stride across the ground, head bent forward as he made straight for his objective; then down on his knees beside the implement, and with fast, strong, hurried, furious wrenching, knocking and twisting with pliers and hammer, do the job, assisted by me doing one item of the affair with another pliers, and accompanied by the boys who, imitating him in every way, would push and pull with immense earnestness. Then, having said what I was

doing *wrong*, would dash off towards some other portion of the farm, where the signal would go up – ' 'E's coming!'

On two occasions a shaft of the roller broke. Curiously enough this was not held against me as these shafts had several times been to the blacksmith for mendings. But actually on the second occasion it was my fault. I had allowed a certain screw to get loose. Harold discovered this and made it clear in no uncertain terms, but did not tell 'E. I had not yet grasped the cardinal fact that a tractor-driver must keep his eye constantly upon all screws. Any one screw out of half a dozen on an agricultural implement is of supreme importance. A screw with its nut at one end looks rather like a spiral-fluted miniature Doric column such as upholds the Parthenon; and if it falls out it may do damage proportionate to the fall of a column. This is what I had to get into my head. All screws must be *tight*, and when you have tightened them then tighten them some

more. I have often thought to myself – well that's tight enough, anyway. But no, tug at it and you can improve it. It doesn't seem necessary but it is; for the shaking of the instrument that it is holding together is equal to your strength in tightening the screw. Hence the tractor-driver must not content himself with looking ahead and watching his implement behind, but must keep his eye on all screws. He need not, as far as I can see, keep bobbing his head backwards and forwards *all* the time as some men do, but he must at intervals really test his joints. Thus then I write down this rule and nail and screw it into my head – though many people think that my head itself has a screw loose.

10

'USE YOUR BRAINS'

At the best of times it was not easy to follow the orders given by 'E in the morning. I often had to get him to repeat them or would ask someone else who happened to have heard – preferably Dick. The latter experienced a certain difficulty himself in taking his orders and said to me that he simply seized upon 'the main outline' of what had been said and carried on from there. Dick's manner while receiving orders was a perpetually repeated comedy. He regarded 'E as his mortal enemy, and when near him lost all his natural gaiety and good humour, becoming at once glum and silent. In the morning he would arrive and make for the stable without glancing his head towards 'E. While going towards it or coming from it, he would receive instructions, but he never took the slightest notice. Had he heard? I used to wonder at first. He had heard all right but merely refused to look in the direction from which the instructions proceeded. Or, out on the field, I would see him being told to do something. He would start off before 'E had finished speaking, his head bent very slightly in one direction which showed that he was really hearing the words that were now addressed to the back of his head.

As I say, I did not always find my orders easy to follow. Sometimes I did not understand what 'E had actually said, and sometimes when I did I still wasn't sure of the moves referred to. For instance one morning it was – 'Take the cultivator back to the centre field, then drag the field you cultivated yesterday. The drags are in the field next to the house. Put one each on they ones that have slides, then take 'ee up to the field. You'll find a pole by the straw rick in the beanfield. When you've finished there get the roller and do the wheat field.' Straightforward enough perhaps, provided I remembered all the geographical designations and the tactics

involved. Seizing the main outline, I went along hoping things would clear up as I went on and saw the objects that had been mentioned. I reached the field where he said the drags were. But *slides*? Ah yes, I saw that two of the four drags if turned over became *sledges* so that you could pull them along across roads and so on. So I turned them over and put the other ones on top. This entailed removing the long pole connecting the four, which enlightened me as to the necessity of that other pole he had alluded to, a smaller one for present use, to be found in the beanfield. There it was; I got it and coupled up and went to the far field to be dragged.

That done the next thing was to get the roller and do the winter-wheat field. I found the roller, but how couple-up without assistance? While backing the tractor you cannot hold up the shaft of the roller, and one's arm isn't long enough to reach the ground when you get into position. Such elementary improvisation as was here needed flummoxed me – again there was no

obvious rule of thumb. But come! I said to myself, use your ingenuity! So I looked in the box and found that the hammer was long enough to serve as a prop. And it did do perfectly well in this capacity. But while coupling-up, that is to say while keeping one foot gently on the clutch, the left hand on the steering-wheel, and the trunk bent backwards so that the right arm can reach right down on the roller-shaft, I wondered why some armchair agricultural strategists imagine that tractor-driving is just a question of sitting down all day.

Having then taken the roller to the winter-wheat field I carried on there for some time. This field was beside the track running up through the centre of the farm, and suddenly the Van appeared coming down it. From the Van an arm, 'E's arm, was outstretched – pointing. What was it pointing at? I looked down at the roller. One piece had disappeared! Then I saw that piece at the far end of the field, sitting there quietly by itself. I had been star-gazing. A minute later and

on turning a corner I would have seen it; but 'E, with his pointing arm, always appeared at the psychological moment.

His eye would discern one's smallest wrong-doing from some way off. A few days later I was chain-harrowing a pasture when the Van appeared. It looked as if it were passing on but it swerved and came towards me and the Arm pointed at my chain-harrow. A link had come undone and hence a portion of the chains was crumpled. Typical of me, I couldn't help feeling, not to have noticed. Then 'E lodged another complaint. I had been seen yesterday – one is always detected – getting water from a certain big house near this field. 'Waste of juice,' he said, 'going right over there when there is a trough in the field. Use your brains!' I could not see the force of this, since you can take a tractor to a trough but you can't make it drink unless you have a filler with you.

While going on with my harrowing I thought over that admonition – 'Use your brains.' I am not a brainy man in any marked degree and have never passed for one, though my capacity to use what brains I possess and to pick the brains of others is second to none. Still, brains was not the right word as used by 'E. I suggest that the word Ingenuity would better fit the case. I possess some Imagination; that is I can occasionally see what is there: but I have little Invention, which is the power to see what is not there. And I fancy that the faculty of invention goes with the faculty of ingenuity and improvisation. But these things are also a matter of habit and experience. An extremely brainy farmer is not likely to be much better and could quite easily be much worse than a stupid man who is born to the tradition, does what he has seen his father do, and which he has been made to do from an early age. The overcoming of mechanical and other difficulties will come to him quite naturally, ingenuity will be second- if not first-nature. What would puzzle me will be simply obvious to him. For what is obvious is not a question of brains but of training.

At a certain gold-mining district in Africa the natives were accustomed to fill buckets with earth and carry them to the inspection yard. One day the British overseer introduced wheelbarrows for use instead of buckets. The natives looked glum at the prospect, and on returning the overseer found them *carrying* the wheelbarrows on their heads. It was not obvious to them what function the wheels would perform. It is obvious to me when I write a letter or a book where I should put a fullstop. It is not in the least obvious to agricultural labourers. When using the first person singular it is my *habit* to write it with a capital I. It is not their habit. They very often use a small i, as in French or German, since it seems less egotistic.

The boss of the farm which I have written about in Part One was a member of the Home Guard. One day he turned up at a meeting at which several proper military men, including an ex-colonel and major, were present. He found them in a quandary. They had wished to move the large desk which was at one end of the room, to the other. But how accomplish this? There seemed no solution. It was not obvious to the Army. Then Agriculture came in. 'The very man we want!' they cried, much relieved at sight of the boss. 'We were wondering how we could move this desk to over there.' To astounded to speak, he said nothing. In complete silence he walked over to the desk, removed the top portion to the floor, carried the two other portions to the required place in two movements, and then placed the first piece again where it fitted. The job was done, the problem solved – amidst the applause of an enlightened Army.

Thus I saw that I must form the habit of ingenuity and improvisation. I was shocked into doing so. Let me no longer, I said to myself, be one of those people who can't do things for themselves, but have to get others to 'do for them' as the phrase goes. I date that resolution from the moment when I had found myself flummoxed by that simple coupling job with the roller. So the next time I found my tractor in need of water I did take it to the trough – and used my *hat* as a filler.

11

OPERATIONS IN PROGRESS

We were into May now, a most beautiful May, but I cannot say that I noticed it much, beyond an occasional glance at the turnout. Nor did anyone else. It is your townsman who is conscious of the seasons and who talks about spring. The agricultural labourer does not notice it. He does not think in terms of months or seasons. He sees it in terms of work. This will have to be done now, then that; it is drilling time, or harrowing and cultivating time, ploughing time, hoeing time, hay-making time, harvest time, and so on – the New Year being in October. He does not know the names of the flowers so well as the country-loving townsman. He does not rejoice in the spring nor become melancholy in the autumn. The scent of hay is not grateful to him. And never, never does he think about 'the summer holidays'!

I could see four operations going forward from a certain high field which I was rolling on 7 May (to take the exact date from my notebook). Away to the left there was a curious activity in progress. A fire was alight under a cauldron. One man, it was 'E, kept poking a stick in the pot. Beside him the shepherd sat upright with a lamb in his lap. Dick was in general attendance. It was rather a lowering day, and the scene appeared as a mixture between an illustration in *Alice in Wonderland* and the Three Witches on the Blasted Heath stirring that remarkable pot boiling twenty-three separate ingredients. Having to ask for certain instructions, I approached and found that they were cutting off the lambs' tails – a bonus of threepence each going to Robert.

On another field Harold was planting potatoes with 'E's daughter and one boy. No more assistance was necessary, for a potato-planter was being used. It is a contraption fitted to the plough – in this case a three-furrow. One person sits on the plough and drops potatoes on to a sort of conveyor-belt which passes round with pockets to hold potatoes and then channels each

into one of the three furrows which are opened and covered at the same time – a remarkably neat affair. A tractor-driver, with two assistants or one, can sow a three- or four-acre field in a day. Remembering what it was like planting by hand, I certainly applauded it, and I am wondering when we shall see a picker-up of potatoes.

Further off I could see the land girls couching. Couch grass is an irrepressible and desperate weed. With hugely spreading roots it clings to the fields. You cultivate the field, drag it, chain-harrow it, pulling up enough couch to build a rick – which you then burn in bundles and lines. But you can get more up – and then more. I refuse to use space in writing about it, but I had plenty to do with the stuff, both in getting it up and burning it when I wasn't using the tractor. It was a job which went on all the time – a ceaseless couch-battle. It is the farmer's curse. But I gather from a neighbour of mine that it has non-agricultural merits of a pleasing character. A

great fellow in the use of herbs, he told me that if you cook some couch-roots you can cure lumbago. But this may not be universal, I fear. He seemed particularly sensitive to roots. Once when he got boils he dug up some dock-roots, ate them, and never had boils again.

How much has to be done to a field before its bed is fit for sowing! Ploughed twice perhaps; cultivated first one way then criss-cross; dragged twice; chain-harrowed and rolled; the couch burnt. Does the general public realize that all this is done to that field seen from the road, looking so silent, so deserted, as if no one ever went near it? Does the man on the road know that it has to be scratched and beaten and turned over like a rug, and scorched and burnt and knocked about? Does he know that before we can live even by bread alone, before bread can begin at all, all this must be done? I did not, when I was a man on the road and in the train.

The carter was busy drilling clover-seed in a field of young corn. The clover would not

come up with the corn, of course. It would follow after the field had been harvested – a new fresh green push between the ruined stalks.

Thus I could see work progressing all around me, while I also was doing my share. I was well in the centre of my world now, and my main feeling was that of being privileged to be there.

I commanded a view also of another field – the hundred-acre which we had drilled in April. It was no longer brown. It had turned green. The field was carrying on by itself. No clumps of men on it as during the drilling time, no carts and sacks and tractors, no operations. But it was the silence of vast schemes not discerned by the eye, not heard; invisible, inaudible, and, it would seem, motionless; yet all in motion, a lofty design being built up, and exchanges made between water and air – that which is fluid being made solid, and that which is solid being made soft.

12

WHILE 'MAKING A SHOW'

I was surprised at the amount of rolling that had to be done, especially on grass and young corn. When taking the heavy roller, not to mention the wheels of the tractor, across the tender shoots of corn, it made me smile to think how the conscientious citizen out for a day in the country will edge his way beside such a field lest he tread on 'the young corn'. It is a bit of a paradox, certainly, that by crushing down the supposedly feeble green ribbons with a heavy roller you thereby make them fit to stand up all the better. But of course the ground is thus made firm, which gives the corn a steady grip, and as for the effect of the roller on the shoots, they are too soft to be injured by something hard, and we all know that elasticity of body, even of the body politic, overcomes all things.

With regard to chain-harrowing the green fields, I had previously thought that pastures were just pastures off which the cattle fed, and that was all there was to it. But no, you cannot leave them alone, they also must be cultivated. The cow-droppings must be spread, otherwise you get a 'sour' patch; too rich. The innumerable mole-hills must be knocked over and dispersed, otherwise your pasture will quite soon disappear altogether, owing to this mole ploughing. The grass itself must be scraped so as to let the air in. Hence this work which looks so uneconomic, pays in the end. For after all, what is this green field but milk, cream, butter, and cheese?

Thus these days passed quickly. Some severe-minded persons say that tractor-driving is boring. I did not find it so. I have, of course, had to do some long fool-proof jobs on big fields, but if it was boring it was not as boring as some other jobs on a farm that have to be done. Moreover, on such occasions one can remain more or less physically fresh and therefore mentally fresh, which makes all the difference. In any case, during these early days of mine there was no question of the time dragging while I grappled with my preliminary and consecutive difficulties and mishaps. It was the other way round, my object was always to get something done, to make a show before anything went wrong – before the Van appeared. One day I had been told to roll a certain field. There was a breakage in the morning and I did not get on to the job before early afternoon. Could I do it now in four hours? I wondered. I just managed it. All the time I was fighting against Space – so Time fled.

Above I have used the phrase 'make a show'. It is an amusing one, so I repeat it. Whenever I started to do any job in company with Dick, he always said – 'Don't you think it would be better to do it this way – *it will make a better show*.' That was my idea also, whether with him or by myself, to make the best impression. And I often used to think how differently I would do certain jobs if I were my own master, with no consideration save the nature of the job itself. Sometimes I would go slow, doing a given piece very thoroughly, since no one would come and say – 'Haven't you finished yet?' I would skimp another field which really didn't need much attention, since no one would say – 'Look, you have left out that piece!' Vast indeed would be the difference. But for the moment I want 'to make a show'. Having got stuck in a gate one day and thus wasted time, I was late in getting started on a field which I had to roll. So in order to make the best show in the remaining hour at my disposal, I went up and down the field instead of round it. In due course 'E appeared and told me I was doing it the wrong way, and that I should have gone round since I would not then punish the corn by unnecessary turnings. I did not explain that I had gone up and down merely to make a *better show*.

Apart from any reasons just suggested as to why there was nothing boring about tractor-driving for me, it was often extremely pleasant on many occasions. It was sometimes necessary to take the tractor with some instrument from one end of the farm to the other. This meant quite a long round-about journey across fields, through gates, along leafy lanes and byways – delightful. Anyone who has experienced stooping or standing for hours at one stationary job understands the difference only too well, and if thus engaged will cast envious eyes at the tractor-driver passing by on his unmonotonous way. And there were some fields that it was a joy to roll. There was a lovely forty-acre field called the Park, where the soil was very soft, and when I rolled the corn I experienced no noise, no clatter, no bumping, no dust. Perched on my comfortable seat, with no animal to bully and shout at, I could glance now and then at the beautiful parky view around, at the gleam and sheen upon the meadows and the groves, at the chestnut trees with their Maytime torches, at the sequestered House beyond with its Old Garden enwalled from the world's woe.

I must add that at other times it was quite the opposite, and I became thoroughly fed-up with the roller. There were some very stony and uneven fields which I rolled after dragging, when there would be an unholy clatter all the time, and dust would cover me and blind me. On days like that the coming of dinner hour was a great moment, when I stopped and the clatter and rattling ceased, then switched off the engine so that its noise and belch also ceased, and a

great calm fell suddenly upon the scene. Turning my back on the tractor I would walk away in the delicious silence towards some good spot for my meal. On a day in May I had it beside a chestnut tree. It displayed a magnificent show of flowers, and when the breeze blew, the petals floated down quite startlingly like a shower of snow. The tree was very large and old. I went and stood under it. A massive trunk. The few holes in the thick canopy of leaves looked like blue stars. I do not think anything in Nature is more mysterious or more effective than a big tree. It is not only that so much proceeds from so little, though this aspect of it is a supreme exemplar of Nature's method of turning thin air into hard and lofty substance: there is something more about a great tree. Standing under this one and looking up, with knitted concentration, quite baffled, I got the impression that it emanated – Goodness. It stood there firmly like a noble Thought, which, if understood, would save the world.

During these dinner hours that so briefly dashed past, when I sat beside a tree like that, I often remembered the Forest of Arden where it was so inviting 'under the shade of melancholy boughs to lose and neglect the creeping hours of time'. That phrase has often haunted me. Not very pleasantly perhaps; for being lazy by nature, I am afraid of idleness, and have never been happy when neglecting time. But now that time was no longer my own I could think with guiltless longing how wonderful it would be to lie down under such a tree, and, neglecting all things, dream my life away.

13

A FREE DAY

On the following Monday I turned up at the yard as usual just after 7 a.m. No one had yet arrived. Some ten minutes passed and still no one appeared. Going to the dairy where work was in full swing, I found 'E there. He was surprised to see me – for it was Whit-Monday, a holiday! I hadn't realized it. We had worked through Good Friday and I had heard no mention about a holiday on Whit-Monday – nor did I realize that it was Whit-Monday. What a break! Yet, how frantic the thought that I had *got up* out of bed when I could have remained there – a most bitter thought. For this early rising was the very devil. I have never been a late riser and have always held before myself the ideal of early rising, if not the practice. But it is one thing to rise at seven and another at a quarter to six, work all day and get back by six in the evening, and then do the same thing again next week. That was now my routine. I lived in a bungalow 'in the wilds' again, though with some near and very kind neighbours. It was twenty minutes' ride down to work, and at least three-quarters of an hour uphill back. I could not therefore rise later than five forty-five, for I had to have breakfast, shave, prepare two lots of sandwiched meals (three if there was overtime), and get down to the farm. As I never succeeded in going to bed before eleven, every single morning's getting up was a little battle. My alarm-clock would go off and I would have to tear my eyes open. Then I would *not* get up, not at once. I always held back till it meant a rush afterwards. I would lie there, facing Time, as it were, feeling that if I lay quite still perhaps I could hold Time, get it to stop, as a man might hold the end of a hose and keep the water back.

Thus I fumed at the thought on Whit-Monday that I had missed the chance of not having to do this. How different was my life now from what it had been! Most of my work had been of a free-lance kind. In those days I never knew when Whit-Monday was coming or when it had come. Once, in my very early days, I remember being asked would I like to dine with certain friends 'tomorrow'. I couldn't think what was on and it was only after I had excused myself that I found that 'tomorrow' was Christmas Day. Week-ends meant nothing to me. Now I was privileged to know what these things mean to others who are owned by masters for nearly every day all the year round.

So now I had the gift of a whole free day. I could enter another world for a change, the world of books. You will never hear me, having done 'an honest day's work', denigrating intellectuals as such. To work day in and day out with the mind only, and never with the body, is as

unsatisfactory as to work only with the body – granted. But to sneer at intellectuality is madness. If a person does not develop his mind he is denying his humanity. For there are only two really human traits – the heart and the intellect. To the extent to which a man does not develop his mind (hence also his heart), he is unhuman, not a man, unmanly – however much he may be a 'he-man'. Since being in the agricultural world, no subject has so continuously and so spontaneously presented itself to me as the problem of education. Up till now the powerful Few have not wished to encourage the Many to become aware of Mind, and most obligingly, the Many have therefore despised it and sneered at 'book-learning'. But we have to pay so dearly for the faculty of mind that if we do not make the best of it, we might just as well be animals. This gift is our specific means of becoming more – *alive*. Two things are essential to the real life of man, and neither can be supplied by Act of Parliament: love and intelligence – all else is the machinery of life.

14

A HARROWING DAY

If getting up early was a curse, the ride down to work was a blessing. It was often an inspiration. I have always loved movement, whether on bicycle, skate, ski, car, or train. Yet perhaps the bicycle is best of all – on a long slope downhill. Add to this an early summer morning, and you have entered heaven. The houses are asleep, and the people have not entered the kingdom, they will not enter it; but the Gate is open, and the fair place lies before you, unstained, unshamed.

My journey took me straight through the village, past the post office, the grocery shop, the forge, the rectory, the inn. A great copper-beech rose behind the rectory wall, and on the left stood a row of chestnut trees whose mid-May blossoms held up their brief lights until they went out, and over the way a laburnum, till then absolutely insignificant and unnoticed, now aristocratically rose up to pay its dues and taxes, a flaming fountain of yellow flower, further enlightened by the morning rays.

Arriving in the farmyard, did I find 'E in a pleasing frame of mind? Hardly. On the Tuesday morning I made straight for the oil-can, meaning to fill it – for seeing to the oiling of an engine is one of my strong points. But he yelled across the yard to me to put it down, that it was no good, that it leaked, and he wouldn't have it used, not by me 'nor the King of Honolulu, nor anyone'.

This unexpected display of wit and learning rather eased the atmosphere in the yard and the others tended to relax their features somewhat. After I had got my oil I wanted some petrol, for which purpose I had a special bottle. All the tins were empty, so it was necessary to get some out of the tank in the lorry. This could be accomplished by sticking a rubber pipe into the tank. You could achieve a flow if you sucked your end for a minute or so. True, this meant petrol in the mouth, but you could spit it out. The operation looks a trifle absurd, and 'E, watching me kneeling down and sucking away at the rubber tube, loosened up and laughed, saying – 'Collis is drinking beer,' and laughed some more. As a wisecrack, no great claims could be made for it perhaps, but the sight of 'E laughing caused a further relaxation amongst those present, and something in the nature of mirth swept perceptibly across the yard.

How about mishaps these days? Well I made a point of examining the plugs now before starting up. They very often needed cleaning, and it saved a lot of time in the end. Indeed I became a champion taker-out and dismantler of plugs in quick time (never even dropping the little screw on top!). This meant, by the way, that a clean hand became a thing of the past for me. I have always had a partiality for clean hands and clean feet. Though often going without a bath for a month now, I still never went to bed without washing my feet. But my ideal of clean hands suffered modification. I actually started my agricultural career wearing gloves, and kept it up for some time. I quite abandoned this now, for you cannot deal with nuts and screws with gloves on. And now – such are the tricks of human psychology – I became proud of my grimy hands. They were real workman's hands. Once, later, when I was pulling beans with Harold on a wet day, our hands became very clean. He looked at his in disgust and said – 'No one wouldn't think I done no work!' And I began to appreciate the real meaning of Edward Carpenter's remark – 'I confess,' he wrote in his Autobiography, 'I love to see a *dirty hand*.'

Though plugs no longer troubled me, other things cropped up of course. Water sometimes got into the forty-gallon paraffin tank in the yard, and subsequently into my tank. This meant a stoppage after a few hundred yards. But I soon learnt to deal with that, though it meant stopping every ten minutes to clean out the glass basin under the tank. Unfortunately, when anything went wrong with the magneto I was done. I could only gape at it, fumbling without the slightest confidence that I could detect what was wrong.

One day, though the plugs seemed all right, I couldn't start up at all, couldn't get a spark out of her (machines are feminine). Harold came over, and we tried everything for over an hour. There was no chance of making a show before the Van arrived. I hoped it would arrive while Harold was with me also unsuccessful in diagnosis, and I knew that 'E himself would not know what was wrong, for his knowledge of machinery was very superficial. But the Van did not appear by the time Harold had given in, and I went off to get hold of Jimmy, hoping it would not appear before I had returned with him. But it did. Just as we approached the tractor 'E drove up, and got out in a fury, waving his hands about, refusing to listen to any explanation or excuse on my part, and saying 'You might as well go home!' We then proceeded to the tractor and Jimmy dismantled the magneto and found the trouble. Impressed by the complication of the work, which took us some time, 'E calmed down considerably. When the Van had gone away again, Jimmy said – 'He do fly up in the air, don't he!' And then added, greatly to my comfort, 'We've all been through it.'

Later in the day Harold asked me what that trouble had been which we had failed to detect,

and I explained. But I was surprised that he had not asked Jimmy who must have passed by him on his way back. The fact is they would not have spoken about this, for they seldom spoke to each other, Jimmy being far more resourceful when confronted by any real mechanical difficulty.

Jimmy, under thirty I should say, was a very cheerful fellow, and equally good-looking. Everyone was glad when he appeared on the scene, his smiling face and pleasant turn of greeting warmed up the temperature a lot. He did not very often appear, for when he was not lorry-driving he nearly always, except during the heavy seasons, managed to work in the barn, doing this or that, no one knew what, and they resented it of course. For he was able to get away with it. He was in a powerful position, for he was the man whom 'E was always falling back upon. All the others were amateur mechanics, which is all right up to a point, but modern farm

machinery calls for a genuine engineer on the premises. He regarded himself as a cut above the others, despising them for their obsequiousness. He didn't belong to the agricultural milieu. He felt superior. And as a human being he was superior. They didn't approve of him, but liked to see his cheerful face all the same.

Before going off, 'E had told me to go next to a certain field and drag it for couch. On arriving I found him and the carter there engaged in manuring. The harrow was in the middle of the field, and I went over to it and began to couple-up. I was in doubt as to which pin would fit this instrument, and was bending over the thing when suddenly a small tempest of a man's body struck against me, an arm shot past me into the tractor floor, grasped the chain, pulled it violently back, hurling several things with it on to the ground, and the voice of the carter using the customary expletives, said something unprintable. He fixed the chain to the

harrow and then went away. But his violence, his apparent rage! Why? I asked myself, why this unpleasantness over what was by no means a momentous matter? I was far from amused at this incident.

It was a small field so I soon finished this job and went away with relief to the other field which I had not begun in the morning. I hadn't been there very long when Robert came up beckoning to me, and started yelling. My dog, it appeared, had just been seen going after his sheep on the Down. Now, my dog didn't run after sheep as a rule and in any case I had seen him a minute ago. But Robert insisted, shouting at the top of his voice, that he had been seen by Harold who had reported it. So I went and looked but could see no sign of him near the sheep. On returning I saw him coming out of the hedge in the field I was working on. He may of course have been on the Down, but was unlikely to have run after the sheep much if at all, and I

reflected upon how colossal and critical a thing can be made to seem if you shout loud enough.

However, before the day was out Robert had cause to thank me. A number of the sheep escaped through a gap in the hedge and began to spread out all over the place. I noticed this, but I couldn't find Robert anywhere. So I drove them back myself, and filled up the gap. I did not experience any difficulty in getting them *all* to go in the necessary one direction and through the hole. For there is one pleasing peculiarity about sheep. If you can get a small bunch of them moving towards a given corner, the rest will follow as if the whole lot were tied together with invisible strings – and they will all rush blindly through the gap like water out of the drain in a bath. I wonder was it sheep, rather than swine, that rushed down that steep place into the sea?

While rolling this field, a very bumpy and stony one, I could see some distance off a lovely rich green field gleaming in the sunshine, all quiet on the agricultural front, and I suddenly

wished I could be back in the old days when I could look at such a field seeing only its beauty and peace, and perhaps sit in it knowing nothing of irate farmers and men – a sudden nostalgia owing to my as yet unconsolidated position here, and my immersion in mechanics, my pushing and pulling with bolts and screws, spanners and hammers, plugs and carburettors, and the clatter and rattle of the roller.

15

BEAUTY THROUGH THE DUST

Though it was June now there still remained some work to be done on fields which were to carry roots. It was worth glancing at the transformation of the fields around. The clover, from ankle-deep, was now knee-deep in rich, dark lusciousness – hay-making being round the corner. A field that recently had only showed lines of burning couch was now covered with a bright green sheet. The field in which sheep were earlier folded was now being ploughed by Harold and dragged and rolled by me. And I was amazed by the good crop of corn now coming up on another field which had seemed to me incredibly stony. 'Some seeds fell upon stony ground' – and did very well, it seems. Up to a point stones are an advantage, I learn, in terms of drainage. Yet looking at such a field earlier, so hard, so dry, so massively stony, the uninstructed spectator might well be pardoned for wondering how so tender a thing as a seed could derive nourishment there and cover it all with silky greens.

There in a corner stood the thresher covered up. How inactive it looked, how dead: yet capable of springing into intense liveliness as were the grass-covered drags and chain harrows lying about here and there like old ugly and forgotten thoughts. Over the hedge was a huge straw-rick: I had helped to put it there. And as I looked round and considered each field in turn, I was surprised to find that I had had dealings with every one of them – which gave me great satisfaction.

The sheep shearing was now in full swing, the large bales of wool being hung up in the barn. It was done by machine shears which completed the whole job in a week. 'E was one of the shearers. Hence it was a week held in the highest esteem by the staff. 'I wish it was three months,' said one of them to me, 'for then you know where 'E is all day.' A great advantage. No fear of the Van suddenly appearing. Especially at lunch hour. Officially we had half an hour off for lunch between nine-thirty and ten o'clock; and 'E had a way of appearing just when you had

sat down for this delightful break, or were about to do so. The staff hated this. They liked to be found working, even though the break was legitimate. It seemed to give a bad impression to be found by the Van sitting down and eating – and of course no boss is ever seen eating. He often arrived just as we were taking that extra five minutes at the end. If he appeared in the middle it spoilt the break, for you couldn't enjoy your food while receiving instructions and holding conference, and you couldn't settle down again comfortably till he was out of sight. It was therefore delightful to have a whole week with the knowledge that the Van would *not* appear, knowing precisely where 'E was – shearing sheep in the barn.

I was on the last lap of the dragging and rolling now. It was very hot and the ground dry, so that the dust rose in clouds behind the harrow, and the roller was deafening. But at intervals I noticed that the weather was magnificent. The days were gleaming in a manner more often

heard about than seen in June, and the surrounding fields and skies were shining with signs and answers and promises and prophecies and praise. The roller clattered, the dust rose, and the tractor gave choking trouble at intervals, but I could not help being aware of that glitter and that gleam. And I marvelled at the thought of night coming soon, the mighty opposite, when all that radiance would go and all those colours pass. A common experience, night following day? Yet we may doubt if between the pram and the bath-chair we will ever see anything more fantastic than this change. Every dawn is the re-enactment of the world's genesis, and the rising up of the light is the rising up of life. Hence in the radiance of the sunshine men shrink from murder. On days like these I could well understand Macbeth calling upon night to scarf up the tender eye of pitiful day, and with its bloody and invisible hand cancel and tear to pieces that great bond which kept him pale.

16

WHILE COUCHING

Some of the meadows were now ready for cutting, so I took the tractor down to the yard to Jimmy, who would now take over. The cutter was power-driven straight from the power-take-off of the tractor. It is therefore a much larger and stronger affair than the ordinary cutter. It was certainly a formidable looking apparatus to fix up. It was necessary to remove half the floor of the tractor and join it to the cutter which has something like fifteen parts – shafts, pulleys, engine, blade, bed. A business of terrific screw-tightening and bolt-fixing. Had I been told to do the job (I was merely Jimmy's assistant) I would have been stumped by the jig-saw; but it didn't seem difficult as each part, taken separately, found its place. What struck me most about the mechanic's operations was that if a hole on the mudguard, say, wouldn't meet the hole in a given shaft by any amount of pressure, then he didn't give in but simply *made* another hole, piercing one by holding it in a vice in the barn. Again if, as so often happened, a screw was too big and would not fix into a given hold and no other screw would perform this office, he didn't give way to lamentation but put it in the vice and filed it off until it did fit. All very, obvious to the initiated, no doubt; and once more I saw that the great principle for a mechanic is to have *resource*, and a sufficient number of tools and gadgets to make that resource practicable . . . I have just said that Jimmy did not lament. I mean not practically. But verbally his lamentations were so frequent and despairing that I imagined he was hopelessly floored every time. But not a bit of it. He addressed recalcitrant screws and bolts as if they had hearts, cajoling and cursing them; but not, I soon discovered, with any feeling that they ever had the upper hand.

When I had sharpened the cutter-knives, I took a horse and cart and went to gather up some couch, for Jimmy was going to handle the cutter – at which I was sorry but relieved, for how would I handle any breakdown of that 'menagerie'? It was very pleasant with the horse and cart in the sunshine – always how pleasant going along quietly in the sun with a cart! And how different today working coatless in the warmth than weighed down with clothes in the cold – to me all the difference in the world! But not shared by the others. They preferred the winter, on the simple ground, they said, that the hours were shorter, half an hour later in the morning and off at five instead of half past in the evening. The heat of summer was regarded as a nuisance – whereas I'd rather have it than champagne. It was not surprising that the sun could give them little pleasure, since they wore underclothes, even pants, all the year round – so that one of the

real joys of life, the specific one open to them, namely physical work in the sunshine, was turned into discomfort! As for working without a shirt – at this place it was quite daring to go without a hat. This sort of thing is not the wisdom of the ages: it is merely convention. In some particulars, of course, they are extremely wise with regard to clothing for certain activities, and I find that a case, even a strong case, can be made out for braces – though not on all occasions. But for the most part it is just a question of fashion. You do what the others do, and no one will break the fashion for the sake of comfort or pleasure. For nothing is so strong, so oppressive, so enchainingly tyrannical as the power of fashion. Almost anything can be done, anything could be done, and done daily and calmly, if it is the fashion. Then the mind turns the fashion into a *moral*. Robert was deeply shocked on one occasion when two land girls rolled up their dungarees above their knees on a hot day. 'E himself was far more broad-minded.

During this hay-cutting period I did a good deal of couching, in company with Alf and his boy who were newcomers. (I'm not bothering to put in surnames. For in practice I have a good working rule-of-thumb method in this matter. I call a gentleman, after knowing him a bit, simply 'Jones'; I call a lower-middle-class person 'Mr Jones', otherwise he is indignant, for he regards the Mr as his only title to fame; and with the working man I take a flying leap as soon as possible to the Christian name.) I don't know how Alf would have been described before Dickens, but now one can simply say that he had a Dickensian appearance and countenance, and leave it at that. Even his cap was Dickensian, even the back of his cap. He was a town worker really, from building and other trades, and was trying his hand at agriculture for the first time. He groused even more than land workers, but was more independent, and much less hard working. In the old days I had heard about the British working man always taking it easy and

'resting on his spade'. Perhaps this is true of the town worker. At the beginning of the war I did some A.R.P. work in Kent amongst a few labourers who were not agricultural. In the digging of a shelter I found that my pace was much too fast, especially for a wonderful man called Knight whose flow of tongue was unexampled in my experience. He required frequent intervals for a breather and some talk. 'The two bottom evils in the world, brother,' he would say, 'are the purse and the female,' and he welcomed as many stoppages as possible to develop this and other themes. But as soon as I found myself amongst agricultural labourers I saw that their pace was much faster and steadier, and that stoppages, if any, were furtive and seldom lasted longer than the lighting of a cigarette. Alf was finding the difference very marked, and gave me amazing examples of easy work and easy money for other trades. And it was clear that Alf's boy, about fifteen, had reached the conclusion that one shouldn't work at all on any account. All the same

Alf was a nervous and inferior little man, and more apprehensive than anyone else at the approach of 'E. He worked in a feverish, jerky, busy manner. He pursed his lips, continually blowing outwards as if exhaling invisible smoke; it was evidently habitual, an unconscious technique to give the impression of earnest concentration and hard work going forward at full steam ahead.

When I joined him he had already decided to quit. ' 'Taint good enough,' he said. 'Don't do nothing 'ere but work, look-see. No one won't speak to you on this 'ere joint. Nothing but blank work for arf the money wot you get in the town. The missus can't stand it 'ere with them neighbours wot don't say a word, and I won't 'ave her locked up in no 'ome.' This tribute to agricultural and village life was followed by an expression of gratitude that I alone addressed him in a friendly manner. But I think this was only because I had taken the trouble to find

out his Christian name. I said something about the others not being interested in things outside. He said that this was owing to 'the bloke wot nurses 'em, they get so as they loses 'art'. At this point the Van appeared at the other side of the hedge, and stopped for a minute while 'E regarded us with no enthusiasm, then shouted across, 'I don't want it raked up but picked up' – a distinction which, when analysed by us, yielded no clear idea as to what we were doing wrong.

I asked Alf whether in the days of unemployment he had been unemployed. He said no, he always found it easy to get work. But many couldn't, I said. He insisted that they didn't want it, that they were better off without it, especially with a large family when the 'Benefit' would amount to about three pounds. I mention this, not because 'better off' has any meaning there, but because this is the sort of remark workers make about themselves. And it is undoubtedly true that when the level of wages and the level of unemployment pay were nearly the same, as was sometimes the case, many preferred not to work. Only people who are ignorant of what work really is, and ignorant of human nature, can be surprised or shocked at this. Those who like their work are the only people who like working. We tend to forget how much work is unlikeable. We used to get it done at the point of the starvation bayonet. Terror of starvation is now a thing of the past. If the spur of necessity is entirely removed, much basic work will simply not be done – unless enforced. My knowledge of the working man is riskily unexhaustive, but what has struck me most forcibly is the fact that he now worries about money much less than the middle classes do. Money affairs really *haunt* the middle-class person. A sudden loss of job or income is a fearful blow, a family catastrophe, the break up of the whole machinery of life. But ever since unemployment achieved considerable dimensions the working man has felt increasingly secure. In the days when there wasn't a great deal of unemployment and the State left every man to look after himself, the fear of losing your job was often a nightmare (this, as short a time ago as, say, the publication of Galsworthy's *Silver Box*). When things got bad enough to be dangerous, Unemployment Benefit or the Dole was brought in and the *dread* of not being able to find a job and the next meal vanished. Then if a job fell through, the workman would say, to my astonishment I have heard him say it with the greatest cheerfulness (before the war-boom in work) – 'Well I'll go down to the "Labour" tomorrow and see if there is anything I fancy.' If there was nothing he fancied he would take the Benefit.

If the reader feels that the exceptions that disprove the above rule, if it is a rule, are just as important as the rule itself, I shall not disagree with him. I am content to make the one observation that the working people today, if not less greedy for money, are less anxious about it than the middle classes, and are less afraid of being broken – or 'broke'. Many of the latter receive a good deal of their income from investments. This brings with it nowadays a terrible feeling of insecurity – for, as Rebecca West has observed, there is a great difference between getting your money from some strange invisible source like investments, and getting it for definite work done or goods produced. In the latter case you do feel in unsettled times that your source of income may dry up. True, while things are all right, the middle-class person has more than the labourer. But this only makes him the more anxious. And even that little extra cash which he gets is spent to support visions and apparitions and ghosts of reality, and to wind round him scarves and veils of illusion, which he calls 'keeping up appearances'. When money fails or

lessens he cannot cope with the situation, he is terrified of the Appearances disappearing. The machinery of his life breaks down, he is broken. But the labourer gets the Benefit and can cope. The onus really falls upon 'the wife' who 'makes do' a bit more. Middle-class people cannot make do, they are stuck in their fantastic swamp. Indeed fantastic: the labourer, accustomed to living within his means, is astonished and bewildered at hearing people with more means than himself speaking about '*my overdraft at the bank*'. He lives in a world mercifully oblivious of such nonsense and such failure in the art of life.

Up till this he had also been free from another word – *taxes*. Now that it is coming into his ken he is highly indignant. 'I'm not going to do no overtime,' he frequently declares, on the ground of paying Income Tax if he does. The tax is always spoken of as if it were equal to the amount earned! I'm told it hurt their pride to be taxed – though I don't follow this. Certainly

they seem to prefer to make less money than pay a small tax. They prefer to marry in a hurry rather than pay a bachelor-tax, as is now virtually the case. The Beveridge business means a lot more paying out; and as insecurity is not their chief fear, one meets with no wild enthusiasm for the scheme. Actually, one never hears it discussed or even mentioned, indeed many seem not to have heard of it. It will be interesting to see how the working man takes to it when he comes in practice to realize its full implications. Accustomed to regard the State as something absolutely external, whose business it is to look after him and pay for his children's education and so on, he may not relish joining the privileged classes whose main privilege it is to pay taxes and to regard the State as part of themselves. But according to a section of the Press he is supposed to be clamouring for it. For all I know this may be true of the working man in the towns; and of course it is still not thought proper to consider the countryman as actually existing. 'A fortnight's

holiday is now universal,' writes Sir Richard Livingstone, calmly turning his back on the whole agricultural world, just as a man called Commander Campbell never misses an opportunity to tell the twelve million listeners of the Brains Trust that their Christmas dinner, or any dinner, is entirely due – to the Merchant Navy.

17

MASTERS AND MEN; A VIEW OF FARMERS

How hard it is to see the whole while merely grappling with the part! I had done a great many things to this field, but what interest had it for me after a few hours' work on the couch? I was just 'burning couch'. The labourer is too close to the earth to see the earth, to glimpse the whole or even the glittering of the part. As for Alf, it was just 'this bloody couch'. His knowledge of agriculture was as limited as his interest in it. He referred to Robert as 'the sheep man'. Once when we were spreading some caving-compost he had no notion that he was doing anything except throwing down some wet mushy straw to please 'the old man', and when I said it was manure he said – 'Oh, it's manure, is it?' While Jimmy was cutting grass on the neighbouring field, Alf thought he was cutting corn. And once he remarked to me – 'The old man don't do much farming, dun 'e? Just removing this 'ere couch.' He could see no relation between this couch-destruction and the preparation of a seed-bed, nor could he visualize any previous work on the other silent fields.

Sometimes Dick joined us, and his presence always enlivened the atmosphere by his humorously exaggerated grousing and take-offs of 'E. 'I hope you are making a good show!' we would hear as he approached. On such occasions I heard nothing good of agriculture. I enjoyed this, for I like unearnest people, and easily suit my mood to theirs. In fact, I like to grouse with a grouser. I don't like to spoil things by appearing too conscientious to a grouser or too slack to a non-grouser, just as I don't like to be too sincere in the presence of an insincere person, and, I may add, just as often lie to liars.

Sometimes 'E also joined with the couching, for there was nothing he was above doing himself. The Van! – and if it was near the end of the day we wondered if his object would be to

finish the field, which would mean going a bit past the hour for 'shutting out'. And we didn't like that, though it was the natural thing to do – to finish a job even though it meant an extra fifteen minutes. How often I have thought of this business of masters and men, arising both from my own experience and from what I have heard from others. The labourers don't think about the master. For he seldom thinks about them. They are to him simply 'labour'. 'I haven't got the labour,' he will say, not colleagues, not assistants, not even labourers. If a job is finished at five-fifteen instead of five-thirty, he doesn't say 'That's all right boys, we'll call it a day,' thus making it easy for himself next time he wants that extra quarter of an hour. Oh no, he says Go and do so and so. He can't bear the idea of losing that time; think of 'the money' I'm throwing away, he feels.

It is sometimes put forward that farmers on the whole are not amongst the choicest spirits

of mankind. It is represented that they are mean, permanently disgruntled, hard, unsympathetic, greedy, and lacking in idealism and interest in the world. If there is truth in some of this, as seems likely owing to the frequency of the charge, it cannot be the fault of the farmers. That is obvious, since you and I, so vastly free from these faults, on becoming farmers tomorrow, would in due course have to be included in the charge, if it is true.

It is the effect of the Earth.

The Sea has a good effect upon men. On the sea we are *travellers*; we voyage in an element of alien mystery which belongs not to us but to fish, and where no man trespasses without fear of prosecution. He who ploughs the main does really plough in fear and praise, does really feel the mystery; so that even the humblest seaman becomes fascinated and cries 'Back to the Sea!' if he goes away from it.

The influence of the Air is often good. When an airman speaks we hear the language of the Ideal, either open or disguised; and some attain the perspective of pity and love.

The spirit of the ancient Earth is sterner. Hoary with cruel taxation from morning to night she exacts a singleness of purpose that shall not waver and shall not tire. Her demands are not only too great but too constant to allow those who battle with her any relaxation, any contemplation, any ideology, any interest in the spirit and the mind. She cannot permit her servant to get lost in reverie like a sea watchman, nor to hold the world in proportion like an airman. He must not pause beside Beauty. He must not open the book of Learning. He must not pay homage to Art. He shall be kept submerged in his great task by perpetual apprehension of failure and ruin.

18

WORK ON A RAINY DAY

A series of breakages were holding up the hay-cutting, and I was glad not to be involved in it. Also some wet days came on. A good farmer is never at a loss to know what to do with his men on a wet day, and 'E had plenty of handy jobs waiting down in the barn and shed – oiling machines, doing repairs, sack-tidying, mixing artificial. I spent one morning removing sacks of beans. They had been left too long and were splitting at the bottom. I mention this job, for now in actual practice, I did really *spill the beans*. But the most usual job was mixing artificial – so much potash with so much sulphate of ammonia. We poured it out on the floor, crunched it up, and mixed it. Some of the mixture seemed to make a remarkable potion, burning boots badly (Alf had his soles destroyed), and I wondered whether it wasn't all a bit too scientific. Often 'E would give his instructions regarding the proportions to be mixed, and then go away. We all heard his words (perhaps four of us), but when we got down to it no one was sure whether he had said, say, half a hundredweight of potash to a hundredweight of ammonia, or more or less of each, or phosphate as well. In due course 'E would return and say we were doing it wrong, he had said less of one and more of the other. But curiously enough, he didn't seem to mind very much.

I did much of this with Alf alone. He seemed to like doing the sack-lifting or to dislike my doing it. I don't know which; anyway, he always refused assistance and even seemed to want to do most of the shovelling. It took us an hour and a half to mix and bag up a pile of manure.

Once when there was an awkward three-quarters of an hour to go, we lessened the next pile by informal proportions, without, I felt sure, making the slightest difference to the yield of the ultimate crop.

But Alf didn't like working in the barn. It was too close to 'E. One afternoon it was half-raining. After dinner, as it looked like clearing, I went up to the field and carried on with the couch (not trying to burn it of course, but to cart it away). It began to rain a bit more but still not much. Now, as a general rule, if there is a drop of rain the English labourer (as opposed to other nationalities I am told) rushes for his raincoat and stops outdoor work on the spot – so much so that some farmers dare not be seen putting on a coat themselves if a shower threatens, in case there is a general cessation of work on the job in hand. But out came Alf now. Seeing that the rain wasn't much, he had made a bee-line for the stable, got the cart and hastened away from the barn up to my field. He was considerably amused at his own haste and determination to get clear of the barn, and kept repeating, 'I weren't going to stay down there with 'e if I could 'elp it. 'E won't find me going down there, rain or no rain. It's better up 'ere. Peace and quiet 'ere, looksee. No one don't get me to go down there this afternoon, we're better off up 'ere.' Observing my amusement at this, he repeated it over and over again with variations every five minutes for the first hour and a half. Sometimes I thought he was going to introduce a new element into the conversation, but no, it would just be – ''E don't get me to go down there if I can 'elp it. Don't want no work in that there barn with 'e around. Better up 'ere looksee.'

The Saturday mornings were long, for we knocked off, not at twelve-thirty but at one-thirty. This made our lunch hour an important meal and break. On one Saturday morning many of us were working at different jobs within visible proximity: Alf and myself spreading some caving compost; Dick over the way carting hurdles for Robert; the carter loading hay; Harold using the tractor. We were all about to break off for lunch at 9.30 when the Van was seen approaching. Better wait till 'E's gone, was the general feeling, so we went on working. He approached Alf and had something to say about his method of getting the straw loose, then over to me, finding that there was room for improvement in my scheme of distribution. He then passed over to Harold with whom he remained long in converse. But he'll be off soon, we thought, and carried on. He left Harold and went over to the carter. Then over to Robert where he remained some time in conference, all of us still working on, and then back again to say something more to Harold. Finally he moved off stage left, and when the Van was out of sight we all sat down – a most memorable break.

Dick was always in a tremendous hurry to be off, on every day, but especially on Saturdays, to see his girl. This morning he had been told to carry three wagon loads of straw to a given place. He loudly declared to us that he could fit in one load and a half, at most two, certainly not three if he were to make a getaway on time. So with a stream of suitable language he assured us that he would get two loads and no more – and he stuck to it, passing us eventually on his way down to the stable with time enough in hand to make his exit and then catch his bus. Meanwhile I carried on with Alf and Harold. 'Speed one-thirty,' they said. 'Speed one o'clock,' I said, since by one o'clock one could sight land, as it were.

It might fairly be asked how 'Patriotism' works in with all this, and 'putting all they have into the land', and 'willing work for the war effort', and 'splendid national service', and other B.B.C. phrases. Not very well really. I mean the phrases don't fit in too well, for the agricultural

labourer, in war as in peace, is cut off from the world. He lives on a desert island. He is cast on a far shore. Upon him all the world rests: yet that world is to him a dream, and they are dream figures that he sees from his field passing on the road. They pay no heed to him, they think of him and thank him not at all. Who can blame him for not being able to think in national terms? Patriotism is not an unreal thing even when one's locality is not immediately threatened, it can be felt in masses such as you get in factories (or can it?). But not on the wide field, not amongst the cows, not under the pressure of the egoism of farmers. The labourer has nothing to prime him save his own ego and its persistent claims for a little freedom and pleasure.

19

WHAT A WEED IS

It became hot again, though with occasional showers which held up the hour of haymaking. I was called now to a different job – that of hoeing some very small kale shoots in a very dirty field.

In towns men have become so far removed from the soil that when we hear that a man has *soiled* his hands we know that he is suspected of crime. But in the country soil is the acme of cleanliness and is only regarded as *dirty* if it has weeds on it. (And of course soil is so far from being dirty that if you cut your hand it is a good tip to plug the wound with a decent piece of earth, when it heals in no time.) What is a weed exactly? It is any plant which impedes or competes with any other particular plant we are interested in. It can be a 'flower'. Would you not call the scarlet pimpernel a flower? or the eyebright? or the poppy? But a field of kale, though it glitter with the scarlet, the red, the blue, the yellow and other shades of pretty flowers, is disgustingly dirty to the agricultural eye, and would still be considered as such though the rose, the lily, or the daffodil lifted their petals to the sun.

A weed may be considered as an exemplar of the paradox that the good that we would we do not, and the evil that we would not that we do. We do our best to care for the good plants, we spurn the evil weeds; but before we know where we are, the latter have sprung up unbidden and choked our plants. No one puts weeds amongst the kale, and yet they appear; while no kale would appear unless we put it there. Knock out the weeds, and after a shower they will rise up again. Knock out your plant, and even replant it, and it will die. In a word, weeds are tough plants, and this is doubtless why we cannot eat them, and why those we can eat are delicate and

not fit for competition. Hence it is considered that only a lunatic will treat weeds as garlands. That is why King Lear, blasted in the storm, was found with docks, hemlock, nettles, darnel, and rank fumiter in his hair.

Thus hoeing is of great importance; otherwise many a field of kale, swedes, or mangolds will become submerged and all your work will be undone. Weeds should be treated, said William Cobbett, exactly as the Duke of Wellington treated the faction called the Whigs in 1828. But I fear I must acknowledge that there were times when I treated some of the smaller ones in the manner of Lord Nelson who deliberately turned a blind eye on another occasion.

The kale shoots were miserably small and weak looking, and it was impossible to believe that anything could come of them. 'Best thing 'e could do would be to plough them in, I allow,' was Robert's comment when he saw the field. But 'E knew better. So I carried on at what seemed a hopeless job. The ground was hard, the hoe light and blunt, and I made very little show. When 'E appeared and looked at my 'cut' he said that if I were doing it on a piece-work basis I would do a good deal more. You're telling me, I felt inclined to reply. For no one in his senses on the staff of any farm would go at the pace of professional piece-workers. These latter gentlemen provide an intimidating spectacle. Every yard covered is so much £.s.d. They know nothing of back-ache, having developed rubber spines. Time never drags for them, space being their only concern. They choose this method of work, preferring to go hard during certain months so as to be independent during others, and their own masters at all times. Some never take off, since work normally can be found all the year round: hedging and ditching by the chain in winter, sowing by the acre in April, dipping sheep by the score in May, hiling by the acre in harvest-time, thatching by the square, dressing mangolds by the acre or load, then hedging again. It would seem therefore that a farmer would be well advised to employ piece-workers for a job like hoeing, at any rate. But there is one snag, for their sole object is to cover so much space, and this can be done quickest by skimping the work and leaving in the smaller weeds. Thus the farmer, having paid a lot, finds the weeds still coming up in plenty – certainly here 'not worth the money'.

The day-labourer is careful not to compete with the pace of piece-workers. Given a certain job to do, for instance, he makes sure of not doing too much on the first day; for if he takes a big cut and does a particularly good day's work, he will be expected to do likewise tomorrow. He is not going to expose himself to the phrase 'you haven't done much today, have you?' if he can help it, when the boss appears. When 'E came out to me he said, 'Give me the hoe and I'll show you,' and then proceeded to give a demonstration which left nothing to be desired in either thoroughness or speed. He carried on for two minutes and then went off. The implication being that I should imitate this pace for the rest of the day. All bosses and foremen perform this exhibition, and while no one has the heart to spoil their comedy, it is held in derision by all the men.

20

THE REAL INEQUALITY

Again the fresh beauty of the morning! The yellow flaming flag of the laburnum falls to the ground; the gorgeous candelabra of the chestnut trees have long since guttered and gone out. All effected at the rate of theatrical scene-shifting, it seems, as I cycle through the passing show. But the copper-beech in the rectory garden reminds me of the constancy of time. Its great trunk rooted in history; its leaves bathed in the memory of a thousand summers; the sunless branches in its tented shade; the slow dripping of the raindrops down into the glorious gloom of the soaking sod – are in themselves the Remembrance of Things Past.

. . . Thus in the early morning is the heart raised and the head cleared, as one steps on to the field of kale. And for an hour or so it is possible to remain in this frame of mind. But not for many hours. The morning goes well enough, but the afternoon sees a different man; the monotony of the task (give me that tractor again!), and the aching of the back, begin to numb the mind until it gradually stops working altogether, like a watch breaking down, and by the time evening approaches you feel little better than a rubbish heap of rotting thoughts, so that a hollow ghost stands where in the radiance of the morning had stood the living man. By that time one idea seemed the only true happiness on earth – the idea of just *sitting down*. Merely to get on to my bicycle and sit down on it – will I ever forget the pleasure! Yet I shall, that's the queer thing. There is nothing we forget so quickly as physical sensations – look how quickly people forgot what they felt when being bombed, and how women forget the labour of child-birth. In the years to come I shall often wish I were on the field, even the hoeing field. But for how *long* at a stretch? I will not remember what it was like, what the conditions for being on the field are. I shall never then be able to experience the excessive pleasure of sitting down, or of eating, for no man can force himself willingly – unless he owns a small farm – to work on beyond what he feels endurable.

This particular field was at its worst stage, the kale being small and the weeds large, so that they often both came up together. Alf joined me now and kept calling it ''ospital work'. He would plug along for a quarter of an hour perhaps, then say – 'Well, it'll soon be Christmas'; then have another go and soon stop again and say – 'Anyway it'll soon be Christmas'. Then he'd say 'I must go and see a man about a dog' and disappear for a short time. Farm work, he said, made you need plenty of sleep. I asked him what time he went to bed, and he said eight-thirty, sometimes nine, and often eight. He spoke of conditions in the professions, the sociality and

also 'good grub in them canteens, not wot it is 'ere, where you get nothing to eat' (true word in war-time on the land!). Often enough, he said, the time is well spread out, there being an hour and a half for dinner, and a break for tea in the afternoon – ah, if there were a break for tea while hoeing! Would *money* thereby be lost? Personally, I think not.

Sometimes it was necessary to stoop down on one's knees in order to deal with some of the plants by finger. I mentioned to Alf that I felt rheumatism in my knees when I did this. Let me hand down his remedy to posterity. Whenever he got rheumatism, he said, in knees, elbow, or anywhere else, he simply rubbed in petrol and in a short time was cured.

This field was near to 'E's house, which had plenty of windows looking out over the farm. Alf didn't like them a bit, didn't approve of windows. 'You know why 'e's put them there,' he said, 'to see wot's going on. That's wot they're there for.' A little far-fetched, I thought, as an

architectural critique, since one top window would do as a spy-hole. Still it is true that many farmers do like to have their houses built on the highest point, so that they can see without being seen. It is natural. And effective. They may never look from the windows, but the worker in the field feels uncomfortable if he is in sight of them – great eyes watching him if he sits down or makes an early getaway. For if the boss isn't there, the family is, and one or other member will notice and tell.

While riding home I reflected upon Alf's time of going to bed between eight and nine o'clock. And this tallies more or less with the bedtime of other agricultural labourers, though some make it a fairly regular nine-thirty. It is necessary if they are to rise early. That is to say they have no free time. This difference in length between the working hours of those on the land and those in the towns, is what has impressed me most; nothing, absolutely nothing, has impressed

me more than this; and when I compare the hours of work put in by these agricultural labourers and those put in by professional men known to me, I say – Here is the *real* Inequality. It is not Wages; it is not Housing; it is not Education which is the bottom inequality, but the distribution of working hours. If the planners improve housing, pay, and education without tackling this matter, then the mental and spiritual life of the agricultural workers will not advance one step.

Recently in a public speech, Mr Ellis Smith, M.P., said that 'There is no reason why, at the end of hostilities, anyone should have to work more than six hours a day for a five-day week.' We need not suppose that he was thinking of agriculture or had ever heard of it; and to say that there is no reason why this should not be achieved immediately after the war is an amusingly empty phrase on the plane of practical politics; but as a general statement it is sound, and must be true. For every year we go on saving labour; and to save labour and yet keep the labourers working the same hours as before is an unendurable absurdity.

It is clear that the world would be saved if all men did work they loved doing. Such men have no time for quarrelling, for fighting, or for money-mania. There will always be few such men. We can never aim to build a society composed of such. But we could aim towards the ideal of work which engages nearly the whole man. In some factories today men use just – one finger. Not the body, not the mind – just one finger! But there is an occupation which can engage nearly the whole man and which if there were time given for the development of the mind, would satisfy the psychological needs of hundreds of thousands of people. This is agriculture. It could provide scope for bodily, mental and spiritual development. These are bald statements. I do not seek to embellish them, they are unquestionable.

When I got home I heard John Barbirolli conducting Beethoven's Seventh Symphony, over the air. What was agriculture for, it seemed to me, except that such a thing as that symphony and the playing of it should be made possible? To make bread so that it shall be possible for mankind to have more than bread and hear the scripture of the kings; to listen to a Beethoven, a Sibelius, a Tchaikovsky, uttering some far message of paradox and joy.

21

HAYMAKING AND COMBUSTION

The weather now made it possible for us to plunge into haymaking. I was soon to become thoroughly implicated in hay. Our first field was composed of sainfoin – for nowadays meadows are seldom composed of a miscellanea of grasses; they are crops. We went out and

drew up in the field with full modern equipment, and went hard at it, the motor cars dashing full steam ahead. For hay is no longer *carried*; it is swept in. Two cars each with an attached sweep, feeding an elevator without cessation, can gather up fifteen to twenty acres in a day. All done in a great hurry. None of the scented peace and quiet which we used to associate with haymaking. The agricultural labourer seldom praises anything, or admits that he enjoyed anything in the way of work; and none, save the old, object to the introduction of any mechanical device. But haymaking provided an exception to this – here at any rate. One and all, they not only hated the present job, but glorified the past. 'We made *hay* in they days,' they said. It was regarded as a kind of holiday time then, their families in the field, great picnics, not to mention lots of beer flowing. Actually and truly a merry time. Now all swept away by the hay-sweep.

Thus we went ahead. The cars were driven by 'E's daughter and one of the boys. The carter kept the tiddler going across the field, the sails of its wheel sweeping up the swathes into long mounds convenient for taking up by the sweeps. Harold, Alf, Dick, and Jimmy received the hay at the foot of the elevator, while Robert built the rick assisted by myself and 'E or a land girl.

I speedily found that ricking under these conditions was no picnic. If four men on the ground are piling the grass on to the elevator, the man receiving it at the top has plenty to hand on. If I stood too near or there was a wind the stuff fell on my head – and at the end of the season I calculated that I had received about fifty acres of hay on my hat. I found that the material, from a hauling-about point of view, was more like wire than my former conception of hay. This was real exercise – but far from boring! Harold, who though officially the tractor-driver, was always one of the best workers at any other job he did, liked to have his game with me. He set the pace at heaving the hay on to the elevator, and catching my eye, would, with a broad grin, in unison with the others, send up a succession of small haycocks in an endeavour to submerge me. On one occasion later on, when we had to build a new wing on to our rick and I was the only person at all near the elevator, a special effort was made to drown me. It was nearly successful, for failing to remove the first lot, the subsequent waterfall came on top of me and I almost disappeared. But by sheer force I rose above the surface, and both on this occasion and on all others managed to keep my head above hay.

Making hay seems to me to be about the most tricky of all the agricultural operations. A weight of decision rests upon the farmer as upon a general in a campaign. If the hay gets a lot of rain it will be spoilt, as everyone knows, though I did not realize until I experienced it that it gets so black that you look like a chimney-sweep after dealing with it. It can be spoilt even easier by sunshine, a thing I had not realized at all; for if it gets too much of it, all the good will be scorched out. And if, in order to avoid this, you lift it too soon and it is slightly green, then the rick may move away, disappear from the field altogether: its means of locomotion being the same as that of an engine – internal combustion. It will begin to heat, getting hotter and hotter until it explodes, catches fire and is seen no more. Such is the marvellous chemistry of the earth, that if we play with her we play with fire.

It happened that our first rick caused trouble in this manner. It had seemed dry enough, but next day we found that it was getting extremely hot. So much so that ultimate combustion was feared. In order to prevent this and let the air in, we dug a hole from the top right down through it. The odour was most remarkable – like very strong strawberries, I thought. But no comparison will describe its richness – at another time I thought it smelt like beer. We took turns with

the hay knife, jumping down into the smoking crater. As we got lower we found it very hot down there, and none of us could stand it for more than a few minutes, and we came up pouring with perspiration. It was a fine morning but with a very cold wind, and the change of temperature after one's shift at this strange mining operation was quite alarming from a chill-catching point of view. We dug two of these shafts, and before building on top again, laid hurdles across the pit-heads. Just before this was done I got down into the shaft we had finished first, being rather fascinated by it. While I was down there Robert began to put a hurdle across the top. I pretended not to notice this until he had put it on. Then I shouted out as if fearfully alarmed at my caged condition, and 'E, much amused, said 'Collis has got left behind!' 'Let him bide!' shouted Robert, pretending to be angry. 'Let him bide! Some volks are better down under, I allow,' and threw a bit of hay on top of the hurdle, at which I shouted – 'Hey, Robert,

I'm suffocating!' At which, with a great show of relenting, he opened the hurdle for me to climb out, saying – 'I reckon we can't afford to lose 'e quite yet', and so I emerged amidst general laughter. For, if work was going forward all right, 'E was by no means averse to a bit of fun, and actually liked an agreeable atmosphere far more than others realized, and was totally unaware of the nervous atmosphere he himself created. (He had two sons, as I have mentioned, and one of them, Reggie, inherited his father's suppressed sense of fun, while the other, John, afraid of being left behind in life's struggle, was in such deadly bossing earnest that it was with consternation that one watched him.)

Our next rick was also slightly damp, but this time we were taking no chances and made two holes in the middle as we built. This was done by filling two sacks tight with hay and building on top of them, raising them as we rose. By this method two clean clear shafts were made

right through the rick, up which the heat could pass. While building, one or other of the sacks continually kept getting submerged and difficult to find. It is sometimes customary to call such a sack 'the old man', and 'E himself, quite aware that he was often referred to by this appellation, added another light touch when a sack got submerged by saying 'the old man is deaf and dumb, 'e don't say nothing when you tread on him'. And subsequently I would ask – 'Where has the old man got to now? I must rescue him.'

This particular dampness we were guarding against was owing to rain that had come on since dealing with the first rick – combustion can also be caused this way. There were constant stoppages, one of the sweeps breaking down every quarter of an hour, the engine for driving the elevator breaking down, and the elevator itself having a stoppage. The wetness of the hay itself tripped up the sweeping, and Robert declared that had four horses been used instead of the power-cutter (which had broken down several times) we could have carried it by now, dry and all.

22

COLLOQUY ON THE RICK

The reading public is so accustomed these days to hear praise of the countryman – the swing in this direction taking place before the war broke out – that it is almost a shock to find that this is not yet realized by country labourers themselves. There are still bitter feelings on the score that the townsman looks down on them. A number of us were couching on the following Saturday morning, before the dew had dried on the next hay field, and the subject came up. Some derogatory remarks were made concerning Jimmy, because they were annoyed that he always seemed to get out of doing jobs such as this 'ere couching. They began to refer to him as 'a town bloke' and to say that he had no right here at all! This led to the complaint, made by Harold, that before the war the town folk 'wouldn't look at you, now they love you', owing to present importance of food grown in England. It was clear that they thought that the present praise was mere lip-laudation caused by the war.

Would 'E want us to go on after dinner today? – that was now the great question. There was a tremendous distaste for working on Saturday afternoon. No one knew what he intended – no one ever knew anything in advance. All said – 'I'm not coming out after dinner, I'm not doing no work on Saturday afternoons' – Alf being even more emphatic in his declared determination

that he would not return after dinner. Yet, in the event, he did – and brought his tea with him. So did all the others – for none trusted the other to stick to his word.

It surprised me that, hay being what it is, feelings about overtime should be strong. But they did not seem to think about the hay, nor to be even vaguely aware that three of the most fearful battles that the world has ever known were at the moment in progress. As for myself, I had brought out a certain amount to eat for dinner, but nothing for tea. That made a gloomy prospect – for whenever I was caught in this way, it never occurred to 'E to ask if I had enough food or bring me out any if I had not, unless I definitely asked him, and then he would bring out a very small piece of cheese and a very plain piece of bread. On this occasion I asked Dick to bring me back something, and he said he would but didn't – for his mother was not in. However, Alf brought me out some chocolate.

We carried a clover field that afternoon and evening. It was the biggest job I had done to date, whether with hay or with anything else, for we did not finish before nine, and there were no accidental stoppages. A seven-hour fall of hay from the elevator to be hauled round, and a steady rainfall of clover-leaves with it. This latter was a part of the business I hadn't bargained for, the downfall of small, dry leaves which comes with clover – and I had not yet properly developed the one and only possible technique against this, namely the tight silk handkerchief round the neck, met by a tightly zipp-fastened shirt, and well topped with hat.

While I stood there on the rising rick the thought crossed my mind that if a painter were to come into the field and sit down and start making a picture of this 'rural scene', I would feel it to be a vast impertinence. And I thought of the picture eventually hanging at an Exhibition to which excessively men-about-town, and women-about-town, totally removed and uninterested in the immediate reality, would come and appraise the picture and see the labourers in terms of paint.

Presently Robert all of a sudden shouted across to me – 'Before the war you wouldn't be on this rick, and if you'd seen I and t'others working here, you'd have thought us a lot of mugs, I allow.' Then he added – 'I think after the war we should change jobs and I'll take my ease.'

'Well,' I said, 'I'd like to see you take on my job which seems so easy, but you don't know what it is.' (For I thought I had concealed the fact that I used a pen.)

'Oh yes I do,' he shouted, 'it's a p–'

'What's that?' I asked, not making out what he had said (it sounded like pig or pork or something).

'A poit, a writer!' he yelled. 'I could go out into that field,' he continued at the top of his voice, 'and write a hundred pages as good as any, but I wouldn't do it. It's too easy. I wouldn't do it. If I did on it, at the end of the day my fingers *would tingle with shame*.'

I turned and looked at 'E who was laughing. Whenever Robert had an outbreak of any kind, 'E always kept up a continuous over-emphatic nervous laugh, in order to keep the matter on a humorous footing.

'Robert wouldn't take no easy money,' he said.

I admit that this sudden attack – though it was really in the nature of an exhibition – rather nonplussed me. I would have liked to advance a more comprehensive philosophy of art than that put forward by Robert, but did not feel equal to doing so under the noise of the elevator, even if I could have found any words that would have been intelligible. Moreover, I was so

subdued to what I worked in at the moment, that I could not help feeling a certain justice in his attitude, and I only said feebly, 'there is a good deal in that', to which he roared back – 'there is far too much in it!'

I felt, however, that I could not quite let the matter rest there, so reducing the terms of the Argument from literature to science, I said that the man who sat down (that deplorable position) and invented the elevator, for instance, had his uses.

But this mute, inglorious Milton was not prepared to lend his support to this view; having already disposed of Literature, he now swept Science aside with a single phrase – 'It took more brain to put it together than to invent it, I allow,' he said.

Since becoming submerged in the land I had frequently reflected upon how great is the difference between what the man on the road sees and the man in the field experiences. From the road, how delightful the sowing of that hundred-acre stretch of land appears; how calm, how leisurely. The tractors are quietly going round with their drills, the horse standing with the wagon-load of sacks is half asleep, the group of men in the middle are conversing at ease, a man is bending over a sack in no haste. Enter the field, draw close. The boss is in a state of great anxiety owing to the threat of rain, the horse won't stand still without being yelled at, the man bending over the sack is in difficulties about getting the grain into a too small bucket and is late in having the stuff ready to feed the approaching tractors, the driver in front being in a great hurry because the one behind is catching him up – the operations proceed amidst flurry, speed, noise, haste, anxiety. From the road, how easy and pleasant it looks on the hayfield; the hay-sweep gently coming in with its nice little bundles, the pitchers throwing the hay on to the elevator with no trouble or effort, the men on the rick in an easy rhythm of leisurely movement, two men chatting together. Enter the field, draw close. The bundles are huge, the sweep has come in too soon and the hay won't come out for the pitchers without tugging, the receivers on the rick are more exhausted than the pitcher below since while hauling with all their might they stand on an unfirm floor; and the men who are chatting are simply saying – 'How's the time going?' 'Only three-thirty, I reckon.'

What the man on the road sees is not the immediate reality any more than when, with the wind blowing away from us, we see an aeroplane hovering like a hawk silently above some trees, or another glamorously glittering in the sky, innocent as heaven's cherubim horsed on the sightless couriers of the air.

Yet here we must pause. The man on the road does not see the immediate reality: he does see something which they in the field do not see, he knows something that they do not know. He sees the Whole. He may see only enough to call it picturesque. The artist is the man on the road with vision. He truly sees the whole, he perceives the Divine Harmony. His task is to reveal the whole to those who are submerged in the part, to unveil the harmony which is really on earth, and thus lessen the burden of life. He does not know that those two men are only asking each other the time, for he sees them in the light of Eternity; and though they may be in hell, he seeks to show that they are also in heaven.

I recently came upon a quotation and comment made by my brother Maurice Collis which deals with this theme. He quoted from the art connoisseur, Mr Max Friedlander, as saying – 'Art creates a second world in which I am not an actor but a spectator, and that world resembles

Paradise.' And my brother goes on to add that 'this provides the most valid reason for the existence of art, which can unveil us Paradise while we are yet on earth'. I would prefer to phrase this with a slight difference and to go a step farther, in company with the great mystic Boehme who said – 'Paradise is still in the world, but man is not in Paradise until he is born again.' We should not say that art creates a *second world*, but rather that the artist uncovers the real world into which we could enter. We should not say that through him we may, *while yet on earth*, see Heaven, for we shall never find heaven save when we are on Earth. It is here. It can be seen when the eye is purged to see it. Sometimes in the stainless, shameless hours of early day, we realize this. As we cycle through the village, which is not awake and never awake to the Great Possibility that lies before it, we become aware that all sins have been forgiven and that Paradise is daily offered to mankind. The artist works for the time when men's vision shall be so purified, that seeing through the outer vesture, they shall have the strength to grasp the farther goal.

But while standing under the elevator, it was not with any feeling of surprise that I heard a man shout at me that his fingers would tingle with shame if he applied them to the task of Shakespeare or Plato. For if I, who by the chance of opportunity can see round the corner of a hay-rick, could nevertheless in the extremities of toil become so submerged in the Part as to think a painter's appearance an impertinence, how much more understandable is the attitude of men who are never in a position to see the Whole. Indeed, I am well content to have such remarks suddenly hurled at me; and, through me, at other artists, so that we may re-examine our place, accept our responsibility, and be true to our function in the scheme.

23

TYPICAL SCENES

On the Monday, when we broke off for dinner, Robert produced a cake which he had brought out for me from his wife, possibly feeling that he had overdone it on the Saturday, or out of good nature, having witnessed the lack of tea I had had (no one having offered me as much as a slice). The business of actually passing the cake over to me was tricky, for it had to be achieved without anyone observing it. That would never have done: a proceeding so unusual and extraordinary would have led to gossip. To me it didn't seem so unnatural as all that, and, always a good receiver, I gave him pleasure by showing great pleasure at seeing it.

After dinner there was a hold-up owing to the breakdown of the battery in one of the hay-sweep cars. The current had to be transferred from the other car. Jimmy was late. 'Where is he

to?' they asked, feeling helpless without him. Everyone seemed to have some idea how to do it, no one a clear idea, and experiments failed. Harold put forward one school of thought, Dick another, while Reggie and John fiddled with this and that, peering closely at the gadgets with unexampled concentration. Wires were strung between the two cars and there was a great deal of trial and error – chiefly error. Harold wound away at the crank furiously. 'E said – 'I don't profess to know. I've too many other things to think about.' Robert advanced a decided suggestion of some sort, but no one took any notice of it, and he strolled to the hedge and carefully examined a hurdle blocking a hole. I stood beside him and made some remark sympathetically indicative of sage council rejected, and he gave me to understand that his patience was nearly exhausted. And so it went on until the mechanic eventually appeared, with that confident smile belonging to genuine engineers in a world given over to ignorance. And sure enough in a few minutes the job was done and the lifeless car was suddenly reborn.

As we went towards the rick, Robert pronounced on the folly of having machines, upon

the waste of time they caused, while with horses the whole thing would be half-done by now; and ended by declaring that if he was a farmer he would let all machines 'go to hell'. 'All except your tractor,' I remarked to Harold. 'I don't want it,' he said quickly. He didn't mean that he didn't want it, but said so for the benefit of the company, because the tractor-driver is generally regarded as having a soft job 'sitting on his behind all day'; and since Harold did not see the matter in this light he wished to disclaim any desire to cling to his heavy burden.

We carried on. This particular afternoon was the hottest we had during the fourteen ricks we put up; in fact I have subsequently set any other gruelling job against this as a measuring rod of the just endurable. My longing for tea-hour cannot by any technical device be brought before the reader nor even felt by me now as I write.

The military were stationed in the neighbourhood, and after dinner an officer came into the field, took a prong, and joined the pitchers at the elevator and continued all the afternoon. At length it was tea-time, which was always heralded by the approach of 'E's other daughter or

wife or both coming out with tea for the family. 'E did not make any remark of any kind to this voluntary helper, nor offer him tea. He was pleased that he had come, appreciated it, and felt grateful; but he was incapable of so simple a social gesture as that of offering refreshment.

It took us only another hour after tea to finish the rick. But today this did not mean that the final raking-up, the horse-raking, was finished, which was Dick's job. Now Dick's ruling idea was always to stop as soon as possible, but today it looked as if we would stop and go home while he alone remained to finish off the horse-raking. He was much perturbed by the enormity of this possibility. Would 'the old man' want him to finish? he wondered; and the job would take some time for he had only half-covered the field.

'Shall I shut out now?' he asked.

'E hesitated an instant and then said that he *didn't mind if he didn't finish*, meaning that he did mind but would not press him to continue.

Dick thereupon said that he would *just as soon stop*, meaning that he would infinitely prefer not to go on.

And he did stop.

There were compensations for working on the rick. A wise man will keep on firm ground if he can help it. Harold never had been on the rick and said he never would – I think he was chiefly afraid of giddiness. Still, I prefer the rick, for the simple reason that I like rising. When beside some trees it is pleasant to become level with the branches, and one gradually gets a good view of the surroundings, of that quiet field, that green hill far away, that village church growing from the grove. But we were too far from the sea to catch sight of it. And that is what I

missed. If only we were by the sea! I constantly thought, nothing would matter, no work would seem too long, no crisis would be upsetting. Mountains that stride down to the sea! cornfields cliffed by the shore: summer in the sky and winter on the waves: the sun-path laid across the dawning deep: the ridged and raving waste enstormed: the dark, cold winter dusk when far, far away on the horizon a long huge black wall of cloud is reared, and just below it soft red rays beam out as from the gateway to another and a brighter land where all is happiness and every tear is wiped away! – thus my mind's eye conjured the sealess scene. For I was born by the sea, and lived by it, and heard from my bedroom window its unfaltering fall upon Killiney Beach. And though I care nothing about immortality, and nothing about what happens to my bones, I do respond with all my heart to the wild and sweeping poetry in Timon's frantic apostrophe to himself – 'Presently prepare thy grave; Lie where the light foam of the sea may beat Thy gravestone daily.'

24

DEPARTURE OF ALF

A few rainy days held us up, and on approaching Alf one morning, his first words were 'I've 'atched out'. He had given notice to quit. I was surprised at this, for though he had always said he was going to give notice, he was wonderful at not sticking to his word. Since he always said that he was not going to work overtime but invariably did, I thought his decision to give notice would remain strictly in the realm of the imagination. But evidently he had had words of a sufficiently stimulating nature with the carter to give him the necessary impetus to quit the agricultural world.

This particular contretemps can hardly be blamed on the carter. Alf had developed a habit of getting down to the stable, when he had a horse and cart, on the tick of five-thirty. Now the carter had to unharness and take the horses out to the field, and needed about ten minutes in hand. He couldn't get away on time when Alf only arrived in the stable at five-thirty. Alf's reason for not arriving earlier was clear and deliberate. He was afraid of being given an extra job by 'E to fill in the ten minutes, which might work out into fifteen or twenty minutes before he could get off. 'I'm not going down yet,' he would say, 'I don't want no new job. 'E'll be there, and 'e'll find me something. It don't do to go down too soon. Better up 'ere, looksee.' But this meant being finally turned on and cursed by the carter – which proved too much for Alf. So at last he gave notice.

He did not leave his cottage straightaway, and as he had often pressed me to look in, I did so one day. His wife, I found, had him well in hand. 'Don't speak with your mouth full,' she said to him, to my embarrassment. She was a regular town person and said how much she missed 'our street'. The neighbours had 'got her down proper' by spying on her and telling things against her to the tradesmen. But his tea was the curious thing. She only allowed him new potatoes and bread.

He said he would let me know where he went when they departed. But he went without a word, no one knew where, for he left no address – on account of bills it was said.

Thus passed Alf from the agricultural scene, a town worker who found that after all land workers do not live luxuriously on 'the fat of the land'. That idiotic phrase is still heard in war as in peace, and I was glad to see a man, accustomed to the canteen-fed factory life, find out how

he liked instead the piece of bread and cheese in the rain by the straw-rick. His departure was pronounced on with a certain glee by the others. He had come to the wrong place, they felt, for a soft job. It is natural for the countryman to enjoy seeing a townsman find the work too much. 'A counter-jumper' is a term, often used, carrying considerable contempt. Not that it was used to describe Alf, who did not belong to that class, but they regarded him more or less with amusement.

25

MY OWN RICK

The rain passed and we continued to parcel up large fields of hay into neat solids. It is very satisfactory to look at a finished field, at the solid ricks in which all the hay is now encompassed, and the ground itself looking like a well-swept floor. (There were no stray bits left on the field at this farm, no waste; even straggling wisps were collected and elaborately added to the rick at the last minute.) When the sun begins to slant after tea, the stacks achieve a wonderfully clear-cut appearance, and seen from a distance cast shadows that seem themselves substantial.

It gave me much pleasure to look at a stack standing in a field, and be able to say to myself – 'I put that there, or helped to put it there.' Still more so, very much more so, if I had actually been the rick-builder. And, in truth, Robert did permit me to build one before we had done our fourteen. In a jocular way he had said that he would make me build one, and this had whetted my ambition, and seizing a favourable opportunity, I held him to it. I was extremely lucky. We had done several fields with short hay and a strong wind. I got a field with good long hay and no wind. Robert did not wish me to succeed. But he did not hinder me at all; on the contrary, he helped me in every way, adopting a fatherly manner as the best attitude. The others were anxious that I should succeed in order that Robert would be annoyed. And so, from the ground I received many signs and gestures indicative of the state of my corners and walls, with shouts of 'harder! harder!' when I was not making the perpendicular, and 'not so hard!' when I was going out too far. The thing in building is to get your walls up straight, which I found easier to understand than to do, since there is a strong psychological feeling against putting the hay *out* – one always feels it will fall over, not realizing how strongly it will be bound by the hay that goes behind it (for hay binds like brambles, as you find quick enough when you try to take it out). This tendency against the perpendicular is most strong at the corners when it is most necessary to oppose it and be bold. The great thing, I found, was to put two helpings at the corners, and not be faced with the psychologically distressing sight of a *sloping margin*. However, all went well, and I roofed it in the approved Gothic style. It needed no props – and, believe it who will, 'E was heard to say – 'One of the best ricks we've done.' It was on the highest level of the field, and so as we went away in the evening when it was getting dark, it looked wonderful, to me, against the sky – all those untidy bundles that I had been dealing with throughout the day now compressed into a pure solid, the pointed roof traced blackly and with geometrical straightness and

sharpness against the light. Going away from it, down the sloping field with the others, I tried not to turn my head too often to have a look at it.

These were long days. By the time I had pushed my bicycle back up the hill, it was generally just in time to hear the Nine o'Clock News – news a thousand miles away. It would be eleven o'clock before I got into bed. Here was a real occasion of taking the weight off my feet – which had been on my feet for over fifteen hours – and doing so was a definite sensation, wonderful. Full days; happy days; days free from indulgence, free from choice, free from domesticity, free from dreams, free from lost hours, unrewarded labours, mistaken projects. How many men is each man composed of? How many men am I! It is a far cry from this to Bloomsbury where I lived seven years. A far cry from that field to the British Museum Reading Room in which I passed so many hours in search for truth. Hours ill-spent? – I searched for the truth and did not

find it. But if I find it here it is because I sought it there. If now I look upon the common earth and read the Riddle, I had to forge my weapon first, and wait and wander till my hour should come.

One night I woke up at two a.m. (I looked at my watch) and moved away the books that I had put on a chair beside my bed; for in forking away the hay I was afraid that I would fork away the books as well, and either lose or damage them. So I piled them together under the chair out of reach both of the falling hay and of my prong. I did this with serious deliberation, being quite awake enough to note the time, but also feeling certain that hay was falling and that I was experiencing some difficulty in not damaging the books; in fact I dared not dig my prong in properly because of them. And sure enough in the morning, when I woke up fully, I found my books piled up under the chair safely out of reach of any hay that might fall.

26

MEDITATION WHILE SINGLING MANGOLDS

The period between haymaking and harvest is rather an uncomfortable one. We are between two worlds, as it were, one dead, the other as yet powerless to be born. Slack off then? Pause in well-doing? Far from it. Now is the time to get down to the remainder of the hoeing before it is too late.

There was certainly still plenty to be done here on fields of kale, swedes, and mangolds. In fact it was only now that we began to single the mangolds. The shoots, sown by drill, come up close together in long lines. They cannot be left like that but must be given room to expand – that is they must be singled. About a foot must be left between each shoot. Thus while hoeing weeds away you also hoe out a vast number of plants – a wholesale destruction which gives one an uneasy feeling, for what good can come of these miserable little shoots you have left at such a great distance from each other? Frequently the shoots grow in pairs, and as it is impossible to use the hoe for separation it is necessary to stoop right down and separate them with your fingers. Thus singling is hoeing multiplied. I have not written enthusiastically about hoeing, though actually at times I have enjoyed it. I cannot remember any time having enjoyed singling mangolds, and as I frequently had to do many hours of this alone, I again began to feel time drag. And again I was shocked at the contrast of my attitude now towards the clock with what it had been in the old days. For I used to think then that all I needed was time to get on with my work, and money so as to be able to do that work. For me the money was time. For the business man time is money. For the hoer money is not time nor is time money; to him time is simply an enemy. And when we go a step further and enter prison, we are confronted with the most terrible phrase known to man – *doing time.*

Still, while performing jobs of this sort I have come closer to understanding the history of mankind. How easy it is, I said to myself one day, how easy while singling mangolds to understand the rise and fall of civilizations!

How did it all start? Who conceived the town, the city, the metropolis? Into whose mind first sprang the idea of the machine? Who first framed the fabric, turned the wheel of civilization? The countryman, of course. He was the first townsman, the first mechanic, the first industrialist. It was he who dreamt the dream of conquering Nature and of escaping from her. He built London and New York.

He stood on the field, spade in hand, trying to till the soil. A hard job with only that imple-

ment. So he invented a horse-movable spade – the plough. He stood amongst the ripened corn with a sickle. He could improve on that, so he made the scythe; and he went on improving all his devices in his conquest of nature – he was the first mechanic. And as he toiled in the fields, often covered with mud, or wet, or freezing cold, or his back splitting as he stooped over the mangolds, he began to think how wonderful it would be to get away from this struggle, to escape altogether from Nature. So he devised something more than a village, he built a large number of houses with intervening paths – a town. He went further – he conceived the idea of the Great City. How marvellous it would be, he thought, to make a place so vast in extent that you could not even see the soil, to make the paths therein so smooth and clean that you would not get a speck of dirt on clothes or boots, to see delicate women walking along who did not know the difference between a bangle and a mangold, to have lights turned on by a switch and hot water by a tap, to have shops making a blaze of light in the darkness, to enter glorious buildings in which you would find entertainment and instruction, and great churches like jewels so that the eyes of those who gazed on them grew dim.

Gradually the edifice of civilization was set up – in the image of the countryman's desire as he stood on the desolate field. But as the years passed and generation succeeded generation the townsman began to forget that he had come from the country, and the countryman that he had made the town. And because the people in the towns were more comfortable and better looking and with wider interests than those in the country, they began to feel more important and to despise the very people upon whom they relied for three meals every day. And because they felt important and began to look it, the countrymen themselves were impressed and thought them wonderful. As the process went on it was the man in the *street*, the man in the city, the *citizen*, who came to be regarded as the only person who counted, while queer derogatory names were found for the men in the fields. The citizens multiplied immensely, became far more powerful than the peasants, and decreed that town wages should be much higher than country wages. Seeing how matters stood, many agriculturists cried, 'Away from the land!' shook the mud off their boots, and joined the citizens.

But as time went on a strange unease began to afflict the people in the towns. As they walked through the everlasting streets they began to pine for the open fields, for the blessed sun, for the realities and simple joys they had left behind. They began to declare that civilization was rotten at the core and perished at the roots, and that nothing could save it except a great Unindustrial Revolution. Not only citizens, but 'City Men' began to say in their cups that their work was a farce and that they would rather 'keep a pig'. Intellectualists insisted that they were 'really peasants at heart'. A cry of 'Back to the Land' went up, not from those on the land but from those in the towns.

And when at last they returned to the soil from whence they had come, they often found that it was no longer there. Their neglect had brought about such appalling erosion that Gobi and Libyan deserts now confronted their astonished gaze, while in other places whole cities were washed away by rivers swollen with water pouring from despoiled and abandoned forests.

Thus my meditation as I stooped over the mangolds. The same conception had occurred to me forcibly earlier in the year when one evening I suddenly felt a great desire to visit a town and dine in an expensive hotel. Changing my clothes suitably I went in. I found a very nice hotel. So great is the difference between the agricultural world and the world outside – a strange, dream-

like, picnic of a world it looks from the field – that I blinkingly looked round at the lounge as if seeing such a place for the first time. The good lighting, the polished floor, the groups of clean and well-dressed amiable-looking people held my attention. I poked round the place, and finding a bathroom, entered it. Overcome by the cleanliness of the room I thought it would be grand to have a bath – and I had one. True, there was no bath-towel; but the bath-mat seemed to me startlingly clean and it would do – and it did very well. It was now time for dinner and I entered the dining-room and sat down. I was greatly taken with the spotless table-cloth, the seven pieces of cutlery (I counted them), the vase with the roses in it, the perfect floor, the panelled walls, the electric candlesticks. The other tables were occupied by miscellaneous people, all looking well set up, pleased, and expectant. Waiters began to come round, dressed in white jackets and black trousers. Four courses were brought to me with great expedition. I examined each plate in turn

– very nice, one with a picture of water-cress on it. I looked round at the smiling faces of the people, all wearing expressions not seen outside; and at a waiter bending over a group with the deeply knowing and confidential smile of a man who can produce wine. I looked at the foods that were brought to me – some meat, peas, greens, and potatoes. Doubtless they came from the land, but it hardly occurred to me to make the connection, certainly no one else in the room did so: the food simply came – no, not even from the kitchen – from behind the screen from which the waiters, like magicians, emerged again and again. For this, I saw, was a dream place, not subject to reality. If a ploughman, I reflected, were to come into this room suddenly, as such, he would be thrown out, or 'asked to leave'. And that would be right. I would be the first to cast the first stone at him. It would be an unforgiveable intrusion. For he would have broken the spell, destroyed the film and the fantasy of the agreed illusion, infringed upon the dream

mankind has dreamt on the bitter field – this escape from Nature, this shelter from the storm, this palace, this paradise.

The whole thing was so fantastic and delightful, and knowing that a bus would soon be due outside, I kept a firm watch on myself (like a man over-drinking) lest I linger for ever here and become lost to the agricultural world. However, I pulled myself together and went out into the pouring darkness and caught the bus and then took my bicycle for a final part of the journey. I was soon passing our farmyard, which adjoined the road. There it was – deserted, silent, a pocket of gloom, a nonentity of a place, something to pass by. Was it really possible, I asked myself, that this slushy yard, so humble, so lacking in all the props and appointments of Power, was yet the foundation of society? Yet so it was. Upon this the fabric rested, upon this was erected all that glittered and all that shone; and I knew that the lighted palace from which I had come where the Figures paced on the polished floor, and the Magicians emerged with food from behind the screens, could not otherwise exist at all. I got off my bicycle and gazed into the farmyard – at the stable door, the pile of manure, the muddy pool, the old binder in the corner, the oil-cans and sacks, the three wagons and the two carts under the shelter. I peered at these things through the dreary dank of the dripping darkness, with some intensity, as if aware that here only, in this place, and in such guise, could I find the roots of grandeur and the keys of life.

27

A CRITICAL MOMENT

Most of my hoeing was done in company with others. Working at this job in company is not only better for the labourers but better for the farmer – far more ground is covered by a worker in company with others than if alone. The spirit of competition always enters into it, for no one likes to be left behind if the work is being done in paralleled rows as is usual. Thus the pace is according to the fastest worker. And if just two people are taking a couple of rows there is the same tendency to compete – no one knows why. Once I did this absolutely deliberately. One of 'E's daughters often came out into the fields, and also imitated her father in every particular. Finding myself on a parallel row with her, I worked during the greater part of a morning at an absurd rate, continually passing her as I went up and down the rows.

Harold, Dick and I did a good deal of hoeing together. 'Anyway, it's a bit of a change and break for you,' I said to Harold. 'Yes, but the wrong kind of change,' he replied. All the same he

always worked the quickest at this job as at many others. We were working now on a field along which the main track ran. Hence the approach of the Van was easily seen. When it was discerned approaching, our pace would quicken; not too fast, since that would look bad, too obvious; but appreciably, while we asked 'Is 'E going to stop?' If the van stopped then we might expect 'E to alight and come across, look on, make a criticism, and possibly join us. This was always a critical moment when the Van was seen – 'Will 'E stop, join us, and spoil the morning?' became the great question. One occasion was rather amusing. Harold, Dick and myself were going along our rows side by side across the field. Our cut reached to about the middle of the field, when normally we would turn about. We were working towards the track when the Van appeared coming up, and then stopped. 'E got out and went over into the next field to speak to Robert, and there he remained for some time. We couldn't see him, but had to suppose that he could see us. At last he appeared again. Would he now come over to us? But no, he got into the van. But it didn't start off at once; evidently he was watching us. We were still working towards the track, towards him. We came to the end of our cut. We should now have stopped, picked our new rows and gone back. But Harold said 'Keep on, don't stop, keep on; if 'e sees us stop 'e'll come over, sure thing. Keep on and 'e'll be off.' And though we had come to the end of our cut we kept going now on ground which we had already hoed ('E wouldn't be able to notice this at the distance), and continued keeping on until the crisis passed and 'E got back into the van and did at last b off.

28

LABOURERS AND MARRIAGE

In the mornings and during the early part of the afternoon at this time there were more than the three of us, for we were generally joined by the land girls from the dairies. At this farm the land girls seldom stayed long, new ones always coming and going; and for that reason it is difficult for me to include them in my canvass, as it were, in spite of the friends I have made, especially one. If it were asked what the Land Army did during the war, the answer is quite simple – they got the milk for the nation. Of course they did a great deal else as well – and would the potatoes have been lifted without them? – but the main fact is this that the nation would hardly have got its milk without their help.

Thus in company hoeing went much better, for there is nothing like chat for passing the

time. I sometimes wonder whether economists, sociologists, heavy-weight philosophers, and world meliorists pay enough attention to the ordinary remarks of ordinary people. In the course of conversation, a land girl (who was in love with Dick) said to Harold – 'Oh you've nothing to worry about. You're married. You have all you want.' A perfectly simple and straightforward statement which was received by Harold without the slightest demur. It is worth bearing in mind the simple desires and natural aims of people, especially women. For whatever unfeminine feminists may preach, women, the most sophisticated as well as the most simple, invariably say sooner or later – 'All I want is to make a home.' The modern publicist who feels it necessary to make it quite clear that of course he doesn't imagine that 'women's place is the home' might just as well say that of course women don't really produce children. (It is the phrase that is wrong, and the conditions, not the actuality.) The idea that women could actually bear children without at the same time being particularly interested in and gifted for dealing with the machinery of keeping them going (often called home life), ought to be too silly ever to be discussed. There is also a lesser difference between men and women – namely that women are more human than men. For that reason they find it difficult to endure non-personal, wholly objective work when performed alone. Thus agriculture (except on the stock side) is nearly as unsuitable for women as is nautical work. In spite of the fact that they are so much stronger than men in many ways, and because of that extra muscle which physiologists say is situated at the base of their tongues, agriculture will remain alien to them until far more people work on the land – for *indifference to the object* gets a woman down much easier than a man.

But Harold, beyond saying that he would like a thousand pounds a year, did not demur in the least to the statement that, being married, he had everything he wanted (he had courted his wife for eight years). For this is true of many men as well as women. It is especially true amongst the working classes generally, and still more so among agricultural labourers, all of whom always marry – it is simply not done not to have a wife. And for them, as for the working class as a whole, there is no marriage problem, no sex problem, no domestic problem. For the most part the woman simply toes the line, she has no other course. Or there may be harmony. Or she may be the stronger and have the upper hand. But there is no great over-conscious problem made of the situation. They dare not think about it for there is no escape. When things are bad they are terrible – for there isn't the hard cash to separate. On this score I have sometimes come upon the greatest bitterness in connection with the actuality here of one law for the rich and another for the poor.

On the whole, however, there is no time for the refinements of domestic infelicity any more than for the leisured infelicities. I have often thought how far removed this world here is from what one might call the Virginia Woolf world of upper-middle-class frustration, time to think (without effect), time to dream (without pleasure), time to feel wasted and lost: what can a bit more money do to make up for this! And, we may add, in the agricultural world there is very little time for the young men to indulge in refined vices. Hence Buchmanism would be inconceivable amongst them. Mr Buchman (sometimes called Dr), was an American psychologist who in the name of religion gathered round him a huge following of university students to confess their private vices. Such introspection is unknown to the young man who gets up at six-thirty every morning and is hard at it till six-thirty in the evening. (Also the religious idealism that genuinely accompanied Buchmanistic confessions is foreign to him.)

Moreover, they do not read. Readers who read a great deal as a matter of course can hardly realize the state of mind of those who don't read at all. It is very different, doubtless. Reading – especially novels – makes us all far more conscious of ourselves and of other people and of our emotions and situations and reactions. We are not conscious about everything in the absurd degree presupposed in novels, we do not dream of emphasizing life in that way; but when we read about problems which approximate to our own we then brood upon our own. The non-readers are nothing like as aware of their feelings as they would be if they read about the emotions of others and the domestic problems of invented characters – though I sometimes wish that they were a little more conscious of their unconscious, for an obvious motive disguised by a trumpery reason is irritating. I am inclined to think that a non-reader takes life easier if less fully. A neighbour of mine enjoys a drink at the pub. But if I ask him to come out he often has to

excuse himself at the last minute – his wife having stopped it, being afraid of him getting into mischief. I doubt if this annoys him much, however, or if he lets it get him down, or asks himself whether he has married the right woman and so on. Not being steeped in books which touch on problems of this kind, he probably doesn't think about it at all. Life doesn't present itself in the form that it does to those whose minds are broadened and often corrupted by reading. I never heard my companions make a psychological generalization about life or women or marriage, and if I ever did so few of them took the slightest interest. The most they will run to in this direction is, to quote Robert for instance – 'She'll always come home on Saturday night'; or, to quote Harold concerning a certain girl who had an extra affair – 'If she done it once she'll do it again,' indeed he kept repeating this much to the annoyance of the girl's friend – 'If she done it once she'll do it again.' I never heard him make any other generalization of any kind, and I

doubt if he ran to more than this sovereign idea that if she done it once she'll do it again. Dick did like reading and was much more alive to the world and the possibilities of life than most of the others; and talking of girls he said – 'I don't like the kind of girl you go out with three times, and then – "How's your father?"'

It is right here that farmers themselves, alone in the British community, know how to choose their wives. They are the only people who show wisdom in this matter. Thus in the agricultural world there is no such thing as a nagging wife. The farmer's position is extremely favourable for keeping her down. He is up early; he is on the move incessantly; he is always grappling with difficulties and anxieties; he is invariably in a hurry; he is continually let down by man and nature; there is nothing abstract or invisible about his work, it can be so clearly seen, it is hugely writ; he is tired and hungry at the end of his hard day's work. This puts him into an impregnable position. You can hardly be petty with a man thus fortressed. You can't suggest that a little pleasure would be nice, since he forgoes pleasures, the hard-working, careful man. The only thing to do is to out-do him in virtue and also renounce relaxation. This is the line taken by farmers' wives, and one wonders whether the nation, while handing bouquets to the men for the work done, fully realizes the part played by the wives.

William Cobbett, wise in everything, provides here also the prototype of how to choose your wife as a farmer. He spotted her in New Brunswick. 'It was dead of winter, and, of course, the snow several feet deep on the ground, and the weather piercing cold. In about three mornings after I had first seen her I had got two young men to join me in my walk; and our road lay by the house of her father and mother. It was hardly light, but she was out in the snow, scrubbing out a washing-tub. "That's the girl for me," I said, when we had got out of her hearing.' In due course they married and lived happily ever after.

29

HOEING WITH 'E

When we had finished this particular field of kale and swedes – how quickly the scene had changed since I had dragged it, chain-harrowed it, cultivated it, rolled it, couched it! – we were sent off to another stretch of kale at the far end of the farm. We assembled and looked round – there was about eleven acres of it. The kale was submerged in a mass of thistles, mutton-docks, and charlock. How could we make any impression on such a field?

we wondered. Harold said that the only sensible thing to do would be to plough it in. I wondered; for that is exactly what Robert had said about the former one I had been on – ''E should plough it in, it won't come to no good letting it bide, I allow.' But in a few weeks it had risen up quite well.

The farmer who knows his job is careful not to take advice from his men. When in a quandary concerning the best place to build a rick in view of subsequent threshing, 'E occasionally asked Robert what he thought about it; but on the whole he was superbly independent. He would have pleased old William Cobbett who, in a little-known book on forestry, remarks upon how foolish it is for a boss ever to consult his men before making a decision. 'Let me exhort you,' he wrote, 'to give simple and positive *orders*, and never, no, never to encourage, by your hesitation, even your bailiff or gardener so much as to *offer* you *advice*.' And again, 'Above all things, avoid asking their *advice*, and even telling them your *intentions*. If you do this, even with the foreman, they will all soon become *councillors*. They will deliberate ten times a day; and those who deliberate know not any sense in the word *obedience*. As many hands as you like, but only one *head*.'

This field was well situated, miles off the track of general inspection, and we had a pleasant time that morning, Harold, Dick and myself. It was very hot, and during the dinner-hour I procured a bottle of beer which we could tap during the afternoon. Thus the three of us started off in a good frame of mind, and having chosen a sensible 'cut' which would make the best show, we did not intend to over-do it.

We had the field to ourselves except for the carter who had now come to broadcast artificial, but was out of sight over the rill. But in a very short time we saw the van draw up outside the gate. 'The Van!' said Harold, 'The Van!' said Dick. And all of us became very interested in our hoeing. 'I reckon 'E's going over to the carter,' said Harold. But at that moment the Van did a terrible thing, it *came into the field*, and the gate was closed behind. 'That means he's going to stay,' said Dick. 'I bet he's coming to hoe with us,' I said; and sure enough in a moment we saw him, hoe in hand, coming across to join us! And without any greeting or the slightest attempt at a *bonhomie* approach, he joined us in silence, and a great silence fell as we worked. I tried to humanize the situation slightly by saying that I wished that the mutton-docks were mutton chops. This decimal point of a joke was taken up by 'E who added another one per cent of humour to the idea. And Harold laughed, though Dick preserved a dead silence. Not being able to think of any further motif for conversation we relapsed into silence again, which was not broken till 'E suddenly reprimanded Dick for his slack way of hoeing – 'You might as well leave the field as do it that way,' he said, which brought the bitter rejoinder from Dick about 'no appreciation if he did well', and a further rejoinder from 'E saying – 'If I speak civil to you I expect you to speak civil to me,' for he was convinced that he himself always spoke civilly, and as a matter of fact Dick was generally more uncivil to him than he to Dick.

Meanwhile the beer was in the hedge. It was permissible at this farm, during a hot afternoon, not to stop working, but at intervals to take a swill of lemonade or cold tea. So I said to Harold – 'It makes one thirsty, this heat,' and when we got to the bottom of our row he went and had a drink from the bottle, whispering to me on return 'that's saved my life'. Dick and I did likewise on coming down again, each saying loudly 'nothing like cold tea for a thirst', feeling that the word beer would sound too much in the nature of a planned debauchery. By this time the carter

had come near us on his errand with the artificial, having made it snappy since the arrival of the Van. He observed this drinking of the beer, and though he knew that I always had a beer-bottle with me normally for cold tea, he was aware from fifty yards off that it was beer we were having, not tea. How he knew this I cannot say, but I was informed afterwards that he did know it. He was knowledgeable about beer. 'There's nothing 'e don't know about beer,' they said.

At last five-thirty arrived, and we had had very nearly four hours of this without a break. On the tick of that hour the three of us stopped dead, and 'E had to stop also and go off to the van. Had we not done so we knew that we would have gone over the time. So we simply 'shutout' abruptly, without comment.

30

THE LABOURER'S THEORY OF KNOWLEDGE

If any farmers happen to read this book they may feel that I have only given one side of the picture. This may be true. But since most books on the land are written by farmers, land-owners, or agricultural specialists, I shall be glad indeed if through me the labourer's view finds expression. At the same time I can hardly help being also alive to the other side. Nothing would induce me to take on the job of running a farm of my own with its attendant responsibility and appalling anxiety. I know well enough that time, for instance, is seen from exactly the opposite end by the boss – he is always *behind*, he must husband every minute. And I know perfectly well that all labourers will take the fullest possible advantage of a weak man. All men, and all women even more so, are bullies. Precisely to the degree in which a person is weak, advantage will be taken by the other side; whether between labourer and boss, or husband and wife, or parent and child, or master and pupil, or governor and governed. I always see this fact of human behaviour wih the clarity of an image. I see it in the form of a spring of great elasticity. If much pressure is exerted against that spring it can be held right down. If no pressure is exerted against it, it will go out and out and out. It is not good to keep it right down. It is not good to let it expand right out. We are all afraid of that spring. In their fear some men try to keep it right down – with bad results. Others exert only a tiny nervous pressure – and are swept away. The

thing is to hold a reasonable balance. This image may not be clear or useful to others, but I take a chance with it, since it is clear and useful to me.

There is an interesting remark which I have often heard here and elsewhere, not uncommon anywhere when some boss or foreman is mentioned. 'The trouble is,' they say, ''e's so *ignorant.*' By this they do not mean that he lacks knowledge. They mean that he lacks *manners.* It is a significant remark. For what is manners? Manners is psychology. It is the understanding of the simple psychological needs of other people. It is homage paid to the strikingly simple fact that people like you to address them amiably, to show appreciation, and to say thank you at intervals. If a man does not know this and act upon it he is called *ignorant* by labourers under him. That is their philosophy of education. I recommend it to the educational pundits who are shocked at the existence of those schools that really do understand the importance of teaching

manners. If I were not afraid of holding up my narrative I would enjoy nothing better than to dig down to the further fundamentals involved here. I shall content myself with observing that when we go one step further we find that manners lead to *morals.*

Let a farmer then, I would say, exert a reasonable pressure upon the spring, with the applied psychology of a good manner, throwing in many a 'thank you', many a greeting, many a word of praise (it need not always be sincere), not to mention occasional sympathetic inquiry regarding a man's mishap or trouble. The grossest advantage would be taken of such behaviour. It would be taken once. It need not be twice. For the farmer could then afford to pounce upon any man, with real fury, and could do so with ten times more force and effect than if his normal behaviour was unamiable. I would myself make it a rule to pounce whenever the occasion justified it, even if I didn't feel angry. And to any man, 'the soul of good nature', who feels himself to

be an exception to my generalizations about bullies, I would say that those who intend to accomplish anything in this world should try to control their good temper just as others should control their bad temper. And should anyone wish to be reminded of a delightful and classic example of just how to deal with the insolence of mankind, he can find it in Mr A. G. Street's *Farmer's Glory*, when a certain labourer thinks he can easily force the young boss's hand, but is given notice instead.

31

LACK OF COOPERATION

During the following days we had the field to ourselves, without any appearance of the Van. Conversation included discussion concerning the hour at which we received our money every Saturday fortnight. The word Wages, by the way, is never used unless it is preceded by the adjective 'higher'. It is always 'I've come for my money' or 'here's your money'. The words *my money* are felt to carry the idea of *my rights* better than Wages. Yet the latter word is a much nicer one. There is a touch of poetry in it. Preachers used to say that the wages of sin were death. That was good rhetoric, so no one questioned it. Had the preacher said that the salary of sin or the fees of sin were death, he would never have got away with it.

The time at which we received our pay was between six and seven on the Saturday. (This business varies enormously from farm to farm.) It was a very unpopular hour. They couldn't go out unless they got back early. And their wives were without shopping money: or so they said – probably untruly. For they surely cannot live up to the hilt like that. I mean except in some cases it cannot be necessary. Yet it may be true. True when the wages were twelve shillings a week; true now that they are three pounds and ten shillings; true if they were ten pounds; while we all know that the thousand-a-year man is very hard up – for here is another 'spring'. However, it is a trait very pleasing to employers.

They could easily have had the hour altered if all of them had become vocally indignant in unison and refused to be paid at that hour. They did not do so. For lack of cooperation was most emphatic. They never combined. They did not stand by one another nor trust one another. Each of them complained to me about the lack of cooperation of the others, making also some denigrating remarks concerning either the behaviour or ability of so and so. Their unsolidarity was quite remarkable. Neither in small matters nor large did they dream of acting together. And if on a Saturday morning 'E was away they were careful not to knock off a little early lest someone would tell the tale.

There is a tendency amongst some passionate middle-class meliorists to give the working-class man virtues he does not possess. For instance, they emphasize his capacity for 'warm friendship'. This would be strange if it were true. For friendship rises from developed emotions and developed understanding. But I have not found it to be true. Indeed the very idea of *affection* almost seemed foreign and uncalled for. And even when a man leaves and goes off somewhere else he seldom bothers to say good-bye to his mates – he just packs up and disappears. No letter communication follows, no answers to letters if written – I have sometimes thought that this attitude amounted to a sort of melancholy sense of the folly of attachments in a shifting world. I was rather amused one day later on, during harvest, when a schoolboy of about seventeen who had joined us was going off next day. He came out into the field in the evening and stood around, wanting to say good-bye to people. But no one knew what he was getting at.

If there was lack of friendship there was no lack of civility. No matter what anyone might say about anyone else, there was absolutely no open hostility. I was sometimes surprised at their double-facedness. But the same thing in higher circles is called tact and diplomacy. In this capacity I have often thought that my companions displayed the greatest mastery, acting on occasion with a discretion worthy of a Cabinet Minister.

32

DICK AND EDUCATION; HAROLD AND VILLAGE LIFE

Harold now went off on another job, while Dick and I carried on. When Dick was in the company of 'E he was silent; when in general company he humorously groused; and when alone with me he would give vent to his ambition to see the world and know things and study. He had a terror of becoming like older men on the land he saw around. Desire to see the world is luckily rare amongst agricultural labourers. We were near a beautiful village by the sea, but I met no one here who had ever adventured so far. As for wanting to study – well that is still rare anywhere. Dick did desire it. He used to learn a little German every evening. He was eager to acquire knowledge. Were it not for the existence of Mr H. G. Wells it would be extremely

difficult to know what book to lend such a man; but there is the *Outline of History*, so I lent him that, which he read twice. Here was the perfect example of the young man for whom there were no educational facilities in the villages. No chance given, no encouragement. He was not talented, not exceptionally gifted at all, and with little will-power and no real passion for learning. He wished to develop himself, that is all – and might quite easily be prevented from doing so by circumstances. In fact he was exactly the kind of person with whom educationalists are concerned. No one need bother about the man of great talent, the man of genius, the man of will. Such men thrive on resistance, on difficulties, on enemies; whether thrown on the rocks or the cushions of life, they triumph in the end. If this is not wholly true, it is truest in the realm of knowledge and literature, when the reading of *one* good book will set him on fire, and nothing will stop his advance. There is little need to help or encourage him. But the man of

small will-power and small talent and mild desire for development needs all the help that can be given, and years of it. Otherwise circumstances prove too much for him, and he gives up. His work stops him, his girl stops him. In Dick's case, however, his girl was his chief source of encouragement, and it is conceivable that she may keep it up.

The actual handing of the *Outline* to him was certainly a process demanding discretion. It would never do, we felt, to be seen with the book. And my edition was large enough to fill a big haversack. I brought it out to the field and at the end of the day we went by the side of a hedge to make the transference from my bag to his. Just at that moment Robert passed. He shyed slightly at the sight of the volume, rather like a horse alarmed at something. But he was not indignant. 'You've got summat to get on with there, I allow,' he said in rather a low and hurried manner, and passed on.

Then Dick went off to something else and Harold came back, and I worked with him for some days. He had lived in this village all his life and was content to remain there and bring up his family in the same place. He had no more desire to venture beyond it than into the realms of the mind, and he said, though not boastfully, that he never read anything whatever – and though I believe in the mind I do not forget that such men are the strong pillars of this world. But he was not uncritical of village life as it now is. He spoke of his boyhood, which was not so long ago, when there was a good deal of life in the village, with games and expeditions sponsored by the Squire. For some years that has been a thing of the past, and the lads hang about with nothing to do. It is the old story. In the old days Inequality and Aristocracy, the Lord of the Manor or the Squire considering it his duty to give life to the village: then the ousting of Aristocracy and the trumpeted entrance of Democracy, until the man whose motto had been *noblesse*

oblige in relation to all the villagers, now has the greatest difficulty in getting a single attendant to come in *and oblige* with a little housework. He is no longer able to think about the life of the village, and the villagers are unable to give life to it themselves. The French revolutionists went in for Liberty, Equality, and Fraternity. Since then a good deal of Liberty and Equality have been established. Has that led to more Fraternity? Do we all now embrace as brothers under the wings of Equality? No. There is less Fraternity. Each man is now out for himself and for higher wages. No doubt it is only a transition stage. We can hope for better days. The moral is clear: the people must have *leaders*. Every village must have a leader. If the old ones have perished to make way for democracy, then the sooner democracy supplies new ones the sooner we shall get out of this wretched transition stage. But it is clear that leaders cannot be sent into the village from outside. This is something that cannot be *planned*. You cannot farm from Whitehall, it is

reiterated, you cannot cultivate the soil. Neither can you cultivate the soul. It would be as absurd to try and plan a Village Revival as a Religious Rebirth or an Artistic Renaissance. It must be done by the village itself. A village will cohere under a leading personality who belongs to the place. Otherwise it will remain incoherent.

From where we worked we could look down upon the Manor House. One old lady lived in it. She had lived there fifty years. But now it was passing from her hands. It was up for sale. She possessed two outmoded things – goodness and culture. When she passed, would they pass away also? I wondered.

33

FARMERS AND INCOMES; PLEASING CONSIDERATIONS

At length Harold went off again and I carried on alone on this eleven-acre field of kale. Although at first it had seemed a hopeless affair we had managed to make an impression upon it. 'E had told us to leave the charlock and concentrate upon the thistles and mutton-docks. But that was against human nature, it goes too much against the grain to leave part of the weeds like that. For making a good show, apart from any effect upon your employer, has a personal bearing as well, and in a case like this one could not leave in the yellow, thus blurring the work, instead of seeing the green portion which one had done over against the yellow-flagged portion one had not yet tackled. I managed to make quite a considerable impression even by myself, and when 'E appeared he was actually surprised at the progress, and though he had not much hopes in the whole field being finished on account of pressing work elsewhere, he let me carry on – in which I encouraged him, for I liked this job; pardon my inconsistencies about hoeing.

When alone with 'E I always got on with him excellently. And if launched into a chat he would often continue on and on for some time, and not necessarily only upon agricultural topics. But I preferred to get him on to agriculture and thus pick up what I could, including such a pleasing item as that cows sometimes do better on poor hay than on very good hay in so far as, instead of stuffing themselves, they are abstemious and thus keep in better condition. Harold and I had amused ourselves while hoeing by calculating 'E's profits (quite a favourite pastime on

this farm). Taking it piece by piece it had worked out under our hands into a huge sum, for we did not err on the conservative side. And I could not resist the temptation of getting 'E himself on to the subject of financial takings, and learnt, of course, that he had so far made – *nothing*. Such and such a field had cost him £1,000 to prepare (we had calculated that it should yield £3,000) so how could he hope for a profit? I listened fascinated as I always am by farmers explaining how they have not made and cannot make anything. I do not necessarily doubt their word, I have no head for this sort of thing. No one knows what a farmer's income is if he chooses to keep it dark. Very often he is quite as poor as he says he is. He may be extremely rich; but on no account must he ever admit it, since if he does he feels he'll be done down: and his men must not be led to think that he has made a huge profit, for then they might expect a bonus. 'E used to have a small farm, and he said that it paid. So I said, just by way of falling in with his line of talk – 'There's no profit in these big farms.' But he didn't like that. For while he didn't want to be thought rich, neither did he wish to be thought poor and unsuccessful. So he said – 'It does and it doesn't. It depends.'

I continued here for nearly a fortnight. And very pleasant it was. This was hoeing without tears. The kale was large enough not to be tender, while the thistles, docks, and charlock were easy to snip away, and not so numerous as to make progress discouraging. The situation was pleasant, the view good, and the weather perfect. I rode straight to the field in the morning, without first going to the farmyard to receive orders. This made a much shorter journey, ten minutes less, as well as a far more agreeable way of starting the day – no complicated orders from 'E, which might need a repeat, nor sight of the carter with furious lower lip cursing at a horse as he backed it into a wagon. And if I was a little late I didn't worry, for no one would see me – on one occasion I overslept a complete hour without anyone being the wiser. Thus my early morning ride was for once unhurried. Also the approach to this field was delightful. I had to pass up the avenue of a Big Thus (not the Manor House) and along by the garden wall, one of those high, weathered, red-brick walls that recall to mind the spacious days of ancient queens. When I stood beside the kale, hoe in hand, I had a morning view of the quiet fields, the nestling village, and the tree-closed church. And I would think to myself – What better than to be here? what more simple or more sane? Then it seemed strange to me that men are packed in ugly towns. So few here, so many there! What fly they, and what seek? and having sought, what found? What found compared with this! This *is* our first and foremost home beside God's foot-print and his fountain. We stray from it, we stray indeed: roofed and walled, paved and collared, we shut it out!

I spent many smooth and peaceful days here. There was a battered old straw-rick in this field which served as my armchair for meal times. I am very critical of armchairs and consider them more important to felicity than electric light and indoor sanitation. I am frequently amazed at the ineptly called *easy*-chairs which I find in the houses of my friends, chairs tilted back at an angle that used to be reserved solely for a dentist's convenience, so uncomfortable that only an athlete could sit in one, and in which no human being could possibly read or reflect. These chairs always seem to me about the maddest things in the present mad world. I must not expand; but I am free to say that though I do not need a whole straw-stack, it serves admirably as a good working model of what I require. It provides the perfect back and leaves the knees and legs with nothing to do but enjoy themselves. But perhaps I lack backbone; it seems that I do in

comparison with my friends who appear quite pleased with their chairs – and also with my friends here, for these latter will often enough sit bolt upright after hours of hard work, with apparent ease, while I look round carefully for something to lean against. They even seem comfortable leaning on their elbows, a position which to me is the extremity of discomfort.

My meal-time breaks were absolute bliss here – perfection in comfort, temperature, and view. In short, true picnic after picnic. Normally picnics are hell – planned pleasure, a seeking after enjoyment. How attain happiness? Only as a by-product. Only by walking smartly in the opposite direction. Then it can come for half an hour. Here the conditions were given. I was tired and hungry and with only a scheduled time for the break. Hence my bliss.

From these favourable dispositions I looked out upon the agricultural world with anything but a jaundiced eye. I passed in review the lives lived by so many thousands of people who are supposed to be better off – the endless number of those who do what is called clerical work, those who sell things on commission, those who type their lives away, those who sit on summer days in electric light, and multitudes of other slaves of slaves of slaves. I thought also of the artistic world, the painters, the writers, the actors and actresses to whom the word Security is unknown, and to whom steady remuneration for work done would seem like heaven, people compared with whom the agricultural labourer knows nothing of insecurity, nothing of poverty, nothing of hardship, nothing of anxiety. If only the land labourers knew the world beyond the field, I reflected, they would be content with their lot. Whatever their wages, they are always at least two pounds to the good on the townsman; they are not plagued by extras (rather given extra), nor by rent (a Civil Servant in London paying for one room as much as the agricultural labourer's weekly wage), nor by Appearance fees (he spends three pounds a year on clothes for himself). His housing for the most part is extremely good. It seems to me that any further emphasis on wages is less important than on the modification of working hours and educational activity within the villages. Then what an opportunity, what conditions for a sane life!

Another thing about the geographical position of this field was that by taking my bicycle down hill I could reach the village inn. While there is little to be said for beer in the winter, it is really wonderful in the summer combined with dinner after a morning's work. So I sometimes went down there in the middle of the day, taking my sandwiches and cheese (if I had any) with me. It was a pleasant hour. The pub was more delightfully situated than any other I have ever known, it might have been in a book; on one side was an orchard, on the other a copper-beech, while in front was a row of chestnut trees. As I write these lines I think of the pleasant and obliging couple who ran this place, owned by the old father in the background, upright, fine-faced, puritanical, and completely humourless. His daughter loved the place, loved the trees, and hadn't ever the slightest desire to go near a town. What's more – she loved the sun. Thus she stood out, let her stand out here, over against the average white-faced country housewife who has never seen the sun, never heard of it, never sat in it. On a lovely day she itched to close at two p.m. in order to get out into the garden and be in the sun. Her husband was the typical independent Englishman with the greatest contempt for B.B.C. blah, and newspaper talk, and official excuses for lost battles and inefficient organization; the kind of man who though a sergeant in the Home Guard was incapable of taking it either with that seriousness or self-importance which would have endangered his good humour and easy-going friendliness.

Very few people went to the pub at this time of day. All were having hot dinners at home.

All except Giles Winterdrew. I'm not a novelisty sort of person who looks round for 'copy' and sees human beings as 'characters'. But I must mention Giles Winterdrew before leaving, for I suppose he would qualify as a 'character'. He was an old soldier, with a Napoleonic Wars look about him. He was tall and upright, but his joints were almost stuck, and his progress slow, as stick in hand, with set sallow face, he made for the pub every day. He arrived at about noon, stayed till closing time, bought several bottles of beer, and returned home with them. He then went to bed with these bottles and remained there till the next morning when he would again go to the pub, have his drinks, buy more bottles, and go home to bed with them. This was his whole life now. Beer got dearer and dearer and worse and worse, but he still bravely stuck to his disciplined routine. At last, for considerable periods, there was no beer at all. The framework of his life was shattered and he died.

But these days of mine were coming to an end, and on 'E's next appearance I was told to leave off now at this job. I had done about half the field, but there was too much to be done elsewhere, and 'E decided that for me to continue here 'would not be worth the money'.

34

STRANGE JOB ON THE BEANFIELD

Returning to the centre of activity I found most of the staff engaged on a beanfield which was just below the scene of our former operations. It was a peculiar job. In striking and indeed appalling contrast to the beautiful beanfield I had delighted to look at on my neighbour's land at my first farm, this was a miserable spectacle, the beans being so hopelessly under the dominion of thistles and other weeds that they couldn't be cut. We had to pull them up by hand. It was a job long remembered on this farm. Though each of us took three rows it was very slow work harvesting a whole field in this manner. But we went at it hard, pulling up the black bean-stalks, which were lower than the thistles, and making bundles of them. We were joined by 'E, and the pace quickened. He was next to me. 'Pull 'ee?' he cried, 'pull 'ee! it don't do they no harm.' And he dashed ahead, grabbing them up, both hands snatching out to left and right, as if he were picking up gold. I began to get left behind. 'Come on, Mr Collis!' shouted Robert (I was always Mr here with all the men) across from his row, trying to get a rise out of me. 'You're too cunning, biding up there on the kale, thee and thy dog. It be harder work on thease field, I allow.' While Dick, who was working on my left, whispered – 'Make a show, Mr Collis, make a

good show?' and, imitating the actions of 'E who was just in front of him, grabbed at the beans with unexampled zeal. Thus we proceeded at the good work till tea-time and went on after tea. But on one occasion I was alone on the job for an afternoon and was about to go home when 'E came and said he wanted me to go on after tea. 'It's not a one-man job,' I said. I stayed; and later on the others appeared, and I gathered that my remark 'it's not a one-man job' had been repeated and gone round. I still think it was an absolutely sound remark, a critique of the purest reason.

During one hot but windy afternoon there was a snowstorm on this field. It was worth seeing. A blizzard just on this field alone. The wild, whirling flakes did not fall from above, they rose from the ground, for they were not made of snow but of thistledown. It was as good an attempt at an artificial blizzard as anything Hollywood could put over.

The final afternoon was memorable and long remembered by everyone. It poured with rain. Our business was now to tie up the beans into sheaves and stook them. We got drenched to the skin. 'E said that we needn't carry on if we didn't want to, but there was no definite and concerted movement to stop, so we went on. We were through by four o'clock. All of us drenched. Then, did 'E tell us to go home and get a change? No. He just stood round saying nothing and looking unhappy, while groups of us held little committee meetings. 'What are you going to do,' one asked another, and some said – 'I know what I'm going to do!' And without anything being said, we all dispersed. Some returned later and did up to an hour's work, while Harold who lived a good way off returned to put in a quarter of an hour. As for myself, rejoicing for once at my distant habitation, I hadn't the faintest intention of returning. And as I rode home I thought of the ridiculous scene when we had stood around in grave committee after the job was done, 'E saying nothing; and I thought if I wrote it down my word would be doubted.

35

WHILE HILING

It was not till 20 August that the weather permitted us to get down to the corn harvest. Now at last we were off. We all rather quailed before the formidable task ahead – perhaps thirty ricks. So we started in on the binding and hiling (not called stooking in this part of the country). Harold and Jimmy carried on with the two binders, and I found myself on the first day hiling with Dick over against Jimmy's binding.

The binder is an attractive instrument. Especially as seen from a little distance, its gently turning 'sails' noiselessly paddling back the lake of corn. At close quarters the ingenuity of the thing is fascinating. To cut at that rate is in itself an achievement; but also to take up convenient portions of what is being cut, and bind it, and then chuck out the bound sheaf – that is something remarkable. Yes, one feels, the cutting was a straightforward invention perhaps, and the elevating of it upward on a moving canvas: but to have it tied firmly into *separate* parts and then flicked out – how accomplish that with robot fingers? And as a matter of fact the two fingers which do every minute flick out a sheaf, have a rather disturbing effect – there is something too roboty about them.

Having cut the corn down it is necessary to stand it up again. There is hardly a layman who doesn't know about the job of hiling. It may be all he knows about agriculture, but that much he

is aware of, and if he has helped in the fields at any time it is generally at hiling. Yet like all these things it can be done wrong. As the corn will now stand up only if it is propped up by leaning against itself, it will certainly fall over if not treated scientifically. No use doing it in an haphazard manner, for the wind will then lay the sheaves as flat as the cutter did. And the way to avoid this is *not* by clustering a lot of sheaves together – for then the ears won't dry. Not more than six at the most, arranged as a tunnel.

This first field of ours was a small one of barley. Barley is the easiest of all types to handle. It makes a short, light sheaf so that you can take two up, one in each hand with great ease and clump them together. Soft and pleasant to the touch, the bunched ears are like flaxen curls on silky heads.

This was one of the very first fields I had had anything to do with on this farm. I had

couched and harrowed it with horses and with tractor. It was brown earth when I had left it, and as its situation was right away in a corner, I had not seen it since. Now it had changed to this, now the drooping pennants, now the flaxen curls; the transmutation that never falters and that never palls; the seeming simple cycle; the turn again of the hundred-thousand-year-old Wheel.

Next day we hiled wheat. Wheat-sheaves build well, as they are very stiff, but it is less easy to take one up in each hand, owing to their weight – grappling with two at once is fairly hard work. The bound stalks make almost a bundle of canes. People complain that hiling wheat cuts and scratches the arms badly unless you wear a jacket. I did not find this was true. You can hold them away from you, there is no need to clutch them in your arms. But I did find it often very hard on the hands when thistles were bound up in the sheaves – one would get on quicker with gloves. We hiled in couples, each couple taking three rows, and going round the field. Going round it, not up and down. Once when I was hiling alone early one morning I started by going up and down. When the carter came out I was asked, Was I backhanded? – which conveyed nothing to me till I realized that everyone went round and round and not up and down, since all the sheaves are thrown out in one direction, and it facilitates matters to approach from the stalk end.

I soon sampled what it was like hiling oats, for now we got on to a very fine field of oats, the field which had seemed so incredibly stony to me when I had cultivated and harrowed it. I found oat-sheaves to be much the most difficult to deal with. They were huge and top-heavy, and very much inclined to fall over if poorly put together. One technique is more necessary in this case than with any other corn: you must *bump* them down on the ground. Holding one in the left, one in the right hand, you don't just *lean* them together, you bump them down on the ground at the same time as leaning them together, as if you hoped the stalks would stick in the earth like spikes – which in a sense they do, for a much steadier stook is achieved that way.

We made fast progress over these fields; the fairly frequent presence of 'E serving, no doubt, *pour encourager les autres*. The person coupled with him was not envied; nor was it good to be going round anywhere near him, since if he was somewhere behind he would soon be bound to pass, and if the ring was getting small, perhaps get round twice to your once. 'Look where 'e's got to! 'e's down the line already!' someone would say, while everyone kept an apprehensive eye on his progress. On one occasion, after the break for tea, when I was walking towards my hiling companion, who was Dick, I found myself also walking towards 'E who then signed to me to join *him*. Away we went, 'E and I, grabbing at and dragging the sheaves together at great speed – for, seeing there was no help for it, I even quickened the pace for fun, making our progress even more appalling for the others to witness, so that I could imagine them saying – 'Look where the bs have got to!'

'E was certainly a real countryman, descending from a line of farmers; but he was not typical in this matter of pace. No calm, steady, leisurely gait such as we associate with the countryman. Yet pace may be the wrong word. For the curious thing was that Robert always gave an impression of great ease and leisureliness, and yet did his jobs much faster than it appeared. Once when we were all spreading the hiles – that is throwing the stooked sheaves on the ground to dry out after rain – the pace was very swift as we went along forking down the hiles, and I found it difficult to keep up. Robert didn't appear to be making any effort at all, and

moved forward with a casual ease that should mean that he would soon be left behind. He wasn't left behind. He was going slower, but he didn't lose ground – strange. And I frequently saw him build a straw-rick without seeming to exert more effort with his prong than if he were stirring soup.

36

WHILE CARRYING

Now for the carrying. My first experience of this entailed pitching sheaves into the wagons in the field. Dick stood in the wagon loading the sheaves which were pitched up by me on one side and the carter on the other. I had to grasp the technique straightaway. It did not take me long. The sheaves must reach the wagon with stalks pointing outwards, otherwise the loader cannot easily do his job nor the unloaders at the rick do theirs. The thing is to take two sheaves up on your prong and elevate them. The carter took three or four, just to show off and get his side done before mine. Being a very small man he always wished to emphasize his strength. 'Small men,' said Dick, 'have big ideas.' It was quite unnecessary to take up so many at once and it made it more difficult for the receiver. I soon found that I could keep pace with him by simply taking *one* up at a time, since you can do that in a jiffy, while in endeavouring to pick up two or three at a time you often muff the affair and fail to get hold of them with your prong, thus wasting time.

This job of pitching up for the wagons on the field is undoubtedly the easiest of all the harvest operations. The loader's position is not so enviable. For not only does he lack a firm floor, but every minute the wagon is jerked forward by tractor or horse while the driver cries 'Hold tight!' like a bus-conductor in Oxford Street. And the loading is a little art in itself, as a lot of people find to their amazement who have come along in the summer to Help the Farmer in answer to the typically urban ineptitude which exhorted them to Take Your Holidays On The Farm – a slogan met with hoots of derision by every agricultural labourer.

But most of my time was spent either on the rick or pitching to the rick; and thither we will now proceed. After the bed of straw had been laid down, as for any kind of rick except straw itself, the first arrangement of the sheaves surprised me. Robert stood in the middle, putting up what looked like a huge hile. What was the idea of this stooking? I wondered – till I saw the point, which was the obvious one that these bottom ears must be kept up somehow, and the middle filled as compactly as possible.

Until later when we began to use the elevator my job was unloading the wagons and feeding the rick. Quite a reasonable job even at the worst of times. And when the rick is low and you are well above it, not a great deal of effort is required provided the wagon has been built properly – otherwise there is the old intensely irritating difficulty of getting the sheaves loose, no matter what plan you improvise. The pitching on to the rick required another new technique. You cannot chuck them down anyhow, for they must lie with stalks facing outwards and crop inwards, and if they alight the wrong way then the men on the rick will have to turn them over and time be lost. Especially is this necessary, of course, when you are dealing out sheaves to the rick-builder himself. Thus in whatever position you may find them on the wagon, your pitched sheaf should fall the right way round if you wish to promote the greatest convenience for the greatest number of people engaged. This is not difficult. A flick of the wrist, as you pitch, easily

makes the sheaf turn somersaults in the air if that is what is required. It did not take me long to get into this; for it is not true that all agricultural jobs require a lifetime's practice to make perfect.

An instructed spectator can generally single out an amateur by observing one particular – namely the way the prong is held by the left hand. Nearly everyone at first has an inclination to put the left hand round it so that the wrist is pointing out instead of the thumb. But I did not do that now. I did, however, at this time do something else which would have enlightened that spectator as to my unprofessional status, something that seems incredible to me now – *I wore shoes*. The discomfort I went through owing to this unnecessary nonsense, still riles me. Rubber boots, of course, were out of the question. But why shoes? I had the fixed idea that shoes in summer were light and cool and restful. But not only was the endless walking about hiling on

uneven ground anything but comfortable in shoes, but now when I stood on top of the ripe ears of corn, the grain continually got into my shoes, and I had to keep taking them off to empty them, or stand feeling as if I had pebbles under my socks. Nor could I purchase a decent footing in them. And the remedy? Boots of course. I thought boots were stiff, heavy, hot, uncomfortable foot-pinchers. The opposite is true. They are comfort itself. Their weight doesn't matter in the least, the firm footing you get is a delight, and no grain ever gets in. When later I took to boots I never even wore rubber ones again, not even in the winter, for if you get leather ones large enough you can still wear two pairs of socks and thus be as warm as you are firm. One must have a firm footing in this world. A steady base is the first essential in agriculture – as it is also in architecture and in literature.

At no time did one need the broad nailed gripping boot more than when unloading the wagons, for one's footing was often precarious, and it was always a pleasant moment when one reached the floor of the wagon, and could stand once again with ease. We generally had two wagons and one lorry carrying the loads from the field. Thus no sooner was I finished with one lot than another was seen approaching. The unwritten law in this affair is that the rick-builders must 'hold' the carriers. That is to say they must always be ready for the new material sent in from the field. It would be a confession of failure if a wagon is kept waiting while the one in front is still being unloaded. Such a situation would get on the nerves of the rick-makers and also lead to the workers in the field being 'stood up'. On no account must such a calamity occur. Thus if three wagons are going strong the unloaders have to work fast. Sometimes one of us (there being two, myself and the man with the wagon last come in) eased up, and then 'E would become apprehensive of the impending calamity, and say – 'Let's have 'em!' At which Dick's brow, if this was addressed to him, would darken into night. Sometimes 'E would jump on to the wagon from the rick and unload a bit himself, throwing out the sheaves at the rate at which lesser men in lesser spheres deal out cards.

When the load came in on the lorry it meant that I had Jimmy as my mate in pitching. As I have said, he was a distinctly cheering kind of person to have around, his smiling face and good-humoured manner always creating a good atmosphere. He used to call me 'Sunshine'. 'Ah, there is Sunshine,' he would say, as if it were my actual name. I mention this, for I am not the man to miss an opportunity of showing myself in a good light. But I cannot subscribe to the description, I'm afraid. Never before have I been referred to in that way, and I suppose never again – so I'm anxious to record it here. I think I can understand it, though. I'm careful not to lose my temper unless a given situation psychologically demands it (so calculating have I become), any more than I ever allow pride to get in the way of an ultimate aim; and during these rather testing days I believe I almost deliberately kept to a cheerful and even smiling countenance. This may have been so, because subsequently, when actually questioning Jimmy about his appellation (which was far truer as a description of himself, indeed perfect as such), he said that 'it required guts to get up on a rick and smile in that way' – a remark which greatly pleased my vanity. And in all seriousness I took note of the fact that a modicum of even deliberate cheerfulness of expression has considerable effect.

Jimmy's lorry-load was much larger than that which could be put on an ordinary wagon, and it was always with great relief that we at length dug down to the floor. 'The parade' I used to call it, 'my old pal's parade'. He had a way of digging down as soon as possible till he stood

firmly on a piece of the floor, however high around him the rest of the sheaves might be – 'I've already reached your old pal's parade!' he would say, while I was still several feet above it on my side. He liked my names for things. I used to call his lorry 'the green thing', and the wagon that was tractor-driven by Harold as 'Harold's caboodle', and he took a great fancy to this nomenclature for such serious agricultural objects.

37

EARLY MORNING JOBS

Sometimes we started the day by making some thatch. We used a machine for this also. It is a kind of large sewing-machine which sews together the straw with which one feeds it into mats which are rolled up and put away until subsequently the thatch-maker unrolls them across his ricks. At a later period I thatched them myself. As I have never thatched with hand-made ones I cannot make a comparison, but so far the traditional sort seem much better. These machine-made ones are much thinner, and also strong wind easily turns the mats into *sails*, so that after a storm whole sides of thatched ricks are found half ripped off. We certainly made our thatch with a maximum of inefficiency. If you do not feed the machine with an even pressure the result is a mat with gaps in it, thus hopeless in rain. However, like all these things, I suppose that soon machine-made thatch will be well knit, and a sure device found for pinning it down on the rick.

At other times my mornings began very quietly, and there was not much for me to do except pull up some of the charlock that still remained covering the greater part of a field of swedes – for when I came back from that far field of kale I was astonished at the change that had taken place here and there, especially this stretch of charlock like a great yellow rug which had suddenly been spread out. Sometimes I had little more to do than go through various hiled fields and re-erect stooks that had fallen down, or turn them to dry out after rain. Indeed, after there had been a good deal of wind, quite a number of the stooks were down. On a certain oat-field I was pleased to observe that my own lines (I had particularly noted their position) all remained intact, which proved to me that even in this small matter deliberate, careful building pays.

While engaged in this I often came upon a rabbit who rushed out from the centre of a stook. For, instead of a burrow, the creature had found this a lovely ready-made house, warm,

peaceful, and dark. Here might it dwell for ever. As one who often feels a longing to curl up in some little nook like that and shut out the world, forget it and be invisible from it, I was sorry for these deluded rabbits, and used to examine the little nest thus created, laying my hand on the warm patch just vacated, and for a moment almost became, in imagination, the creature.

Later on there were rainy spells before we had carried the oats, and consequently it stayed out a long time. Oats has to be left in stook for a few weeks before carrying, and it cannot be carried wet – whereas you can cut and carry wheat or barley on the same day, while if it rains you can rick wheat even while the water is dripping from it, I was surprised to find. But as none of this applies to oats, constant weather is most important; a lot of sun during harvest being more important than during haymaking – for though you need not make hay while the sun shines and do not want too much of it, the more you have with corn the better. We had no such luck this year. And on one oatfield, at a later date, which I was turning, I found that the ears of different sheaves were stuck together in fraternal embrace. I could not get them apart. It was a remarkable sight. The seeds had already germinated within the damp ears, and had sent out long shoots which, like green pieces of broad twine, were intermingling and clasping each other. A curious and unruly spectacle: as if Nature, unwilling to conform to man's requirements, was eager to cut out the harvesting, the autumn, and the winter, and start the work of spring straight away.

38

SCENES AT THE PUB

Though we did not get through without rain, we had some long, hot spells. Once more I was putting in a very full day, once more enjoying it even when I wasn't enjoying it, so to speak – for I like doing things in extremes. Again the very early rise in order to make enough sandwiches for three meals – and what lack of material there was! being reduced for the most part to fish paste and bread. Again the break for lunch at ten, and the coveted hour for dinner, at which time I counted myself the gainer, for I could sit down at once, wasting no time going home and getting back like the others. Then the long spell before tea at five-thirty. At many farms, when overtime is on, it is customary to stop for tea at five – but not here. The break for tea was the day's great event: it was an event which at certain times on certain days did not seem actually *possible* (a feeling hard to express, but which I frequently had during hoeing, when I caught myself saying to myself, It is hard to believe, but five-thirty will in fact arrive and you will

stop). My thermos kept my tea really hot, and drinking it was like taking whisky then: I mean this in the exact sense that as the first mouthful runs along inside, you *feel* it passing through, warming and bracing you in a manner it never does save after a long interval of exercise. Thus I harp upon these simple themes, not for the first time. For this is one of the main realities of the agricultural life, too dull to refer to often, but more central to one's experience than the peculiar incident and the lofty thought. After tea we all felt surprisingly revived, it was quite remarkable. The next two hours were no effort, and three would not have seemed too long – that is why farmers, who think of their men, stop at five and do two and a half hours afterwards instead of the two after the five-thirty break. Then again up the hill home, and yet another meal. And so to bed, the sheer pleasure of lying down being itself a physical luxury.

But I did not always go straight home. Very often I went with Jimmy and had beer at the

pub. There was a certain inner room – it was called 'upstairs' though it was exactly one step higher than the other rooms – in which darts were not played and where we had song and dance. For women could come into this room, but never went into the darts room, as that is a game reserved for the men. There was a table taking up the greater part of the room, but in the space left at one side we danced, for one man played the accordion. And the enjoyment was quite as great as if we had had the Hall of Mirrors at Versailles at our disposal (if there is such a hall). The atmosphere was distinctly cheerful and there was singing during the dancing and in between whiles. Pressed to sing I had to explain that I couldn't command a single note, but I performed my one and only parlour trick, which was a take-off of a Churchill speech, with Churchillian intonations and rhythms. I made an elaborate job of the thing, putting the man who acted rather as the comedian of the company into the role of a Lord Mayor, whom I could

then address as if at a banquet at the Guildhall. To my astonishment this went down remarkably well, and I had to repeat my *pièce de résistance* again and again throughout the harvest and well beyond it, until 'Churchill' became my nickname. These were great evenings after our day on the field, providing an excellent contrast.

We did not always get this room to ourselves, for the military sometimes came in. One evening there was enacted here a peculiarly national scene. A corporal began to sing certain songs which eventually were felt to be too raw in the presence of womenfolk; and our company ostentatiously moved into another room, after first making some deprecatory remarks. But in a moment the corporal followed in a great state of indignation. He wasn't standing for the remarks that had just been made! He wasn't going to pass over such accusations! He had witnesses and he would have the Law on us, he would have us up for Libel! Very angry indeed, he supported his threats with two statements. The first was financial. 'I could buy this pub,' he kept repeating. 'I could buy this pub, and two like it!' The second drew its strength from domestic values. 'I'm a married man,' he reiterated, 'with a wife and two children.' Having thus established his impregnable position in society, he returned to his threats of Law and Libel.

This was received by my friends very quietly. They had not wished to hurt his feelings, and their one aim was to appease him. With the greatest civility they unsaid everything they had just said, and eventually shook hands with him – not so much in friendliness as in the manner that one tries to pat or soothe an obstreperous dog. The corporal took this with a poor grace, and the incident did not end at this point. The man who had been mainly responsible for the earlier remarks began to feel dissatisfied with himself for climbing down, and subsequently took the corporal outside and threatened to fight him, or did fight him, I'm not sure which. He had been ashamed of his earlier attitude of giving way to the man, and confessed privately to me that he 'liked a bit of a set-to'. Thus here in this corner of England, as anywhere else, was exhibited the national characteristic of appeasement and pugnacity. First appeasement, then pugnacity. If the first is not appreciated, so much the worse for the offender.

What with one thing and another these were great evenings after eleven hours harvesting, and when beer and lots of it was what we needed. In the nineteenth century people got drunk: today no one gets drunk. At least not in the traditional and proper sense as summed up by Plato. It would never do, he said, for a guardian to get drunk and thereby need a guard, and '*not know where he is*'. We were glad to know that we were where we were and not in the field under the eye of 'E. And there was one other great thing in favour of beer at this hour. To take more tea just before bed was not good, but after plenty of beer one could be certain of almost immediate oblivion in the best sense of not knowing where one is.

39

SCENES ON THE RICK

Pitching from the wagons was easy enough while the rick in question was still young. But the time came soon enough when we no longer chucked the sheaves down but began to throw them up. At this stage we often got on to the new wagon-load from the rick, jumping down. Once when I had reached the top of the ladder – which reached to the top of the half-built rick – and was getting off it I lost my balance, seized hold of a sheaf which did not support me, and fell to the ground. Everyone peered over, expecting to see me disabled; but finding that I had achieved little more than a slight cut and bruise, I immediately rose, replaced my hat, and without making any observation whatever, went up the ladder again and started unloading at once, as if I had merely chosen a quick way down to pick up something I had forgotten. This procedure was witnessed with some surprise (as I secretly meant it to be), but all the same I was careful never to slip up again in this manner, and I do not recommend anyone to try and use a top sheaf as a means of support.

When the rick grew really high our work from below became proportionally harder, since we had to throw the sheaves up higher and higher. Sometimes, either owing to bad timing on one's own part or carelessness above, one's sheaf came tumbling down again. But this seldom happened, for if the sheaves go up in proper rotation they need never be muffed at the top if the receivers know their job – that is, simply realize the necessity to give a *bold stab* of the prong into the up-coming sheaf (an almost infallible method, as I found when on occasion I was in that position myself). But sometimes, if there were too few people on the rick and no one was 'built in' on the rising wall, a point was reached when it became necessary to throw the sheaf right up if it was to be caught – an exhausting procedure. 'Come on now, Mr Collis!' shouted Robert at one such time, 'throw they sheaves up thease side. It'll give thee summat to remember when on thy tractor again!' At which I threw one so high that it would have gone right over the rick had he not just spiked it in time – an exhibition received with acclamation by Robert and 'E. But Harold, who was pitching with me, said – 'You haven't done nothing yet.' Having done the same amount as he, I replied – 'Then you can't have done nothing neither' – at which there was some hilarity, and we all continued not doing nothing until the rick was finished.

As there was still a lot to be carried, and as large ricks would save time, 'E decided to use the elevator when the ricks reached a certain height. I don't know whether this is a widespread practice. There is supposed to be a certain wastage of seed that way; but actually when a sheet is

spread out under the elevator, most of the grain which falls out is caught and can be bagged. I was very pleased at this innovation, since when things began to get rather difficult they became exceptionally easy on pushing the moving stairs beside the wagon, and I called the elevator my friend, and it began to be known as 'Collis's friend'.

But this was short-lived. For just at this time some extra helpers came along, and I was called for on the rick, where I remained for most of the rest of the harvest. My job here was fairly equally divided between dealing with this new type of waterfall from the elevator, and binding after Robert. Binding is straightforward enough, and consists chiefly in laying a second layer of sheaves half-over the first layer put down by the rick-maker, other sheaves going behind yours, and so on. Of course if the sheaves are coming down very quickly from the elevator and falling all over the place, it is easy to get flummoxed and to bind loosely and badly. Thus I was always much relieved when a load was finished, thus giving us a few minutes anyway to sort things out if they had got in a mess. Harold, continuing his fun and games with me, always sent as many sheaves as possible up to me as quickly as possible. Having failed to bury me under hay he tried to bury me under sheaves, and certainly they sometimes tumbled down in great quantities. 'I don't think much of this elevator idea!' I said to 'E. He laughed and shouted down to Harold, 'Collis says he's going to withdraw the elevator. He hasn't no use for his friend no more!'

Yet I still liked rising in the world and getting my view. At this time of year one of the most satisfactory of all agricultural sights meets the eye – that of sheep folding a field of clover. I could see them on a thick luxurious field which could have taken a second hay-cut. On one side of the hurdles was the dark green clover, and on the other all of it eaten away by the sheep who had at the same time thoroughly manured the ground. It is a sight which gives one such a feeling of benefits bestowed upon all by this most proper homage to the rule of return.

And I got a good view of the workers out in the field, pitching and loading. It was especially fascinating to observe 'E's boy, John, at work. It was phenomenal. Here anything at all in the nature of leisurely work was absent. His forking up of the sheaves was accomplished at the double. He dashed at them with his prong as if to bayonet them, hurled them up to the loader on the wagon, ran to the next and hurled it up, then jumped on to the tractor, and, before the others were ready on the far side, cried 'Hold tight!', brought the wagon forward a few yards, stopped it, seized his prong, leapt off, and rushed at more sheaves – as if something were biting him. How far this really pleased the parental eye, I don't know, but I suppose it did. But he had one relaxation. If a rabbit suddenly ran out from its hiding place in a stook, he would rush madly after it with his prong, no matter for how far or for how long, forgetting all else. This pursuit was entirely utilitarian of course, and emphatically pro-agricultural and calculated to promote extermination of vermin; but happily it dovetailed remarkably well, I thought, with his psychological requirements.

I was generally sorry when a rick was practically finished and I had to get down. As the roofing grew our plateau naturally became continually narrower so that there was less and less room to work in and the pitchers below had to send up the sheaves slowly. Soon there was only room for two of us, then only for one and Robert would say, rather apologetically, 'Better get down if you will', knowing that I didn't like somehow having to retire as a now useless tool. Once, long before roofing, our rick began to come up against the branches of a tree, which had seemed far

enough away (over a wall) when we had planned our base. While the elevator was going full tilt ahead, Robert asked for a billhook and began hacking away at a branch, and in fact engaged himself for some time at this. My pile of material began to assume proportions. 'Hey, Robert!' I cried. 'You can't start taking up forestry while building a rick! What am I to do with these sheaves?' 'Let they sheaves bide!' he yelled, 'I baint gwine to have thease wold tree interfere with I!' Meanwhile I failed to grapple with the waterfall of sheaves – increased in volume from below for the occasion.

One rick finished, on to the next – with 'E measuring out the space for the bedding of straw (I saw now where that bent head and long cricket-pitch strides came from: the result of perpetually measuring out rick-floors). We generally built almost exactly one and a half a day. I liked it to work out so that we were finishing a rick after tea. For one thing, the intensity of the

agricultural earnestness was relaxed and good humour often prevailed; more people came out then, and we had our land girl from the dairy and the atmosphere was even uproarious at times when Robert yelled about gaps and holes, pretending that I was responsible for them. And this was by far the best time of the day to be high on the rick. That is the hour at which one really does glance round at the view, when the soft lights come on and the hard ways of the world are diminished.

We were now on a field beside that piece of kale I had first hoed, those plants that had seemed so poor in promise. The miserable stalks that I remembered were now as thick as a man's leg and as high as the waist or shoulders – and again I marvelled at the march. We worked very late that evening, and it was an especially lovely one. The wind had gone down completely and all the shapes of earth captured in the yellow rays were sculptured by their shades. The sun

set and the dusk gathered, and with it came a deeper silence, as when a clock stops ticking in a silent room; the clouds had got stuck and would never move again; the new moon stooped down so low above a tree that I could have hung my hat upon its horn. The final tricky part of the rick-making began when, the platform growing very narrow, I had to handle the sheaves with much circumspection. Down below I could see the roads becoming whiter and the fields darker and the woods more sombre, and as I glanced at them it occurred to me that perhaps after all this is how I would prefer to catch sight of Beauty – through the corner of my eye, while immersed in something else, while not seeking her at all.

40

MY FIRST ATTEMPT AT RICK BUILDING

By this time I began to know what a rick is. It is a *solid* cottage. Its bricks are sheaves, its slates are sheaves, and it is filled with the same – on similar lines at Ghenghis Khan built his pyramids of skulls. They stand at this time of the year all over the countryside, and it looks very easy to put them there. But how would I get on, I wondered, if I tried the job of architect? Would my exhibit resemble the leaves of yesteryear? Yet such is my pertinacity and venturesomeness, that I determined to try.

As I had succeeded rather too well with a hay-rick, Robert was none too keen on a further success. Nor were the others, really. It would hardly do to let me get away with it. 'Build it on the sand, you mean,' said Harold, whatever that meant, when the subject came up. 'You'll be losing your job, Robert,' said Jimmy, and Robert not quite liking this even in jest said that 'come threshing' he would be only too glad to hand it over to me. Nor was 'E particularly keen, as my attempt might well hold things up. But he was always very sporting to me in such things. When we had started on a certain barley-rick, a favourable opportunity seemed to offer, and I weighed in on it. Actually it was idiotic to choose barley of all things, since the sheaves are so stumpy and as slippery as glass. However, I started and began going round. Here I made another capital error. I remained standing up, doing the work with my prong, instead of dealing with the sheaves by hand and going round on my knees as Robert frequently did. The corners were my chief difficulty. I had carefully watched Robert dealing with the corners, and I could *teach* how it was done, but to do it in full action without fumbling was another matter. However, I carried on round.

'Go forward with thy left foot!' bellowed Robert loud enough to be heard two fields away.

'Tread 'ee down!' said 'E, my second tutor.

'Keep 'ee closer!' shouted my first instructor.

Baffled by having placed a sheaf too far in I tried to push it out, but another fell on top of it before I could do so, and another bellow came from my foremost guide.

'I though you said - ' I began.

'You're not giving me instructions!' he roared, 'I'm giving them to you.'

'Not so hard this side!' shouted further agricultural advisers from the wagon, who were careful to deliver sheaves in plenty.

Under these ideal conditions I proceeded. The Israelites, we are told in the Bible, were in the deplorable position of having 'to make bricks without straw'. I never understood what straw

had to do with it, nor do I now; but here I was attempting to build with bricks *of straw* and with no cement. My tendency to keep the sheaves too far in became too strong for me, especially on one side, and my rick began to slope inward Gothically as if I were already roofing. Then in a too great effort to check this, my architecture began to take after Giovanni Gambuti who inspired the Leaning Tower of Pisa. Meanwhile the sheaves were handed to me far quicker than I would have ever dared hand them to Robert. And at last, under protest, I was prevailed upon to give in, and must chalk up the truth that I did not succeed in this venture. The pressure was too much. It is a good thing to learn under pressure, no doubt. Bertrand Russell said that his parents taught him to swim by holding him upside-down in deep water; but he added that he could not recommend this as the best method for everyone. In the same way I daresay I could have found easier conditions under which to build my first rick.

41

MEDITATION IN THE OLD GARDEN

We reached our last wheat field now, and only two fields of oats and the hundred-acre barley lay ahead. Owing to a faulty packing of food one morning I had gone short at lunch, not daring to be short at dinner with the afternoon in front. As the morning advanced I began to feel exceedingly hungry, and was afraid even to look at my watch lest its progress would be too discouraging, and refused to give my well-known signal (using arms as clock-hands) to Dick whose sovereign thought was always the progression of time – it ruled his mind like a king. Unfortunately it worked out that it would be possible to finish the rick in the morning if we went on a bit longer than usual – which we did.

Actually I was glad of this because the next field to be tackled was right away at the other side of the farm – beyond the Big House. I saw that I would be able to have my rest and food in the garden. So when the others had gone I took a short cut and made for the Big House and entered the Old Garden. It was not open to the public, but it was open to the private, so to speak. No one seemed to be in residence at the moment. The door through the wall in the garden was not locked and I went in. I sat down on a seat backed by the high wall and fronted by a pool of lawn cliffed by ancient trees. Here I now ate my much postponed meal. I enjoyed it so much that when finished, and with cigarette in hand, I felt a great sense of physical well-being. It is not very often that one gets this feeling after agricultural work, but if the weather has been hot and the work hard-going as opposed to a slow drag, it is possible to feel really well afterwards. When this happens the mind sometimes attains considerable liberty and can move without hindrance. And, in my own case, as I had been doing what is called 'an honest day's work', my mind enjoyed still greater freedom. I could regard phenomena, natural or social, without guilt, without anxiety, without ideas conceived by others, without for a moment having to attain to the condition of that strangest of all birds, the bird with only one wing, Left or Right, the bird that cannot soar upwards and take a bird's-eye view.

In this mood I fell into contemplation of the Old Garden. Aloof in the melancholy shade of history, it gave out peace and cast the ancient spell. How did it come into existence? By some men being rich and others poor, by inequality, by privilege. Entering into the era of equality, shall we then throw them open to the public? The moment we do so they will become – something else. They will no longer be gardens: they will be *parks*. Instantly their essence will evaporate and they will no longer be what they were. We must face the logic; the moment

privilege becomes public it ceases to be privilege, for you cannot have a privileged many – they would not then be privileged. So our question is – Shall we have a privileged few? Well, the many do not like this kind of place anyway; secluded reverie is alien to them, quiet reflection wholly unsought – they prefer the definite peopled park. But they also enjoy on occasion the parade of circumstance and the pomp of power. And I said – Let us not throw everything away in the name of Equality. Let there be privilege! Let there be pride! Let there be palaces though they be built out of the pennies of the poor! The time is coming when the flood-tide of the multitudinous Many shall flow through all the gates and into all the courts of pleasure; but even then, let there be here and there a too favoured Few, so that scattered throughout the land there may yet remain, enwalled from the world's babel, the sequestered place, the pool of silence, the repository of peace, into which the wanderer may come and bathe in the spirit of the past and hold converse with the mighty dead!

While lifted up into this pleasant mood as I sat in the old garden, I heard the distant rumble of wheels. I knew exactly what that sound meant. It was the approach of our wagons making towards that other field which we were to carry in the afternoon, and I must now get up and move out into the *medias res* of agriculture. And as I was happy in my thoughts at this hour, and in this place, so was I happy in *that* thought; for whereas the time had been when the rumble of wagon-wheels would have meant nothing to me save the faint murmur from a world of labour in which I had no share and yet upon which all my ways depended, now, though I might dwell for a brief period in the Old Garden and the Ivory Tower of my soul, I must presently depart from thence, and enter into and take my place at the centre of the world's work. And in this also there was happiness. In this there was freedom.

42

IMPERFECT SCENES

The weather broke. Not badly, but just enough to hold us up and make it necessary to turn the stooks of oats. 'E took hold-ups caused by weather very well, I thought. He didn't let it make him lose his temper. And though we had more to do and fewer of us to do it than at many of the farms round about, we were ahead of most with our harvesting. 'E was respected in the neighbourhood as a man who at any rate got things done. Looking at him, I wondered what such a man would do under complete State Ownership. Would not this strong natural force be lost? Men who are out for themselves in agriculture, and not for the State, do more work and hence serve the State better than those who work for the State. A post as mere Manager would never engage the full force of these men; it would be largely wasted. This would be a bad thing if we go on the assumption that efficiency is the aim of life.

The sun returned and we carried on again after first spreading the hiles. One morning while I was engaged at this I found a dead hare which I picked up and put in my bag to take home for consumption. Next day while we were starting another rick, 'E began to talk about someone having been seen with a hare, the implication being that 'someone with a dog' had caught a hare. 'E was a tenant of the Squire who was much against there being any dogs about that might interfere with his shooting. 'Don't let the Squire see thy dog loose,' Robert had said to me, 'or he'll have him shot, I allow' – for Robert didn't approve of my having a dog as well as he. And now 'E brought up this subject of the hare and said that the Squire would be 'creating'. I said I had picked up a dead hare. He said he 'didn't know nothing about it', but that he had heard but 'wasn't saying nothing' as to who had informed him, but anyway if I wasn't careful the Squire would be *creating*.

I failed to take all this with the proper seriousness, and was inadequately impressed either by the Squire's alleged creative powers or about the hush-hush concerning who told the tale. I knew who must have told (not Robert), but said, with the maximum of indiscretion, 'the only person within sight was Robert'.

It was as if I had put a match to a piece of petrol-soaked paper. Up went Robert in flames. I could hardly blame him, for it was a poor joke on my part; but he certainly got excited, yelling and stamping with rage at this scandalous imputation, finally bringing up the occasion when my dog had been seen worrying his sheep, to which he had a Witness (the same being Harold who now looked appropriately sheepish). I'm no hand at shouting-matches and could say little

under the circumstances except 'the trouble with you Robert is that you can't take a joke' which didn't do much good. 'Joke be b'd,' he said. But the thing then petered out, and I said no more, leaving bad alone, and not trying to add to or quench the flames.

By seven-thirty we had finished the rick, and with half an hour in hand we trekked off to another field and started a rick at once, for some of the others had gone ahead and loaded the wagons. At one time a loaded horse-drawn wagon stood waiting by the rick till we were ready to move it in. When we were ready we found that the horse wasn't. He had decided not to move, just refusing definitely to bring the wagon alongside. 'E got off the rick, went up to the horse, and saying – 'Up you sod!' jabbed the wooden end of his prong into the horse's ribs. It gave a leap forward, snapping the harness in four or five places and breaking clean out of the wagon. 'E gave it several more jabs, though this did nothing to improve the situation, since the

wagon now remained exactly where it was before. Someone had to go and get fresh harness, and a considerable interval elapsed before the wagon at length moved forward under the now docile horse – Harold leading him forward and giving him a friendly pat on the nose and neck.

This brought us to the end of an imperfect day. The following day also closed imperfectly. We were working at a rick near the end of the afternoon when the sky blackened and rain approached. It would be necessary to throw a tarpaulin over the rick. Harold and Dick were feeding the elevator. Suddenly Robert exploded. With extreme fury he yelled down to Dick – *not* saying, Get the tarpaulin, but Why the etc. etc., hadn't he got it? as if Dick had refused to do something he had been told. Dick's gorge rose and he didn't budge – at least not until he was told to do so by 'E. After this had been done and we had put the tarpaulin over the rick, Robert, still in a rage, advanced towards Dick with his prong as if to lay him out, while pronouncing an

oath of the utmost extremity. Dick stood his ground, hurling back a drastic imprecation; while Harold, who was watching the business carefully, placed himself close behind Robert, fully intending to strike him down if he really did raise his hand against Dick. But Robert suddenly put up his prong and walked away.

Thus nerves began to get rather on edge as we neared the end of the harvest. The truth is Robert was afraid of rheumatism if he got caught in that oncoming rain, for on the rick we were not within reach of our coats. It was therefore very irritating not to have the tarpaulin fetched at once instead of having more sheaves sent up on the elevator. Robert was a fairly good-hearted man and he did not bear ill-will towards Dick after this, nor towards me about the hare – in fact he brought out some more cake for me. Indeed there was very little in the nature of sulking at this farm. 'E himself detested sulking and reacted at once when it was exhibited. 'I like a clear atmosphere,' he said, quite convinced that no man ever did more to promote a good atmosphere than he himself. Though Robert was not notable for his sense of humour or fun, he could laugh and I always got a tremendous loud guffaw out of him if I made some grousy kind of joke against something. But 'E, who treated him with great respect, never found him a good listener. Feeling the necessity sometimes to make some kind of remark while waiting between-times on the rick, 'E would speak about the market or the weather or even the war, but Robert hardly ever said more than 'Aye' or 'That's where it is' without looking up. And on a certain occasion when loaders and rickers were all on a level, 'E actually told us a story, and a very good story, about a bull, but Robert neither listened nor laughed, and gazed firmly away into the distance.

Elderly workers have always been critical of the younger generation. It is even more so today. Men who have worked very hard all their lives for a very small wage, now see young men, with a lamentable tendency to enjoy life, working less arduously for a far higher wage and with promises of security and what not in the future. Robert was a very skilled man, invaluable on any farm, who could do a number of jobs a good deal better than younger men; but it was clear to him that a grateful nation was going to repay him by making Dick's life easier than his had been. Elderly working men and women are much less critical of the social system than of the younger generation.

There was twenty minutes in hand before it would be officially time to leave off. So 'E found jobs for us. He instructed me to go to a certain distant field and pull up charlock. By the time I got there I had ten minutes before me, so I stood sheltering from the rain under the hedge and read a weekly paper, coming upon a review by Mr Raymond Postgate about a book on Detective Fiction, in the course of which he remarked that the photographs of the detective-writing authors betrayed, with one exception, definite criminal types: the one exception being thus mentioned, I supposed, so that if any of them reproached him for saying this, he could say it was the other fellow. Thus lost in these incredibly non-agricultural considerations, I now saw that it was five-thirty and I could depart.

But as I went home I reflected upon the situation as it must now present itself to the employer. In the old days wages were so low that it cost three shillings less to keep a man than a horse. Those were the days, he feels. Now he is faced with a heavy wage bill, the difference within one generation being immense. Thus it is only human that he should now feel – as probably he seldom did in the past – that every minute wasted is money spent on nothing. As I write, wages are still going up. It might be a good thing if they stopped now. For the fact is that it will tell

against workers if they go too far. Not only will it make the psychological atmosphere uncomfortable, but after five or six years of increased mechanization and increased knowledge on a farmer's part of how many men he can *do without*, it will not be so easy to get a job on the land if wages are very high. Men who really want to work there, who would love it, may find themselves going round and being told by farmer after farmer that he 'doesn't want no more labour'.

43

THE COMBINE HARVESTER; THE LEISURE STATE

We were now faced with the hundred-acre barley. It had been left too long in any case, so it was quite unnecessary to hile it. If the weather held we could cut and carry at the same time. But it was now late September and 'E decided to hire a combine to do half of it. And this was done. While we cut and carried fifty acres, a combine harvester did the other half.

It is a remarkable machine. A truly triumphant invention. No open-minded person could fail to admire the scientific ingenuity of the men who contrived it. It is a binder and a thresher in one unit. The corn which has been cut and taken up by the binder is taken up but not bound; instead it passes through a threshing operation so that the grain pours straight into a tank which is emptied into sacks and deposited on a lorry once every round of the field. The straw, instead of being ricked, is spread over the field as it comes out by means of a revolving fan like the screw of a ship – so what with the usual binder-sails and this screw behind, the contraption looks like a sort of paddle-steamer whose element is corn. It is very neat: for when you examine it closely it seems astonishing that the job of the bulky thresher can be encompassed in so small a space.

Thus it proceeds round the field, doing two jobs at once: that of cutting and threshing; and knocking out the necessity of three middle ones – carting, ricking, and thatching. An absolute godsend to the small farmer, I reflected, to the man who runs a hundred acres by himself with a son, a daughter, and one or two assistants. But in relation to big farms, I could not help feeling gloomy about its appearance. It is rather as if the Future had arrived before we were ready for it.

It has just been reported that in liberated Ukraine, a girl combine-operator, Vera Panchonko, has received a Badge of Honour for harvesting two hundred and sixty acres in five days.

Let us consider exactly what this means.

There are few subjects harder to think *out* than this of machinery. An honest man will tend to be inconsistent. Even Gandhi, who decided to oppose with the whole force of his mighty spirit the entry of the machine into India, made an exception in favour of Madame Singer's sewing-machine. It is hard to be fully sensible on this subject. I shall tackle it here simply in relation to the land.

The farm labourer, I repeat once again, is a mechanic, always, from the word go, having to deal with nuts and screws and overcome difficulties without help from outside. A very bad mechanic, farmers may complain, lazy, stupid, and careless concerning machines, and needing specialist help in all serious problems. Perhaps; but my point is that mechanism starts on the land; however amateurishly, there we started to conquer nature with ever more ingenious weapons. There the machine is a natural growth, seen at once as the right thing in the right place, and the man who deals with it seen as fully a man – in staring contrast to the man at the conveyor-belt in a factory. The machines have evolved in the country almost as naturally as flowers. First the spade – then the plough. First the rake – then the harrow. First the broadcast of seed (father of the B.B.C.) – then the drill. First the flail – then the thresher. First arm-pitching – then the elevator. First the sickle, then the scythe, then the reaper, then the binder – now the combine.

Each in turn is felt to be grand by those concerned. I have described my first potato-planting and how I would have rejoiced to see a machine-planter and also a better method of unploughing them than the old usages. Both have come along – our attention being fixed, each time, on the matter in hand, without any principle being considered. And now we come to the combine. It has arisen as organically and inevitably as all the others. It is as natural an object as the picturesque thresher – and more admirable.

Yet here we pause. Here we reach a climax in our story. For though the combine has evolved as naturally as the other machines its effect is much greater upon the lives of the labourers. At one stroke it does away with harvesting – save for Vera Panchonko at the wheel. The age-long, centuries-old tradition of harvesting, of gathering up the year's work, is taken away from the labourers. In their place the one big machine. We look across the land for human beings, and we see – one engine. And in its wake the bare field: no ricks meet the eye, and no work for thatchers or threshers.

Gazing across, we try and take in the total situation, and we think it fair to ask – Is this fact a little thing, or is it a big thing? In the old, far away days, the whole village came out to take part in the haymaking and harvest. Bit by bit as wages went up and machinery came in, the villagers had to stay at home. Today the process nears completion, when the labourers themselves, the rick-makers, the thatchers, the general workers will stand afar off while Vera Panchonko alone performs, receiving the applause of the State and the Badge of Honour.

Does this constitute a problem? Hardly, in the eyes of the world, for it is not a utilitarian problem. It is a human concern. And though we are all human, and all seek happiness, we only regard problems in the light of utilitarianism, and to attempt otherwise is a battle lost in advance. The human problem here is simply that harvesting is one of the few really satisfying tasks in the world; it is a shared effort, communal work without being stressed as such, and enjoyed even though this may not be admitted. If it is knocked out, the agricultural profession will suffer on the human side. Gradually each man will come to work more and more on his

own, neither able nor willing to take part at this, that, and the other tasks in company. There is something gloomy, to me, in the project.

Yet, eager to stick to the realities that will not be altered by such opinions, we must carry our inquiry further and ask again – Where are we then with our problem? And the answer is that, assuming the advent of the combine on a big scale, we see labour-saving carried a long step forward. So the real problem now turns out to be – *leisure*. We have reached the Leisure State. But the moment we say that, we know that it is purely theoretical, a mere theorem no more connected with the given situation than a conclusion by Euclid (who died mad). For we have done nothing to increase leisure while increasing the saving of labour. Some of the workers are simply exchanged for metal, while those who are not exchanged continue to work, as I have remarked in relation to the machine-milker, for exactly the same hours as before. I do not com-

plain of this. I make no tirade against it. It is so much in the nature of things. To adjust matters of this kind, entangled as we all are in a thousand economic wires, will be frightfully difficult – on a par with establishing Justice herself in our midst. That's the first point. But there is a still more unfortunate one. It is, quite simply – that no one wants the Leisure State. All we want is work that suits us. Some of us have this. Nearly all farmers have it, and some labourers. These do not mind how long they work. The others want less long hours. But the idea of much leisure is something from which everyone turns in dismay. You can never make *that* a goal! We are quite unfit for it mentally. This was not always so everywhere. It was not so in the island of Typee before the West found and corrupted it. It is so here. We cannot bear idleness, we cannot fill that empty cup with happiness. Owing to the failure of intellectual leadership, the breakdown of religion, and the short-cuts to culture, our minds are now for the most part demoralized; in any

true sense we know nothing, we study nothing, we understand nothing, we see nothing, we listen to nothing, we are incapable of reflection. Hence the hardest toil is a welcome refuge from the horror and tedium of leisure. We loathe a long holiday. We cannot endure pleasure for more than half an hour. Even picnics drive us mad. Agricultural labourers die six months after retiring. Unemployed middle-class people die slowly all their lives. Thus conditioned, where shall we find the *will* to create the Leisure State?

So, without less gloom than before, we turn again and look at the combine. It is splendid. But only from a utilitarian point of view; only for the employers of labour, for a few labourers, and for Vera Panchonko who harvests two hundred and sixty acres in five days.

44

LAST DAYS OF HARVEST

Meanwhile we assembled on the field in order to cut and carry the remaining fifty acres. At 9 a.m. some clouds gathered in the distance. They spread; they came towards us; the entire sky blackened and it began to rain. There was no break to be seen in the sky anywhere, nor likelihood of one. We had come too late. All was lost. Several thousand pounds' worth would go up in smoke, so late was the hour, so lowly drooping were the ears – down nearly to the very ground. After one hour it cleared up completely and did not rain any more for a week. Worth mentioning, I think. It was like a human touch from above: a decision and then a withdrawal. Good luck like this is forgotten sooner than the bad.

I caught a chill just before we reached this last lap, and so had to do this final business for a week in that condition. Between 2 p.m. and 5.30 p.m. I knew exactly what constituted Paradise and could name its precise geographical position. It consisted in lying down in a sunny windless nook at the side of a copse which impinged upon this field. Unfortunately this knowledge was useless to me, since I couldn't go there.

Putting about twelve acres into each rick, we built four, and I began to feel that I knew what a barley sheaf looked like and could do without seeing another for some time. It was evening again when we were finishing and I had a good view of the big field. In the refreshing, sharp, evening air of autumn I compared the change that had taken place since the spring when I had been there drilling at the beginning of my experience at this farm. It seemed a long time ago since I had stood there feeding the oncoming drills, and I remembered how I had grappled with

the horses and wagons and taken off the gate-post, and had had no time for dinner, and how 'E had laughed when I had spoken about the 'little pills of comfort'. How different the scene now, and how much I had experienced since then!

We began to get near the last sheaf. Finally we came to it and pitched it up (we were not using the elevator here), though it nearly fell down again. And as we approached this last sheaf, was there any sense of a grand climax? And when it was pitched up, did someone say – 'Ah, that's the one we've been looking for all this time?' And did 'E say cheerio and give thanks to all and sundry? No. It might have been the first sheaf.

45

BEGINNING WITH THE PLOUGH

The following day was our new year. We must hurry up now and get things ready for the next harvest.

There remained of course the harvesting of the root crops, swedes, mangolds (we didn't grow any sugar-beet), and above all potatoes. These are steady autumn and winter jobs; in the south of England it is often December before all the potatoes are up.

But my eye was on the plough. I was determined to get that into my hands now. And I did. There was an eleven-acre field of stubble, bounded on one side by a hundred-acre stretch of down which was about to be ploughed-up by Harold; and on the other by that field of kale where I had enjoyed working after haymaking – to which 'E now sent me with a tractor and a three-furrow plough. It was set properly for me in advance, for I could not possibly do this myself. And without further instructions I set out with it to that far field, along the out-of-the-way lanes and through the gates, feeling pleased with life – for the plough fascinates me.

I reached my field and set to work. I had taken care to acquaint myself with the general practice in operation, and hoped it would work out for me. First I went round the field marking out a headland ten feet from the hedge, for without a headland you cannot have room to turn at the end of each row. Then I struck out a line across the field about twenty yards from the headland. It was an oblong field with a rise in the middle so that only the top half of the hedge was visible from one end. To assist my preliminary strikings-out I took a stick and put a white envelope on to it, went to the middle of the field, took a careful twenty paces out from the side and stuck in my stick, then went on to the end and hung a handkerchief high in the hedge after

another careful measurement. This striking-out is an important business, for if your line wobbles or had a bad kink in it, you will find it hard not to continue along the same pattern subsequently. So I set the radiator-cap straight towards my flags and tried to keep it there as I advanced. It didn't keep straight, and when I got to the end I expected to find my line very bad. But to my surprise it wasn't too bad at all. How about the second striking-out when a parallel line is essential if there is to be neat workmanship? Again not bad. Indeed I was luckier in these first attempts than in some subsequent ones. All the same it was an error to have put up that guiding-stick in the middle. You need two sticks, Harold pointed out to me later, but not one in the middle – that is only a hindrance. You want one in the hedge and one just a few yards in front of it. Then if you keep those two, the one covering the other, in your eye from the far end, you can get a better line, and are much less likely to curve out or in as you go along.

This done it was only a question of going up and down my lines until I had come near to filling my parallelogram. Since the plough throws the turf over in one direction only you can't avoid working continually inwards on your figure; so when it became too narrow to turn in, I struck out a new line at another parallel of twenty paces, thus being able to go along the narrow lane in one direction only, while using my new line as the other route.

So much for the question of movement. At first I fumbled the question of depth. I went much too shallow. Then I went too deep and broke a share – that is, the end piece which does the spade-work. But I didn't notice this till I had reached the bottom and hitched-up. Luckily I had some extra shares with me – the kind that only need a piece of wood for a pin, plus a bit of cloth to stabilize it. When I broke another I spotted it before I finished the line, being very anxious about the possible wearing out of the stump. It was curious, this share-breaking, for I

was not going really very deep at all, and in fact, later, I had to go less deep than 'E told me to, if I was to preserve my shares. It was not particularly stony ground; but I gathered that there are shares and shares, some given to breaking, some hardly ever breaking.

Apart from this I did not come to grief over anything, and began to feel in command of the situation. But I wondered how the closing up of my first parallelogram would work out. When it became a very narrow lane I saw how far from perfect my striking-out had been. There was a bulge in the middle of the field, and so I found myself finishing the other part before I had finished the middle. The next one was better, but there was room for improvement. My aim was the unbroken single trough which you see running down at given distances across all well-ploughed fields. At dinner-time, at every dinner-time, I walked to another higher field opposite and looked across to examine the work in progress. It looked grand! The troughs didn't seem at

all too bad from there, while the furrows, though inclined to curve at the ends, presented a slice of ploughed land which looked on a par with other ploughed fields. I hoped that I wasn't kidding myself about this and that my turn-over was good enough – for I had by no means *buried* all the stubble completely. There was much green on top of the brown. It was not a clean turn-over. This plough had been left out in all weathers and had not been greased. Thus when I started, the blades were very rusty, and the earth stuck to them. This naturally militates against a clean overturn by the turn-furrow. So I got down at the end of every row and knocked away the clinging earth with a spade and then finished off with a long thin steel knife belonging to Victorian days. (By the way, this was the first time I had used a spade since working on a farm – fitting reply to friends who ask perfunctorily, 'How do you like digging?') It was a long time before the soil ceased to cling to my turn-furrows. But at last they began to brighten, then to shine,

and at last to blaze like silver when on rising from the earth they caught the sun. When I knocked off for dinner I liked to have the plough in such a position that I could see it glittering in that way.

Soon 'E paid a visit and strode across with his famous strides to the portion that I had done. He had a good look at it, up and down, then said – 'That's good enough for I.' I tried not to look too surprised and pleased. He explained that he didn't want the weeds completely buried, because the couch and charlock could not then be so easily harrowed out.

My furrows were inclined to curve at the end for a very simple reason. When you reach the end of the line you must turn the tractor of course, and turn it quickly in order to avoid running into the hedge or getting so close to it that one wheel gets stuck. But just when this turning is necessary you must reach back and pull the rope that connects with the hitching-up apparatus which lifts the blades clear of the earth – and this latter must not be done until you have really reached the end of the line. But there is a strong tendency to start turning the wheel of the tractor too soon, and so you get your curve. Yet this can be overcome by going slow and not getting flustered. The moment I most enjoyed was when, after having swung round from the hedge and got the tractor's right wheel into the groove for going up the next line, I pulled the rope again so that the blades crashed down into the soil once more and immediately that solid substance turned into three fluid waves of earth that rose and fell, and having fallen, lay still again. It is most unfortunate that one is placed in front of the plough with a tractor, for one needs to watch the work for utilitarian reasons and wants to watch it for aesthetic ones. And if you do this for too long at a time while only the left hand guides the tractor, a crook or a bad curve is the result. I did my best to *mend* such curves by treatment each time I reached the place, but though the spot looked obvious from the distance it disappeared as I approached it, of course. On some occasions I threw down a handkerchief to mark it. I should add that in this matter a certain amount depends upon the tractor. A really steady one, not too ancient, will go along with its right wheel in the furrow without need of a guiding hand (especially uphill). Thus I often observed Harold *walking* behind or beside his plough, while the tractor quietly went ahead by itself. A cheering spectacle, I always felt. Man is often the slave of machines, as also of cows and of sheep. But not here.

It might be asked why there is so much fuss made about a straight furrow. Apart from the initial necessity to strike out as straight as possible and make your parallelogram true, why should it matter if lines curve slightly here and there, or even bulge badly at places, seeing that the furrows will presently be knocked to pieces under the harrow? If you ask a farmer this question he will give utilitarian answers: it makes for better harrowing or it saves time. True enough, no doubt; but I think the real reason is aesthetic. It is the tribute that Agriculture pays to Art. It is felt that there is virtue in a straight line, not to be found in one that wobbles even slightly. This calls for concentration and skill. Where there is skill there is art. Where there is art there is passion for the absolute. The straight furrow is the labourer's acknowledgement in the validity of art for art's sake.

46

HORSE PLOUGHING

These were the days! Now I never looked forward to dinner hour nor to knocking off in the evening. (Later, when ploughing in December, I was downright annoyed the way it got dark so soon, and I went on until I couldn't see what I was doing.) I recalled a remark made to me by Morgan at my first farm, when he was engaged in ploughing a pleasant six-acre field. 'I would rather be doing this than anything,' he said. 'I'd rather do this than go to any cinema.' Morgan was not an intellectual, not a man of ideas; he was a very level-headed, unpoetical sort of chap. He was just making a statement. There are some writers today, who, with the cause of agriculture deeply at heart and worried by the very real problem of mechanization, tend to refer to tractor-drivers with a scarcely veiled sneer. Soulless fellows merely 'fiddling about with machines' seems to be their idea of such men. A justified view in some cases. I know a fair number of agricultural workers: for as a member of the Home Guard I met a lot more than those on this farm; some delightful men, but also, I admit, some tractor-drivers who were absolute louts who didn't see an inch further than their nuts and screws. But it is wrong to sneer at tractor-drivers as a body on that account. Anyway, it is not the tractor that is wrong. It is all a question of the attitude of mind brought to the work – it is the attitude of mind every time! The tractor-plough is a superb instrument to look at when stationary, and to manage when in action.

Yet at this very point I want to say a word about horse-plouging. I have had experience of it also. At this stage in my narrative I cannot infringe upon the unity of place and time which I have imposed upon myself, by introducing any lengthy account of an experience elsewhere. But, with the reader's permission, I may say here that I have acted as horse-ploughman elsewhere for a season from September to December, which days were the happiest in my life. If I were asked the straight question whether I would prefer to plough, *always*, with horse or tractor, I might find it difficult to answer, since I very much enjoy working with a tractor and a three-furrow plough. Yet nothing can really compare with the simple, strenuous horse-work. For one thing there is no other physical work to compare with it: there is not a game in the world that can make you feel half so good. And, fascinating as the machine work is, you do not hold the plough. But it is just this *grasping* of the handles of the plough, both arms stretched out fully and often putting out full strengh, that somehow is the very top-notch of satisfaction. Ah, I say, even as I write these lines, give me the plough-handles that I may grip them and strike out across the field! release me from this chair! (for it is so much easier to do a thing than write about it, so much easier to perform than to reveal). And to be able to see your work directly in front of you all the time, to watch your wave rise up and fall to silence in your wake – this you cannot get the other way. But again I say, it is the grasping of the handles for which there is no substitute, no compensation. Then your feet are upon the earth, your hands upon the plough. You seem to be holding more than the plough, and treading across more than this one field: you are holding together the life of mankind, you are walking through the fields of time. This work has always been done. Whatever happens this can be done. Machine-power may fail for fuel. This power will never fail. In the day of calamity, in the day of battle, all men must cease from work and rise to slay. All save the ploughman on the fields of Normandy. When D-Day came and battle raged upon the beaches; when the sky was filled with fighters and the land was lashed with fire, that Nameless Man took out his plough and did his work and turned his furrow in the midst of all. And when the brief hurricane of mortal men had passed, he was still there.

47

WHILE PLOUGHING

Meanwhile the tractor-pulled plough is a very good second best. The exhilaration is not quite of the same kind, but it is exhilarating none the less. It is absurd to denigrate our own amazing creativity. To have a great metal horse in front of you, over which you have complete control, knowing that it will take that steep rise in the field in its stride, while you look back and watch the three waves falling on your ribbed and rolling beach – who could tire of that?

Ever since one memorable day, when standing on a rise in Devon, I saw in a field below the white leaves blowing round a ploughman, I have looked out for seagulls following a plough, for there are few more pleasing sights. I frequently saw them following Harold. Now they would come to me.

But this was anticipating. They did not seem keen on coming in my direction. Instead, I got numerous starlings, rooks, and crows, brown and black birds in whom I had no interest. However, one day the seagulls were kind enough to come over. They didn't do a great deal of swirling round me. But when I reached the end of my row on one occasion I looked back and saw the whole lot of them standing in the furrow right across the field, in perfect line, dressed by the right. I was satisfied with this parade.

Indeed I was well satisfied in every way on this work. The day was too short. Sometimes I had to attend to Harold and give him assistance, for he was ploughing-up the Down over the hedge, and occasionally went right into a hole and could not get out. I had to go over with my tractor and pull him out. Otherwise I carried on happily without any interruption. Here would I gladly remain, I said to myself, islanded from that world which is too much with us; let all men, all women, and all children, do what they like. I've got my tractor, my plough, my field, and am content. Having wandered in the realms of thought, I could bring the roving mind to rest; having journeyed between New York and Warsaw across the countries of the world, I could now discover one patch of ground at home; nor had I any need of games – for here my work was play, my play was work.

This field was on a considerable rise. I could see the village below and a long way across the

land. We plan our habitations; we design; and the result is sometimes good. Yet how often one is struck by the beauties that are undesigned, where there was no prearranged pattern, yet all is pattern. We planned the position of the Manor House; but we could not have hoped to arrange matters so that the red creeper would climb just to catch that last sunset ray, nor so arrange the growth of yellow flowers that they would lean against the high green field beyond. We planned the position of the church, but now it is locked in Nature's arm. I looked down and saw the double beauty of man's deliberations clothed in all the careless forms of earth.

More often I looked upwards at the great cathedral piles of cloud that passed along the winter sky, extravagant and erring shapes radiantly rimmed or quite ensilvered by the sun. Once, a broad shaft of light, let out from the clouds, beamed down upon the distant land. It lit up the ground on which it fell and slowly moved from field to field, from hedge to hedge, as if

looking for something – like a giant searchlight reversed. Then it went out suddenly, as if switched off. The clouds above increased in splendour. Ah, it is a land, a land up there, that does belong to us though raised so high! token of some great happiness that yet shall be fulfilled, the hope and promise written in every heart!

When the dusk fell and I could go on no longer, I often caught the sharp whiff of smell coming from the upturned earth. Scent is a mighty marvel. What it is I do not know. But I knew what this smell was, which is the most intoxicating of all. It was – Fertility: it was life itself coming across to me in pure sensation – the *odour* of eternal resurrection from the dead.

48

VIEW OF THE WHOLE

The mornings were cold and dim now as I cycled through the village, past the copper-beech and the chestnut trees. Their way of life had fallen into the sere and yellow leaf, and then, obedient to the later ruling, no leaves at all. The clawing fingers of the ash, the bare pale branches of the beech, the high tracery of the elms, all spoke of winter. And for us this meant threshing, and lots of it. We must now take down the ricks again.

Put like that, by the way, it does make the combine seem rather obvious, doesn't it? The whole-hogging anti-combiner would have to say that the proper thing to do is to put up ricks in order to take them down. It is the actual logic of that view, I fear. We cannot say that the goal of life is work when the work is not necessary: otherwise, as I think Dr Maude Royden once remarked, instead of getting ten men to dig a trench with spades you could get a hundred to do so with spoons . . . But let me not fall into further speculation on this, but discreetly tiptoe, as Donald McCullough would say, on to the next.

There was certainly enough threshing for us to do, several months' work in fact, after all that harvesting. Thus again we assembled the famous rig-out and got going on the work of separation. Once more we unlocked the elaborate cupboard and took out the bread. Once more the untiring jaw was fed, and the bags bulged behind – ten, twenty, forty, eighty. When the actual day's threshing was over, it didn't mean that we had finished. The machine still went on for a long time dealing with the remaining bits, while we fiddled about clearing up, the lack of a definite thing to do being sometimes quite maddening. I was always glad when we got down to the formidable business of lifting the rows of sacks on to the lorry. As a solo sack-lifter I'm not

only bad but a shirker: but in partnership with a mate I count myself as adept at it – and so never minded this heavy finish.

One morning I accompanied Jimmy in the lorry to the neighbouring town's railway station where we deposited a load of sacks. It was pleasant to find myself amongst the cheerful workers in the station yard and see the place from that inner angle. It was good to put the sacks in the truck. Where are they going? I asked. No one knew. Nor cared. Nor did I. But I was glad to connect them with the truck and have in my mind's eye the continuity from seed to truck and the number of operations that take place between that beginning and this ending when these sacks go away into the blue.

Robert, though rick-maker in general, was after all the shepherd, and it was not convenient for him to come out in the mornings if there was anyone else to do the work. So it happened that I started building the straw-ricks myself. Being an unpractical man, I am at intervals more practical than the practical, and I made a good job of it. Thus Robert didn't need to come out, and when he did late in the afternoon, he didn't interfere with me, but fed the thresher, subordinating the carter to string-cutter.

I was very pleased with this arrangement, of course. I had no assistant on the rick; but it is a fallacy to suppose that two are necessary for straw, just as it is an illusion to suppose that eleven men or even eight are really necessary for threshing. We started with the barley and finished it off first. Very short, light, slippery stuff, but I managed without mishap and without props. Robert, looking at one, said – 'No one could say you can't build a rick now, I allow.' A remark which he need not have made, and which endeared him to me. (Next summer he put no opposition in the way of my making a corn rick – and this time there was no question of failure from start to finish.)

There were some stoppages owing to something going wrong with the thresher. The chief members of the company went down on all fours under it, pushing and grappling with its inner mysteries, all quite beyond me. The good of being on the rick was that I didn't have to busy myself with something or pretend to look wise. Ejaculations would come up from below – 'Let it bide' or 'Leave very well alone' or 'That's some of it, I expect' – this last from 'E. 'That's some of it' was a favourite expression of his. In thus suggesting that *some* of the trouble had been located, he not only encouraged further research but showed a proper scepticism about it being all of it.

The barley finished, we went for the wheat. After a couple of ricks we began to use a trusser. The trusser is a machine which, placed between the thresher and the elevator, ties up the straw into fair-sized sheaves, after which they proceed up the elevator. You can sell straw better that way than loose – (and better still, I believe, when it is baled, that is, parcelled into two-hundredweight bricks). This called for a new technique and 'E expressed doubt as to whether I could do it properly. This put me on my mettle, and I soon got hold of the idea, found it in fact a good deal easier in the end than ricking loose wheatstraw, and up went my buildings, still unpropped. I derived what may seem a childish pleasure in looking round the fields and saying to myself – I put that there; and that; and that. It gave me particular pleasure to see them from the road on a bus when coming back from a visit to London and its vastly different scene. And I wondered whether those who journey up and down the roads notice how today there are two ricks on a field and tomorrow only one in a different place, larger and more light in colour. In

days gone by I would not have noticed it. But from henceforth, wherever I go, through whatever land, I shall know what is going on beyond the hedge, beyond the railway line, and I shall realize the ardours that have been bestowed upon the silent scene by the unwitnessed workmen of the fields.

Again I rejoiced to rise on my pedestal and have a view of the whole. When I was fairly high up I could see over the greater portion of the farm. And as I gazed across, I realized that I had had dealing with every field: there I had harrowed and rolled, there couched, there hoed, there made hay, there drilled, there ploughed – and here now were my ricks. I did not feel a beginner or amateur any longer. I was well on the inside of the wall. I would no longer make idiotic mistakes: not now would I leave a prong lying on the ground or throw it down the wrong way up from a rick; nor walk on the wrong side of a horse and take a gate-post away; nor fail to examine

the plugs of a tractor that wouldn't start; nor be absent-minded about implements I was using; nor drop things as I went across the farm; nor try and lift sacks in the wrong way and put them down untidily; nor start hiling up and down instead of round the field – nor wear shoes! Standing there with the straw waterfall well in hand, I could look down on the company below feeling very much part of the proceedings and by no means an outsider.

I could see from where I stood the changing scene of the unchanging motion of the year. That hay rick over there, like a great cake carefully sliced, had been already half-cut for the cows. That straw-rick in the next field, left over from last year, was steadily getting lower, and like a punctured balloon was shrinking every month more and more until it was but a shadow of its former self. The potatoes had been lifted and clamped beside their field. The mangold field was half-pulled, the once thin red roots were now bulging balls in tinted red and yellow shades that

no potter ever could come near. Beyond that hedge the winter wheat was shining now, so fair, so green against the dark leafless trees and the pale blue winter sky. And in a field of stubble a crop of clover was rising fresh and strong. It was good to see it there, bright witness of the rapid round – green youth beside the stumped and paupered stalks of age; new life climbing on the knees of death; the never resting tireless toil of earth. Down below me the sacks were filling fast. In my mind's eye it was only yesterday that we had sown this field – then the green light; then the yellow; then the brown; and so the fall. Now seeds were pouring out, many times more numerous than those which had been sown. Thus the Circle, thus the Order, confined within the little space before me – type of all of Nature's vast, relentless roll.

And as I stood upon my pile, this year, and the next year, looking across the land, I looked also across the centuries. This was the eternal tale. This did not alter and would not stop. The

historical tapestries hung across the streets of fame, figuring the pride of kings, the frenzy of tyrants, the clash of nations, and the fall of empires, held no meaning here. The same work went on in each country regardless of whatever drama was being staged by the men in cities. So it would continue as surely as Nature continues to unfold in spite of all the roaring wrack beyond the fence. Those men below at work upon the thresher, whom I have not sought to glorify – yet are they not glorified in these natural tasks? – support the conditions for the theatre of history, but they work outside the drama. Civilizations rise, fluctuate, and fall, men reaching out for expression now in one direction, now in another; at one time, turning their gaze towards the perfect commonwealth, the greatest good, the glory of thought, and the rose of art, they raise a noble culture; and at another time riding recklessly on into the bitter darkness of their own night and the cold bleakness of massacre and crime, they are driven shamefully back along the

fields of their pride. But here is the thing that remains constant. Here is the order that does not break, Here shall the husbandmen of all the world, using this device or that, this machine or another, remain obedient to the increase and faithful to the unfolding, from generation to generation and from age to age.

From this lofty stool on which I stood, I looked down upon the Great Highway that led from the cities to the sea. It ran beside our largest field for some distance. All day long and every day the Military dashed past in lorries, in jeeps, in tanks – ceaselessly every day. The clatter of the tanks was something awful. They passed in long lines, these the chariots of our day, their helmeted riders aloft in the turrets. I sometimes lifted my hand in friendly salute, but there was not much response. The division between us was too great for communication. Only a thin fence, but what a gulf! On this side was life everlasting: and over there – History roaring past. It simply passed us by. We were bound upon the field: and their only freedom was the hard, long, ribbon of road, their destiny and their doom. They could not possibly leap the fence and join us. They could not pause in their trampling nor turn aside from their path. They could not break from the bonds of history. They could not pass from that which was temporal to this which was eternal. On and on they clattered, making for the beaches and the sea, for danger, destruction, torment, death. From the field it seemed appalling, fantastic. But the charioteers were not appalled. Truly we *are* such stuff as dreams are made on, entrancingly protected from the agony of truth! Already crowned with the laurels and the bays of sacrifice, they were lifted up into the realm of a dream, raised high above the material world and the earthly clods of care . . . Marvelling at Mankind, I turned my gaze back to the Earth. And presently as often happened late in the afternoon, this traffic ceased. We worked on in the sudden silence. Militarism had faded out – as if it had never been.

INDEX

ACKNOWLEDGEMENTS

The publishers would especially like to thank the following for their assistance (abbreviations as shown in brackets): Chris Beetles Ltd (CB), Garton & Cooke Ltd (G&C), Rowland Hilder (RH), Michael Parkin Fine Art Ltd (MP), Mrs Reynolds Stone (RS), Towner Art Gallery, Eastbourne (TAG), Tryon Gallery Ltd and the Trustees of the Estate of the late C.F. Tunnicliffe (CFT).

COLOUR ILLUSTRATIONS

Gerald Ackermann, R.I.: "*Haymaking at Arundel*" (detail) opp. p. 145 (TAG)

Robert Alexander: "*The Hayrick*" (detail) opp. p. 160 (MP)

Stanley Badmin, R.E., R.W.S.: "*Winter's Sunshine*" (detail) opp. p. 17, "*Storm Over Pole Hill*" (detail) opp. p. 33, "*Old Fashioned Harvest near Luscombe*" (detail) opp. p. 81, "*Harvest*" (detail) opp. p. 88, "*Collecting Grass for Silage in Thundery Weather*" (detail) opp. p. 96, "*The Plough*" (detail) opp. p. 129, "*The First Time Round-Harvest in Wiltshire*" between pps 184-5 (CB)

James Bateman, R.A.: "*The Harvest*" (details) (Art Gallery of South Australia, Adelaide) opp. pps 64 and 89, "*Haytime in the Cotswolds*" (detail) (Southampton City Art Gallery)

Brian Cook: "*South Eastern Survey 1936*" between pps 40-1, "*Farming in England, 1937*" (detail) opp. p. 65, "*England and the Farmer, 1941*" between pps 88-9, "*Corn Country, 1940*" (detail) opp. p. 113. These paintings were jacket designs for books by the same titles, published by B.T. Batsford Ltd and reproduced with their kind permission, courtesy of the artist (MP)

Evelyn Mary Dunbar: "*A 1944 Pastoral – Land Girls Pruning at East Malling*" (detail) opp. p. 41 (Manchester City Art Gallery)

Rowland Hilder, R.I.: "*Oasthouses, Shoreham Valley*" (detail) opp. p. 16, "*Winter, East Anglia*" (detail) opp. p. 40, "*To Enjoy the Fruits of Victory*" – *1944 Poster for National Savings Group* opp. p. 48, "*Lane in Winter*" (detail) opp. p. 49, "*Harvest Time*" (detail) opp. p. 80 (courtesy of the artist)

Lucy Elizabeth Kemp-Welch, R.I.: "*Return From the Fields*" (detail) opp. p. 97 (David Messum Ltd, Marlow)

John Nash: "*Dorset Landscape*" (detail) opp. p. 161 (Tate Gallery)

Eric Ravilious: "*The Downs in Winter*" (detail) opp. p. 112 (TAG © 1987 DACS All rights reserved)

Gilbert Spencer: "*The Progress of Husbandry*" (detail) opp. p. 128 (Tate Gallery)

Harold Swanwick: "*Harrowing near Wilmington*" (detail) opp. p. 144 (TAG)

Charles F. Tunnicliffe, R.A.: "*Ploughing*" opp. p. 32 (CFT/Boots Ltd, Nottingham)

BLACK AND WHITE ILLUSTRATIONS

Stanley Anderson, R.A., R.E.: "*The Farm Hand, 1933*": 2 (G&C), "*The Saddler*": 35 (G&C), "*Trimming Stakes*": 57 (G&C), "*Sheep-dipping, 1935*": 77 (Ashmolean), "*Hyden, the Old Shepherd*": 109 (G&C), "*The Stone Breaker*": 121 (G&C), "*Windswept Corn, 1938*": 150 (G&C), "*The Thatcher*": 157 (G&C), "*The Wayfarer, 1941*": 158 (Ashmolean), "*Clamping Spuds, 1942*": 174 (Ashmolean)

Robert Austin, R.E., R.W.S.: "*Hero's Widow*": 135 (V&A)

Stanley Badmin, R.E., R.W.S.: *New Hop Poles*": 12, "*Evening Light near Sevenoaks, Kent*": 15, "*Swinbrook Bridge, 1931*": 41, "*Farm House in Forth Valley*": 47, "*Tanyard Farm*": 64, "*Farmyard*": 105, "*Study for Farmyard, Alkham*": 124, "*Sorting Potatoes, 1932*": 128, "*The Field Corner, 1929*": 162, "*Darby and Joan Cottage, Essex, 1935*": 166, " *The Old Ash*": 58, "*Warham*": 143 (G&C)

Robert Bevan: "*Farmyard*": 139, "*Landscape*": 185 (V&A)

Paul Drury, R.E.: "*September 1928*": 43, "*Nicol's Farm 1925*": 97 (G&C)

Joan Hassall: Trial proofs for "*Portrait of a Village*" by Frances Brett Young (published by Heinemann): 1, 106, 122, 125, 138, 142, (V&A)

Gertrude Hermes, R.A., R.E.: "*Landscape 1925*": 18 (G&C)

Rowland Hilder, R.I.: Engravings made for various newspapers and "*Farmers' Weekly*": 14, 63, 83, 98, 99, 152, 163, 175, 180, 181 (RH)

Edward Bouverie Hoyton: "*Winter*": 182 (G&C)

Dame Laura Knight, R.A., R.E., R.W.S.: "*Country Corn*": 107 (V&A)

Clare Leighton, R.E.: From "*Four Hedges*": 42, 50, 55. "*Threshing*": 70, "*Rain*": 108. Trial proofs for "*Return of the Native*": 115, 140, 141, 147, 148, 155, 156, 160 (V&A)

Guy Malet: "*A Berkshire Farm 1946*": 95

William Arthur Narbeth: "*Threshing Ttime*": 123 (TAG)

John Nash: "*Cottage*": 94, "*Sheepshearing*": 100 (V&A)

Claughton Pellew: "*The Ricks*": 127 (V&A)

Eric Ravilious (© 1988 DACS All rights reserved).
From Kynoch Press notebook 1933: 44, 165, From Four Proofs for Curzon Press, 1935: 53, From 54 *Conceits*: 72 (TAG)

Reynolds Stone, R.E.:
From "*Boxwood*", 1957 (Monotype Corporation): 81, 132
From Cornwall County Nursing Association Calendar, 1937: 89
From "*Moments of Vision*" by Kenneth Clark (John Murray, 1973): 13

Reynolds Stone (*cont.*)
From "*The Open Air: An Anthology of English Country Life*" by Adrian Bell (Faber & Faber, 1936 – 1st Edition): 23, 101
From "*The Open Air*" (Faber & Faber, 1949 edition): 16, 20, 91, 113
From "*The Other Side of the Alde*" by Kenneth Clark (Warren Editions, 1968): 28, 69
From "*Old English Wines and Cordials*" by T. Read (High House Press, 1938): 29, 45, 46, 136
From "*The Praise and Happinesse of the Countrie-Life*" by Don Antonio de Guevarra (Gregynog Press, 1938): 3
From "*The Old Rectory*" (Warren Editions, 1976): 111
Unpublished c.1956: 133

Graham Sutherland, O.M.: (© DACS/Cosmo Press)
"*Village, 25*": 19, "*Pecken Wood*": 59, "*Number Forty-Nine, 1945*": 126 (G&C)

Robin Tanner, R.E.: *The Gamekeeper's Cottage, 1929*": 22, "*Wiltshire Woodman, 1929*": 25, "*Wiltshire Rickyard, 1939*': 93, "*Allington in Wiltshire, 1927*": 164 (G&C)

Charles Taylor, R.E.: "*Lamberhurst*": 31 (G&C)

Charles F. Tunnicliffe (by courtesy of the Trustees of the C.F. Tunnicliffe Estate)
From "*Both Sides of the Road*" (Collins, 1949) 17, 32, 36, 37, 48, 65, 67, 76, 79, 80, 85, 87, 90, 114, 118, 131, 144, 153, 167, 170, 173, 179
also miscellaneous 33, 34, 49, 62, 66, 68, 82, 102, 129, 149, 168, 172, 176, 177

Frances Unwin: "*The Threshing Machine*": 54 (G&C)

William Washington: "*Winter Fuel*": 60 (V&A)

Ethelbert White, R.W.S.: "*Ploughman's Cottage*": 26 (V&A), "*The Rick Yard, 1926*": 39, "*The Rick*": 117 (V&A)

Abbreviations:
Ashmolean: Department of Prints and Drawings, Department of Western Art, Ashmolean Museum, Oxford; O.M.: Order of Merit; R.A.: Royal Academy; R.E.: Royal Society of Painter-Etchers and Engravers; R.I.: Royal Institute of Painters in Watercolours; R.W.S.: Royal Society of Painters in Watercolours; V&A: Department of Prints and Drawings, Victoria and Albert Museum, London.

Picture research by Jenny de Gex.

·DHF·